ARTIFICIAL INTELLIGENCE AND AUTONOMOUS SHIPPING

This collection of essays critically evaluates the legal framework necessary for the use of autonomous ships in international waters. The work is divided into three parts:

Part 1 evaluates how far national shipping regulation, and the public international law background that lies behind it, may need modification and updating to accommodate the use of autonomous ships on international voyages.

Part 2 evaluates the new legal challenges that autonomous shipping will introduce and the possible need for changes in the insurance market in terms of providing cover for such vessels.

Part 3 analyses international convention regimes dealing with maritime safety and other matters, arguing for specific changes in the existing conventions, such as SOLAS and MARPOL, which would provide the international framework that is necessary for putting autonomous ships into commercial use.

The book also takes the view that amendment of international conventions is important in the case of liability issues, arguing that leaving such matters to national law, particularly issues concerning product liability, could not only restrict or hinder the availability of liability insurance but also hamper the development of technology in this field.

Written by internationally recognised experts in their respective areas, the book offers a holistic approach to the debate on autonomous ships and makes a timely and important contribution to the literature.

Artificial Intelligence and Autonomous Shipping

Developing the International Legal Framework

Edited by
Barış Soyer
and
Andrew Tettenborn

•HART•
OXFORD • LONDON • NEW YORK • NEW DELHI • SYDNEY

HART PUBLISHING

Bloomsbury Publishing Plc

Kemp House, Chawley Park, Cumnor Hill, Oxford, OX2 9PH, UK

1385 Broadway, New York, NY 10018, USA

29 Earlsfort Terrace, Dublin 2, Ireland

HART PUBLISHING, the Hart/Stag logo, BLOOMSBURY and the Diana logo are trademarks of Bloomsbury Publishing Plc

First published in Great Britain 2021

A catalogue record for this book is available from the British Library.

Library of Congress Cataloging-in-Publication data

Names: Soyer, Barış, editor. | Tettenborn, Andrew, editor.

Title: Artificial intelligence and autonomous shipping : developing the international legal framework / edited by Barış Soyer and Andrew Tettenborn.

Description: Oxford, UK ; New York, NY : Hart Publishing, an imprint of Bloomsbury Publishing, 2021. | Includes bibliographical references and index.

Identifiers: LCCN 2021002360 (print) | LCCN 2021002361 (ebook) | ISBN 9781509933358 (hardback) | ISBN 9781509947935 (paperback) | ISBN 9781509933365 (pdf) | ISBN 9781509933372 (Epub)

Subjects: LCSH: Maritime law. | Shipping—Technological innovations. | Ships—Automation. | Marine insurance—Law and legislation. | Marine pollution—Law and legislation. | Law of the sea. | Shipping—Safety regulations. | International Convention for the Prevention of Pollution from Ships (1973) | International Convention for the Safety of Life at Sea (1974 November 1)

Classification: LCC K1150 .A925 2021 (print) | LCC K1150 (ebook) | DDC 343.09/65—dc23

LC record available at https://lccn.loc.gov/2021002360

LC ebook record available at https://lccn.loc.gov/2021002361

ISBN: HB: 978-1-50993-335-8
ePDF: 978-1-50993-336-5
ePub: 978-1-50993-337-2

Typeset by Compuscript Ltd, Shannon

ACKNOWLEDGEMENTS

The idea of writing a book evaluating the legal issues surrounding maritime autonomous surface ships, or MASSs, first surfaced spontaneously during an otherwise dull meeting in June 2018 of Swansea Law School's Institute of Shipping and Trade Law. We shortly afterwards discovered that Roderick Bagshaw and Peter Macdonald Eggers also found the idea fascinating, and were delighted when they enthusiastically agreed to come on board.

We would like to take this opportunity to thank our colleagues at the IISTL for supporting us with useful feedback on key matters, in particular Professor Richard Williams and Dr Iur Bűlent Sőzer. In this context, we need to mention our research assistant, Miss Alicia McKenzie, who has been excellent! Also, we wish to express our enormous appreciation for a number of academics from other institutions who engaged in fruitful and helpful discussions with us on a raft of issues. In this connection our thanks must go in particular to Professor Olivier Cachard (Lorraine University), Professor Lia Athanasiou (Athens University), Professor James Hu (Shanghai Maritime University) and Professor Beiping Chu (Dalian Maritime University).

Last but not least, we are grateful to the editorial team at Hart Publishing, namely Roberta Bassi, and Rosemarie Mearns for giving us fantastic support from beginning to the end!

Needless to say, we are responsible for any errors or omissions.

BS & AT

CONTENTS

THE CONTRIBUTORS

Associate Professor Roderick Bagshaw
Oxford University

Roderick Bagshaw is a Fellow and Tutor in Law of Magdalen College, and holds the post of Associate Professor in the Faculty of Law. He teaches undergraduate courses in Administrative Law and Tort Law, and on the postgraduate BCL Private Law and Fundamental Rights course. Formerly on the Executive Committee of the Society of Legal Scholars and convenor of the Tort Law subject section, his student book on tort law with Nicholas McBride is currently in its sixth edition. He is also one of the editors of *Clerk & Lindsell on Torts.*

Professor Simon Baughen
Professor of Commercial Law, Institute of International Shipping and Trade Law, Swansea University

Professor Simon Baughen has been Professor of Shipping Law in the Department of Shipping and Trade Law at Swansea since 2013, having previously been a Reader at the University of Bristol Law School where he had worked since joining academia in 1989 from practice.

Simon's research interests lie mainly in shipping law, on which he has written extensively over the last 30 years. He is the sole author of the classic student text *Shipping Law*, now in its seventh edition, and took over authorship of *Summerskill on Laytime* in 2013 for its fifth edition; the sixth edition was published in autumn 2018. He is not solely a shipping lawyer, however: he also researches in the field of the interaction between free trade/investment and environmental protection and human rights, and indeed has produced two books on this topic: *International Trade and the Protection of the Environment* in 2007 and *Human Rights and Corporate Wrongs. Closing the Governance Gap*? in 2016.

Dr George Leloudas
Associate Professor of Commercial Law, Institute of International Shipping and Trade Law, Swansea University

Dr Leloudas has been with the Institute of International Shipping and Trade Law (IISTL) at Swansea University since 2011. A graduate of the National and Kapodistrian University of Athens, he holds two LLM degrees (one in Commercial Law from the University of Bristol, and one in Air and Space Law from the Institute of Air and Space Law at McGill) and a PhD from Cambridge obtained in 2009. George's principal research interest is the carriage of passengers and goods by air, but his expertise extends also to multimodal transport, insurance law and the regulation of autonomous transport systems. He has published two monographs, *Risk and Liability in Air Law* and *Air Cargo Insurance* (the latter with Professor Malcolm Clarke of Cambridge University), and a slew of articles on carriage and liability in journals in Britain and worldwide. In addition he acts as one of the editors of *Shawcross and Beaumont on Air Law*, being responsible for the (passenger and cargo) liability chapters of the publication. At Swansea he teaches insurance law, carriage of goods and passengers by air, sea and land, arbitration law and aircraft finance law.

Peter MacDonald Eggers QC
Barrister, 7 King's Bench Walk

Peter MacDonald Eggers QC is a commercial barrister of very wide interests, having switched to the bar from a commercial solicitor's practice in 2000. His very successful practice includes insurance and reinsurance, shipping and transport, energy, commodities, international trade, financial services, professional negligence, and international investment projects. He appears regularly before the Commercial Court, the Court of Appeal and the Supreme Court, and also in commercial and international arbitrations. In 2017, he was appointed a Deputy High Court Judge, assigned to the Queen's Bench Division. Two years later in 2019 he was named Insurance Silk of the Year at the Chambers Bar Awards. In addition to his practice he teaches part-time at UCL and has published widely, perhaps his best-known book being the much-acclaimed *Deceit: The Lie of the Law*.

Professor Barış Soyer
Professor of Commercial and Maritime Law, Director of the Institute of International Shipping and Trade Law, Swansea University

Professor Soyer is Professor of Commercial and Maritime Law and Director of the Institute of International Shipping and Trade Law. A member of the British Maritime Law Association and the British Insurance Law Association, he is the author of *Warranties in Marine Insurance* and *Marine Insurance Fraud*. The former won both the Cavendish Book Prize and the BILA Charitable Trust Book Prize; the latter, the same BILA Prize in 2015. Barış has also published extensively in *Lloyd's Maritime and Commercial Law Quarterly*, the *Journal of Business Law*, the *Cambridge Law Journal*, the *Law Quarterly Review*, the *Torts Law Journal* and *Journal of Contract Law*.

He regularly edits the books produced as a result of Swansea's annual shipping law colloquiums (which he organises); in addition he is on the editorial board of the *Journal of International Maritime Law, Shipping and Trade Law* and *Lloyd's Maritime and Commercial Law Quarterly*. He currently teaches charterparties, carriage by sea and marine insurance on the Swansea LLM programme and acts as director of Commercial, Maritime and International Trade LLMs.

Professor Andrew Tettenborn
Professor of Commercial Law, Institute of International Shipping and Trade Law, Swansea University

Professor Tettenborn has been attached to the IISTL at Swansea Law School since 2010, teaching international trade, aspects of banking and admiralty. He has also taught at the universities of Cambridge, Exeter and Geneva, and held visiting positions in Europe, Australia and the USA. His book with Francis Rose on *Admiralty Claims* came out this year. By way of background, Professor Tettenborn is general editor of *Marsden's Collisions at Sea* and the leading student textbook on commercial law (*Sealy & Hooley's Text, Cases and Materials*, now in its sixth edition).

He has just been appointed editor-in-chief of *Clerk & Lindsell on Torts*. In addition, he has authored numerous articles on commercial law and obligations and sits on the editorial boards of Lloyd's Maritime & Commercial Law Quarterly and the Journal of International Maritime Law.

In addition to his other activities, he is also a member of the committee recently set up in 2020 to produce a draft Commercial Code for England.

Dr Youri van Logchem
Senior Lecturer, Institute of International Shipping and Trade Law, Swansea University

Dr Youri van Logchem is a senior lecturer at the Institute of International Shipping and Trade Law at Swansea University. A graduate of Utrecht University, he was with the Netherlands Institute for the Law of the Sea, where he obtained his PhD, and later worked as a lecturer and researcher in legal theory at Utrecht University, and a Junior Policy Officer at the Hague Institute for the Internationalisation of Law. Youri has also received a number of academic honours, including the Rhodes Academy Submarine Cables Award, and has presented at various conferences around the world.

Youri has published widely in both Europe and the USA. His articles and book chapters have been widely cited before international courts and tribunals. A monograph entitled *The Rights and Obligations of States in Disputed Maritime Areas* is forthcoming with Cambridge University Press. At Swansea he teaches both at the postgraduate and undergraduate level, primarily in the areas of international law of the sea, international energy law, and general public international law.

TABLE OF CASES

European Union Cases

International Court of Justice Cases

International Arbitrations

TABLE OF LEGISLATION

United Kingdom Statutes

United Kingdom Statutory Instruments

Regulatory Codes of Practice/Guidance

Explanatory Notes

Institute Clauses

Cyber Exclusion Clauses

Working Papers

TABLE OF EUROPEAN AND INTERNATIONAL LEGISLATION

EU Directives

EU Regulations

Codes

International Conventions

Introduction

In simple terms, artificial intelligence is the process of simulating human intelligence through machine processes. It dates back at least to the 1950s.[1] In the maritime field, following the successful harnessing of computer technology over more than five decades to operate underwater vehicles remotely for military and scientific purposes,[2] attention turned at the turn of the millennium to the problem of designing vessels with the ability through artificial intelligence to make their own navigational decisions and determine their actions autonomously.

The most influential research programme aimed at developing 'a technical concept for the operation of autonomous merchant vessels' and assessing its 'technical, economic and legal feasibility' arguably was the Maritime Unmanned Navigation through Intelligence Networks (MUNIN) project,[3] co-funded by the European Union.[4] This was a concept study, which ended in August 2015, aimed at identifying the most critical technological, operational and legislative factors that might obstruct the development of autonomous shipping.

Similar studies, mainly driven by engineering and IT firms, have been launched since then with the encouragement and financial support of some Nordic countries. Some of these studies have utilised lessons learned from remote operation in industries such as aviation, space exploration and defence, resulting in the use of interactive smart screens, voice recognition systems, holograms and surveillance drones to monitor and assess onboard operations and conditions around the vessel.[5] The ultimate aim of all these projects was to produce a viable model which could be subjected to actual sea trials. This object was partially achieved in December 2018, when Finnish state-owned ferry operator Finferries, in collaboration with Rolls-Royce, tested the navigation of the world's first fully autonomous ferry, the *Falco*, in the archipelago south of the city of Turku. During the test, the *Falco, a* 54-metre double-ended car ferry, successfully navigated autonomously for about a mile and half. Similarly, Yara and Kongsberg have entered into partnership

[1] S Bringsjford et al, 'Creativity, the Turing Test, and the (Better) Lovelace Test' (2001) 11 *Minds & Machines* 3, at 5.

[2] For example, in the 1970s and 80s the Royal Navy used 'Cutlet', a remotely operated submersible, to recover practice torpedoes and mines. Similarly, remotely operated vehicles have been used to locate many historic shipwrecks, including the RSM *Titanic*; see www.whoi.edu/page.do?pid=83577&tid=3622&cid=130989, accessed 1 July 2020.

[3] See www.unmanned-ship.org/munin/, accessed I July 2020.

[4] See the EU's Seventh Framework Programme, implemented through the agreement SCP2-GA-2012–314286.

[5] See www.iims.org.uk/rolls-royce-reveals-its-vision-for-future-shore-control-centre-for-unmanned-ships/, accessed on 1 July 2020.

to build the world's first autonomous zero emission ship, the *YARA Birkeland*. The vessel, which is planned to operate in the territorial waters of Norway as a 120 TEU container feeder vessel, will function initially as a manned vessel, moving to remote operation in 2021; it is expected to be capable of performing fully autonomous operations from 2022.[6] This is obviously a significant development. Neverthless we must not lose sight of its limited scope: the sole planned function of the *YARA Birkeland* is to operate solely in Norwegian territorial waters, to transport one manufacturer's product along one very specific route to a particular port from which it can then be shipped globally. True, to this limited extent the expectation is that she will provide an economically viable and environmentally friendly alternative to truck transport. But this in no way shows that an economic case has been successfully made for replacing conventional vessels with autonomous vessels more generally, let alone that the technology is ready to operate autonomous vessels on transocean passages. Moreover, even when (or if) the appropriate technology is developed, it is highly likely that not all commercial cargoes will be suitable for autonomous transport. For instance, there may well be continued resistance to the carriage of oil and hazardous cargoes on wholly autonomous vessels, even if it is accepted that vessels carrying such cargoes will be able to rely more on autonomous systems with a reduced number of crew on board.

In addition to the technological challenge of developing the autonomous operation machinery as regards ships, there are equally important shoreside challenges. We need fairly quickly to establish codes and practices to standardise the security, quality and integrity of the data generated by autonomous ship operations. In addition to this there are training requirements; we need a new and different generation of naval architects, technicians and engineers, not to mention new roles in cybersecurity and operational management. But that is only one side of the equation. To make autonomous shipping a reality, the infrastructure in ports needs to be developed in a parallel fashion. For example, shore facilities, such as automated mooring systems and shore power hook-up, will be necessary for autonomous vessels. This may also include high-accuracy positioning systems, better communication infrastructure and other facilities to simplify the critical port approach and departure phases. Ultimately, there will be no way to avoid the need for investment in better shore traffic monitoring systems to simplify onboard sensor systems, and improved VTS and remote pilotage functionalities to support autonomous ships.

The challenge is however not merely technical, but legal and regulatory. True, states naturally have jurisdiction to regulate internal trade and events within their internal waters; but the majority of maritime law principles are of an international character, developed through customary international law and international treaties. Many of these rules operate on the assumption that a human being will be in charge of a vessel. This may or may not matter as regards individual instances: but it means that to make the operation of autonomous vessels a reality outside

[6] Owing to the Covid-19 pandemic the project has been delayed for a considerable amount of time.

internal waters, it is necessary to explore to what extent each existing rule of public and private maritime law (and the law of the sea) may require amendment. International regulators are now aware of this and have begun to take up the challenge. In particular, in 2018 the Maritime Safety Committee (MSC) of the International Maritime Organisation (IMO) agreed to establish a Working Group (the Maritime Autonomous Surface Ships Working Group, or MASSWG) to undertake a scoping exercise; this will aim to identify which of the existing international instruments dealing with maritime safety need amending, and what new legal instruments need to be developed. For the purposes of this exercise, MASSWG has prescribed four degrees of autonomy:[7] 1) ship with automated processes and decision support, but with seafarers on board to operate and control shipboard systems and functions; 2) remotely controlled ships with seafarers on board, but controlled and operated from a distant location; 3) remotely controlled ships without seafarers on board, controlled and operated from a distant location; 4) fully autonomous ships, where the operating system of the ship is able to make decisions and determine actions by itself.

This is a good start. But even when this scoping exercise is complete, there is a long way to go in determining the nature and form of reforms that need to be carried out. That is where this book comes in. Our main objective has been to evaluate rigorously and critically the legal framework necessary for the use of MASSs in international waters. To achieve this end, the book is divided into three parts.

In Part I, we investigate how far current legal principles can support the development of autonomous shipping. This involves asking how far national shipping regulation, and the public international law background that lies behind it, may need modification and updating to accommodate the use of MASSs on international voyages. Accordingly, Chapter One analyses the challenges autonomous vessels pose for the IMO regulatory framework established through conventions such as SOLAS, STCW, ISM, MARPOL and the Collision Regulations. The focus of Chapter Two is on the rights and obligations of states under public international law concerning MASSs. Particularly important here is the 1982 UN Convention on the Law of the Sea (LOSC), and the rules and obligations it imposes on states in their roles as coastal state, flag state and port state. Chapter Three deals with private law aspects of maritime law and offers and examination on the rules relating to salvage, collisions, limitation of liability, pollution liability and other relevant areas, and makes a detailed examination of how suited they are (or are not) to MASS shipping. The aim is to illustrate the difficulties that can arise in terms of apportioning liability and risk on the basis of conventions and practices designed to apply to manned ships, and to suggest a way forward. The last chapter in this part focuses on the relation between the existing contractual and treaty regimes – Hague, Hague-Visby, Hamburg and possibly Rotterdam, as well as various voyage and time charter forms – covering carriage of goods by sea and the issues thrown

[7] MSC 99/WP.9 Annex 1, para 4.

up by the use of unmanned vessels, especially those at levels three and four on the IMO's MASS scale. This issue is vital for the entire insurance and P&I market.

The focus of Part II is rather different. The object here is to evaluate the new legal challenges that MASSs will introduce and the possible need for changes in the insurance market in terms of providing cover for such vessels. This part begins with Chapter Five on the operational and legal challenges that cyber risks pose to autonomous ships. With increasing dependence on such things as cloud computing, satellite communications and the Internet of Things, the management of cyber risks becomes an essential element not only for current operations, but also for the evolution of the industry towards an autonomous paradigm. Having mapped the cyber risk landscape, this chapter seeks to identify the characteristics of cyber risks that call for innovative legal solutions in the context of civil liability. It then passes to an analysis of the applicability of certain shipping conventions to an array of cyber-related incidents, drawing parallels from (for example) the operational and legal management of cyber risks in autonomous cars, a sector arguably more advanced in dealing with cyber risks.

The background to Chapter Six is that the aim of MASSs is, crudely, to replace human power with machines in respect of a large proportion of shipping operations. This means that when things go wrong, this will increasingly be due not to direct human fault, but to the failure of a machine or an algorithm, something that has the potential vastly to increase the relevance of product liability issues. It is these that the chapter seeks to analyse in this connection.

Chapter Seven looks closely at the changes that will need to occur in insurance market so as to provide sufficient cover for MASSs. In particular it investigates whether existing hull wordings may need to be rejigged to take into the account the fact that autonomous operations can raise additional risks not currently contemplated, and whether the focus of liability insurance will remain on P&I Clubs or whether it may move elsewhere with the increased significance of product liability issues.

In Part III, which is composed of Chapter Eight, we deal with the mechanics of the law reform that will need to be carried out to make the use of MASSs a reality. It concludes that a different regulatory process for amending technical rules with regard to safety and manning requirements for such vessels should be followed, as opposed to regulating civil liability issues emerging from the use of such vessels. The chapter also highlights the key elements of such law reform.

The analysis in this book is a comprehensive one. It goes beyond doctrinal legal scrutiny, offering in addition a contextual analysis elaborating the relationship between different compensation regimes, such as various tort and international regimes, taking into account economic and political considerations. There can be no doubt that making the necessary changes to the current legal framework will be a lengthy and at times politically fraught process which will face scrutiny and opposition at every step of the way. We hope that this book makes a small contribution to solving the problems and creating a suitable legal regime for MASSs.

PART I

MASS in the Context of the Existing Legal Framework

1

International Regulation of Shipping and Unmanned Vessels

PROFESSORS SIMON BAUGHEN* AND ANDREW TETTENBORN**

I. Introduction

International regulation of vessels as regards safety, navigation and other matters is primarily achieved through a UN organisation, the International Maritime Organization (IMO), established in 1958 by the Convention on the International Maritime Organization.[1] Its purposes, as mentioned in Article 1(a) of the Convention, are 'to provide machinery for cooperation among governments in the field of governmental regulation and practices relating to technical matters of all kinds affecting shipping engaged in international trade; to encourage and facilitate the general adoption of the highest practicable standards in matters concerning maritime safety, efficiency of navigation and prevention and control of marine pollution from ships'. Today, its primary roles are to promote safe, secure, environmentally sound, efficient and sustainable shipping through cooperation.

The IMO has developed a variety of conventions regulating aspects of international shipping, which are then transposed into national law by state parties to those conventions. Its conventions are subscribed to by 90 per cent of states, representing about 99 per cent of world tonnage. The IMO's principal regulatory conventions comprise eight instruments, most of which are periodically amended:

- The International Convention for the Safety of Life at Sea of 1974 (SOLAS), an instrument that also gives legal force to the International Ship and Port Facility Security Code (ISPS), the International Safety Management Code (ISM), and the Polar Code.

* Professor of Shipping Law, Member of the Institute of International Shipping and Trade Law, Swansea University.

** Professor of Commercial Law, Member of the Institute of International Shipping and Trade Law, Swansea University.

[1] Adoption: 6 March 1948; entry in force: 17 March 1958.

- The International Convention for the Prevention of Pollution from Ships of 1973, as modified by Protocols of 1978 and 1997 (MARPOL).
- The International Convention on Oil Pollution Preparedness, Response and Co-operation of 1969 (OPRC) 1969.
- The International Convention on Standards of Training, Certification and Watchkeeping for Seafarers of 1978 as amended in 1995 and 2010 (STCW).
- The Convention on Facilitation of International Maritime Traffic of 1965 (FAL).
- The International Convention on Maritime Search and Rescue of 1979 (SAR).
- The Convention on the International Regulations for Preventing Collisions at Sea of 1972 (COLREG).
- The Convention for the Suppression of Unlawful Acts Against the Safety of Maritime Navigation of 1988, amended by the 2005 Protocol (SUA).

There are also various IMO civil liability conventions (notably the 1969 and 1992 CLC and the 1992 Fund Conventions, the 2001 Bunker Oil Pollution Convention, and the 2007 Nairobi Wreck Removal Convention), and also the International Labour Organisation's Maritime Labour Convention of 2006.

A. Degrees of Automation

The IMO is currently assessing its existing instruments to see how they might apply to ships with varying degrees of automation, through a regulatory scoping exercise on Maritime Autonomous Surface Ships (MASS). The degrees of autonomy identified for the purpose of the scoping exercise are:

MASS 1: Ship with automated processes and decision support, with seafarers on board to operate and control shipboard systems and functions. Some operations may be automated and at times be unsupervised but with seafarers on board ready to take control.

MASS 2: Remotely controlled ship with seafarers on board, but controlled and operated from another location. The seafarers on board are there to take control if necessary, and to operate the shipboard systems and functions.

MASS 3: Remotely controlled ship without seafarers on board, the vessel being entirely controlled and operated from another location.

MASS 4: Fully autonomous ship, whose operating system is able to make decisions and determine actions by itself.

The key factor differentiating MASS 3 and MASS 4 on this scheme would be the level of operational control exercised by human shore-based controllers.

It is worth noting that other more detailed scales of autonomous operation exist. There is Sheridan's 10-point scale from 1992,[2] running as follows:

1. The computer offers no assistance, human must do it all. (This would equate to MASS 1.)
2. The computer offers a complete set of action alternatives, and/or
3. narrows the selection down to a few, or
4. suggests one, and
5. executes that suggestion if the human approves, or
6. allows the human a restricted time to veto before automatic execution.

(These levels (2)–(6) would fall within the scope of MASS 2–3, depending on whether there was any human being on board the vessel.)

7. The computer executes automatically, then necessarily informs the human, or
8. the computer informs the human after execution only if asked.
   (These are on the border between MASS 3 and 4.)
9. The computer informs human after execution if it, the computer, decides to do so, or
10. The computer decides everything and acts autonomously, ignoring the human.

(These last categories are roughly equivalent to MASS 4.)

There is alternatively a six-point scale set out in the 2017 of the Danish Maritime Law Association, itself adapted from Lloyd's Register. In summary the points can be described thus:

AL0: Manual controlled. Navigation controls or waypoints for course are handled manually. The operator is on board or controls the vessel remotely through radio link. This would seem to be MASS 2, though issues are raised as to how many operators should be on board for a long voyage, and will necessitate examination of, inter alia, the requirements in the MLC requirements and the STCW.

The next levels, described below, see a move to MASS 3 with diminishing navigational input by the onshore operator.

AL 1: Decision support on board. Automatic navigation is possible according to set references and schedule. Course and speed are measured by onboard sensors. The operator sets course as waypoints and determines desired speed. The operator monitors and changes course and speed if necessary.

AL 2: Decision support on board or from shore. Course navigation is achieved through a sequence of waypoints, and the course calculated according to a planned

[2] T. Sheridan, *Telerobotics, Automation, and Human Supervisory Control* (MIT Press, 1992).

schedule. An external system can upload a new schedule. The operator monitors operation and surroundings, and can change course and speed if needed. Suggestions for interventions may be provided by algorithms.

AL 3: Execution by operator on board who monitors and authorises actions. The system recommends navigational actions on the basis of sensor information from the ship and its surroundings. The operator monitors the system's functions and actions, and authorises actions before they are carried out.

AL 4: Execution by operator who monitors and is able to intervene. Decisions on navigation and operational actions are calculated by the system that executes them on the basis of its calculations following approval from the operator. The operator monitors the system's actions, and takes correctional actions as needed. Monitoring may take place from shore.

The next level starts to look like borderline MASS 3–4.

AL 5: Monitored autonomy. Overall decisions regarding navigation and operation are made by the system, which also assesses consequences and risks. Sensors capture relevant information about the surrounding circumstances; the system interprets it, calculates its actions and executes them automatically. The operator is however alerted unless the system is very certain of its interpretation of the surroundings, its own state and of the following calculated actions. Furthermore, general goals are determined by the operator. Monitoring may take place from shore.

Finally there is AL6, equivalent to MASS 4 save that there is a still a human in the navigational process on shore, subject to referral by the system. At MASS 4 one cannot sensibly speak of any person being 'in command' of the vessel.

AL 6: Full autonomy. Overall decisions regarding navigation and operation are made by the system, which also assessws consequences and risks. The system acts on the basis of analysis and calculations of both own actions and any responses to them; moreover, knowledge of past and hypothetical situations is continuously factored in via machine learning. The system makes its own decisions and actions, calculating own capability and predicting the behaviour of surrounding traffic. The operator is alerted in the event that the system fails to determine what to do. General goals may be determined by the system. Any monitoring is from shore.

B. The Approach of the CMI and this Chapter

A recent spreadsheet submitted by the Comite Maritime International (CMI) to the IMO identifies numerous convention provisions which, according to its researches, presuppose or indeed require the existence of a master and/or a crew of some sort on board the vessel.[3] These matters will clearly pose regulatory

[3] Spreadsheet Regarding Conventions, https://comitemaritime.org/work/unmanned-ships/.

challenges in respect of vessels at MASS levels 3 and 4. This chapter seeks to build on this and identify the possible amendments required to the existing regulatory structure (or where necessary to identify areas where completely new regulatory work may be necessary).

One point should be noted. This chapter will not be concerned with the definition of a 'ship'. Instead, we will proceed on the assumption, which we consider justified, that in connection with autonomous vessels, no issue arises over the definition of a 'ship' as regards whether a vessel is manned or not. An uncrewed or partly crewed vessel is just as much a 'ship' as its fully crewed equivalent would be.[4]

C. The Master and the Crew – A Definitional Issue

Throughout the various regulatory schemes there appear frequent references to the position of the 'master' (and sometimes the crew). This has always been based on the assumption, hitherto correct, that every vessel had a master, and that the identification of who fulfilled this role was relatively straightforward. The functions which a master is assumed to perform are several: navigational and command, things connected with cargo handling and carriage, disciplinary, and compliance. However, as soon as we reach autonomy corresponding to the person directly answering to this description at levels MASS 3 and MASS 4 – at least on board the vessel – a question arises: when there is a reference to a 'master', need this by definition refer to a person actually aboard? The answer would seem to be: sometimes.

John Cartner's *The International Law of the Shipmaster*, which is as good a source as any, defines the master as 'a natural person who is responsible for a vessel and all things and persons in it and is responsible for enforcing the maritime laws of the flag state'.[5] This definition does not in terms require him actually to be on board the vessel under his command. Some national legal definitions are to similar effect. In the UK, for example, section 313 of the Merchant Shipping Act 1995 reflects the definition just given: it defines 'master' as 'every person (except a pilot) having command or charge of a ship'. The definition does not require onboard presence and could therefore encompass the shore-based controller (SBC) as remote operator of the vessel. (It is fair to say, however, that by contrast, some national laws do define 'master' in such a way as to require their presence on board the vessel.[6])

[4] B. Sözer, in a report attached to the CMI Working Group on Ship Nomenclature, analysed the definition of the terms in almost 20 key maritime conventions, and none link the definition of ship to the presence of crew on board, http://comitemaritime.org/wp-content/uploads/2018/05/Letter-to-Presidents-of-NMLAs-re-IWG-on-Vessel-Nomenclature-080316.pdf.

[5] Ibid, p. 86.

[6] The CMI sent out a questionnaire on unmanned vessels to the maritime law associations (MLAs) of 19 states. In 'Summary of responses to the CMI questionnaire' the MLAs of Brazil, China, and Croatia stated that the master is defined as a person on board the ship. All 19 MLAs answered that neither the chief pre-programmer of an autonomous ship nor another designated person not immediately involved in the operation of the ship could constitute the master, www.comitemaritime.org/Unmanned-Ships/0,27153,115332,00.html.

If an SBC can be a master, it might seem that this simplifies matters greatly; and indeed to some extent it does. However there remain some problems. An obvious one is that it cannot cover completely autonomous vessels at the level of MASS 4. If there is no human being in charge at all (save perhaps someone on call in case of emergency) and navigation is entirely under the control of pre-programmed artificial intelligence, then clearly there is no person with command or charge.

Furthermore, there may be difficulties even with autonomous ships at level MASS 3 under the control of an SBC. True, on the basis that a land-based master was possible one could shift the master's status landwards to the SBC. However, even this is not quite as simple as it seems.

One problem is that with autonomous vessels, navigational functions will be shared between at least two human participants: the programmer of the software for the vessel's autonomous operation on the voyage, and the actual SBC who monitors her progress and where necessary navigates her by remote control. Who then is master?

We might solve this by choosing the SBC, in that their control is more immediate and hands-on. But if we do, this solution promptly generates another problem: we then get a multiplicity of masters. Assuming three shifts in a 24-hour period, there will be at least three SBCs in control during any one day, if not more (a point that might arise if control is shifted from one onshore centre to another). Furthermore, to make life even more complex, each controller will probably be in remote control of more than one vessel in their shift. This is a far cry from the traditional practice of one ship, one master; traditional definitions become unworkable, and will have to be adjusted.

Thirdly, the master also has non-navigational functions. He is responsible for supervising the loading, stowing and discharge of cargo carried on the vessel; further, while he no longer generally signs bills of lading, he is responsible for ensuring that they are accurate in what they record. These functions will require someone's physical presence at the ports of loading and discharge; since they cannot be assigned to the SBC, they will in practice have to be fulfilled by port agents or employees on the spot. Once again, the problem is one of multiplicity; instead of the regulatory governance of a single individual, we have these regulatory functions split between a variety of different individuals spread throughout the globe in different onshore locations.

Fourthly, the master has a number of disciplinary and compliance functions, for example as regards control of those on board the vessel, control of access to it, obedience to shore authorities, and such matters as automatic authority to engage salvage services.

There seems no doubt that if intolerable uncertainty is to be avoided, these definitional points will need to be resolved in some amendment of the relevant IMO regimes and UNCLOS.

II. The Issues Arising

Unmanned vessels at MASS levels 3 and 4 will face regulatory obstacles in the following areas which will be considered throughout this chapter:

a. manning requirements;
b. references to master, crew and onboard human activity;
c. documentary requirements;
d. vessel construction and design requirements.

The absence of regulations in connection with unmanned vessels will also prove an obstacle to their acceptance by port and coastal states, in particular with regard to standards for software and hardware used in operating unmanned vessels, and in respect of training and certification standards for onshore operators involved in remote operation of vessels. The chapter will conclude with recommendations for clarification, and amendment of the existing regulatory structure to accommodate the operation of unmanned vessels.

A. Manning Requirements

There is no rule of international or treaty law requiring a vessel to be manned in order to be registered; such matters are for flag states to determine, including (subject to what is said below) the acceptability of unmanned vessels. Under Article 91 of the United Nations Convention on the Law of the Sea (UNCLOS), it is for every state 'to fix the conditions for the grant of its nationality to ships, for the registration of ships in its territory, and for the right to fly its flag'.[7] It follows that a state can choose to register unmanned ships, or not to do so, or to set conditions for doing so. Similarly, with port states, UNCLOS does not qualify the rights of states to regulate the admission of vessels to their ports, thus leaving them free in the absence of clear abuse of rights[8] to deny them admission to their internal waters, something which, in the absence of a satisfactory regulatory framework being established through the IMO many states may well elect to do. In practice however this may not be very important in the early phases, since the initial phase of unmanned vessels is likely to be coastal trading within the territorial sea of the

[7] Subject to the existence of a genuine link between the state and the ship. Art 91(2) provides that 'Every State shall issue to ships to which it has granted the right to fly its flag documents to that effect.'

[8] See the general reference in Art 300 'Good faith and abuse of rights: States Parties shall fulfil in good faith the obligations assumed under this Convention and shall exercise the rights, jurisdiction and freedoms recognized in this Convention in a manner which would not constitute an abuse of right.' An unmanned vessel will almost certainly constitute a ship and as such under Art 17 of UNCLOS would have the right of innocent passage through the territorial sea.

flag state – as contemplated for the *Yara Birkeland*, which will be sailing exclusively between ports in Norway, in Norwegian waters.

On manning as such, however, Article 94 of UNCLOS sets out certain duties of the flag state. Paragraph 3 requires every state to:

> Take such measures for ships flying its flag as are necessary to ensure safety at sea with regard, *inter alia*, to: … (b) the manning of ships, labour conditions and the training of crews, taking into account the applicable international instruments.

Paragraph 4 goes on to provide that:

> Such measures shall include those necessary to ensure: … (b) that each ship is in the charge of a master and officers who possess appropriate qualifications, in particular in seamanship, navigation, communications and marine engineering, and that the crew is appropriate in qualification and numbers for the type, size, machinery and equipment of the ship.

Paragraph 5 requires the flag state in taking these measures

> To conform to generally accepted international regulations, procedures and practices and to take any steps which may be necessary to secure their observance.

However, this does not seem as such to rule out registering unmanned vessels. The 'accepted international regulations' referred to in UNCLOS are contained in the IMO Conventions, notably SOLAS (Safety of Life at Sea) and the International Safety Management (ISM) Code. SOLAS in Chapter V, regulation 14, requires, subject to exceptions,[9] that '[f]rom the point of view of the safety of life at sea, all ships shall be sufficiently and efficiently manned'. Similarly the ISM Code requires owners to ensure that ships are 'manned with qualified, certificated and medically fit seafarers in accordance with national and international requirements; and … appropriately manned in order to encompass all aspects of maintaining safe operation on board'.[10] This does not however prescribe any particular level of manning, and does not, it is suggested, require the presence of a crew actually on board (though this might be made explicit in any revision). It is, in other words, left to the flag state to decide what constitutes sufficient and efficient manning, and if a vessel is effectively and safely controlled from shore, the answer may be nil.[11]

[9] Exemptions. Chapter 1. Reg 4(b) allows the flag state to exempt any ship which embodies features of a novel kind from requirements of Chapters II-1, II-2, III and IV. Flag administrations may accept equivalent solutions if satisfied at least as effective as that required by SOLAS.

[10] ISM 6.2.

[11] The responses to the CMI's recent questionnaire on unmanned vessels on this issue, 2.2, showed a majority of MLAs considered that potential inconsistencies should be resolved through measures at IMO level. The British Maritime Law Association stated that Art 94's requirements were not prescriptive and arguably permitted unmanned operation if the relevant ship's autonomous navigation system were sufficiently safe. The French and Irish MLAs considered that UNCLOS would require amendment in order to allow unmanned ships (Fre, Iri). See ch 2 of this book for support for this view. The MLAs of Brazil, Canada and Italy took no position on this issue but considered the wording of Art 94 excluded unmanned operations 'but are hesitant to exclude that a teleological interpretation could not lead to another conclusion'.

Nevertheless, occasionally there is a manning requirement that might be taken to require crew on board, and which may therefore need some kind of amendment. One such is contained in the IMO's Polar Code, which requires ship operators to 'ensure that masters, chief mates and officers in charge of a navigational watch on board ships operating in polar waters shall have completed training to attain the abilities that are appropriate to the capacity to be filled and duties and responsibilities to be taken up, taking into account the provisions of the STCW Convention and the STCW Code …'[12]

B. References to Onboard Human Activity by Master or Crew

In a number of cases Convention regimes refer to, or at least assume, onboard activity by master and crew.

(i) The Master's Duty to Render Assistance

Three conventions impose a personal duty on the master to render assistance to persons in distress at sea. This raises issues as to who, if anyone, will constitute the master, and what would be the content of the obligation in the case of an unmanned ship.

The first of these provisions, all of which are in fairly similar terms, is Art. 98(1) of UNCLOS which imposes the following obligation on the flag state in respect of the obligation of masters of vessels flying its flag to render assistance to ship/crew/passengers when possible:

> Every state shall require the master of a ship flying its flag, *in so far as he can do so without serious danger to the ship* [emphasis added], the crew or the passengers:
>
> (a) to render assistance to any person found at sea in danger of being lost;
> (b) to proceed with all possible speed to the rescue of persons in distress, if informed of their need of assistance, *in so far as such action may reasonably be expected of him* [emphasis added];
> (c) after a collision, to render assistance to the other ship, its crew and its passengers and, where possible, to inform the other ship of the name of his own ship, its port of registry and the nearest port at which it will call.

Similarly, Chapter V, regulation 33 of SOLAS provides that the 'master of *a ship at sea which is in a position to be able to provide assistance* [emphasis added]', on receiving a signal from any source that persons are in distress at sea, is bound to proceed with all speed to their assistance. Article 11 of the 1910 Salvage Convention and Article 10(1) of the 1989 Salvage Convention provide, in similar terms, that 'every master is bound, *so far as he can do so without serious danger to his vessel* [emphasis added] and persons thereon, to render assistance to any person in danger of being lost at sea.'

[12] Polar Code, para 12.2.

The master's obligation to render assistance is thus not absolute and is qualified by the italicised wordings. There seems no reason to think, either, that any of these provisions requires an onboard master, or that they require anything more of a shore-based controller (assuming he would count as master) than that he communicate the need for help to other vessels in the area and to the coastal authorities. This is something which needs to be clarified. The majority of responses of national maritime law associtations to the CMI's 2017 questionnaire stated 'That whereas the mere fact that the ship is unmanned does not discharge the master from providing whatever assistance the ship is capable of, the fact that the ship is unmanned may de facto limit the scope of the duty since it would be limited to what is inter alia technically possible.' By contrast, the view of the French MLA was that a ship which is not technically able to render assistance should not be allowed to sail. The Maltese MLA concluded that the incapability of an unmanned ship to adhere with the requirements to render assistance could preclude it from flying the Maltese flag.[13]

It should be noted that the same seems true of the two assistance obligations imposed under UK municipal law by sections 92 and 93 of the Merchant Shipping Act 1995, requiring a master to render 'such assistance as is practicable' after a collision and, on receiving an aircraft's distress signal at sea, proceed with all speed to provide assistance 'unless he is unable, or in the special circumstances of the case considers it unreasonable or unnecessary, to do so'. Again, it seems clear that any duty to assist would be satisfied by summoning help, and that there is no need for the 'master' to be on board.

(ii) Other Onboard Personnel Operations

Some other regulations under Convention regimes assume the presence of a master or crew on board.

First, there are notification requirements. For example, under MARPOL, Annex V, regulation 10.1, every ship of 12 metres or more in length overall has to display placards which notify the crew and passengers of the disposal requirements for rubbish. Again, SOLAS requires training manuals about the use of escape craft and fire safety to be provided in crew mess-rooms and cabins.[14] Such requirements need not detain us for long in connection with unmanned ships. Clearly they make no sense if there is no one on board; and while they probably would be held not to apply anyway,[15] it would be as well expressly to disapply them.

Secondly, there are requirements for organisation and supervision of evacuation and life-saving. Under SOLAS, for example, there must be a sufficient number of trained persons on board for mustering and assisting untrained persons.[16]

[13] CMI responses to questionnaire, 3.3.

[14] SOLAS III, reg 35; SOLAS, II-2, reg 15.2.3.

[15] If only because an unmanned vessel would not have crew to notify, or crew cabins or mess-rooms where such things were required to be displayed.

[16] SOLAS III, reg 10.

Again, under the Polar Code there are similar provisions about fire and evacuation safety.[17]

Thirdly, there are provisions of the Collision Regulations Convention which seem to imply the presence of a crew. Two are worth mentioning. One is the slew of rules relating to the rules of the road – overtaking situations, crossing situations, etc – contained in Part II. Importantly, the heading to this section states that it applies to vessels 'in sight of one another', a phrase used to distinguish the situation from one where each is aware of the other's presence only, say, by virtue of radar. However it would, to say the least, be somewhat curious to say that two entirely unmanned vessels were 'in sight of one another' when there was no human eye on either vessel to see the other.

If the rules had to be interpreted in the context of autonomous ships, it is to be hoped that this would be done purposively and that vessels would be regarded as 'in sight' of one another if a reasonably observant officer of the watch on each vessel would have seen the other, even if there was no one on board. Nevertheless, there is a great deal to be said for putting the point beyond doubt and extending the definition of 'in sight of each other' accordingly.

The second is rule 5 of the Convention, which requires every vessel at all times to 'maintain a proper look-out by sight and hearing as well as by all available means appropriate in the prevailing circumstances and conditions'. Arguably this requires actual sight and hearing. True, the idea of a lookout by sight might be stretched to cover sight through an onshore computer screen; but it would seem difficult to say that one was maintaining a proper lookout by hearing from the mere presence of a loudspeaker array thousands of miles away, however many microphones were strategically placed on board. There is, it is submitted, an urgent need for measures to be taken to update the Collision Regulations to clarify what amounts to an adequate lookout in the case of autonomous vessels.

(iii) Labour Law and Seafarers

SBCs may undertake many of the functions of the master, but their employment will be entirely shore-bound. The International Labour Organisation's Maritime Labour Convention 2006 deals with the living and working conditions of seafarers, defined in Article 2(f) as 'any person who is employed or engaged or works in any capacity on board a ship to which this Convention applies'. Clearly, the Convention will have no relevance to unmanned ships which have no crew on board. Similarly, the master's lien for wages and disbursements will not be available to the SBC. The lien presupposes some onboard presence on the vessel by the master as part

[17] Notably, para 12.3 of ch 7 (Fire safety/protection): 'The goal of this chapter is to ensure that fire safety systems and appliances are effective and operable, and that means of escape remain available so that persons on board can safely and swiftly escape to the lifeboat and liferaft embarkation deck under the expected environmental conditions.'

of the crew.[18] The provisions in Part III of the Merchant Shipping Act 1995 which apply to 'masters and seamen employed *in* sea-going ships [emphasis added]' will also have no application to the SBC who is not employed in a sea-going ship.

(iv) Ship Security Officers

As currently drafted, the ISPS Convention requires the designation of an onboard security officer responsible to the master.[19]

(v) Watchkeeping Officers

Regulation VII of the STCW Regulations 2010 currently requires watch officers keeping the bridge and engineering watches to be physically present on the bridge or in the engine room as the case may be.[20] In addition there is a requirement for a continuous watch on board while in port over dangerous cargo.[21] These requirements will clearly have to be modified in the case of wholly autonomous vessels.

(vi) Criminal Law and the Master

The master may face criminal charges in respect of his operation of the vessel before the courts of a coastal state. A notorious example of this is the prison sentence imposed by the Spanish Courts on Captain Mangouras, the master of the *Prestige*, in connection with the oil spill from the vessel when it broke up in Spain's exclusive economic zone (EEZ) in 2002. But this liability is also possible in the UK. The master, for example, is criminally liable for oil pollution emanating from his ship,[22] subject to limited defences,[23] for various other environmental wrongdoings[24] and generally for acts done that endanger his ship, other ships or structures, or persons.[25] So, too, the master, together with the owner, is guilty of

[18] See Clarke J in *The Ever Success* [1999] 1 Lloyd's Rep. 824, 832: 'In my judgment the authorities show that a master or a seaman is entitled to wages and thus to a co-extensive maritime lien if he renders the service appropriate to his rank. That is as, say, master, chief engineer or seaman. He must be part of the crew of the ship, but need not necessarily render the service on board the ship or live on board the ship, but the service must be in a real sense referable to the ship and the service must be rendered during a period when the particular claimant can fairly be said to be part of the crew of the ship.' The SBC cannot be said to be part of the crew of the ship, as there is no crew.

[19] See ISPS Code, Art 1.6. 'Ship security officer means the person *on board the ship* [emphasis added], accountable to the master, designated by the company as responsible for the security of the ship, including implementation and maintenance of the ship security plan, and for liaison with the company security officer and port facility security officers.'

[20] See regs VII/2, VII/24, VII/64, VII/65, VII/71.

[21] See reg VII/105.

[22] Merchant Shipping Act 1995, s 131.

[23] See s 132.

[24] See ss 135–36.

[25] See s 58(2).

an offence if a ship which is in a port in the UK, or is a UK ship and is in any other port, is dangerously unsafe,[26] and also for failure to carry an oil record book in a UK ship.[27] Discharges of oil into the sea when done with (i) intent, (ii) recklessly, or (iii) with serious negligence attract the highest penal sanctions, with the owner and master liable for a fine of up to £250,000.[28] It should be noted that unmanned ships make it much harder for a port state to get hold of the functional equivalent of the master, who may be located in a distant state.[29]

C. Documentary Requirements

A variety of documentary obligations fall on the master under various international conventions. MARPOL provides reporting obligations in the event of oil spills and requires the keeping of various record books,[30] with detailed provisions for their filling-out.[31] So, too, there are detailed documentary requirements contained in the FAL Convention,[32] the Polar Code,[33] the SOLAS Convention,[34] the STCW Convention[35] and the ISM Convention.[36]

The IMO civil liability conventions in force, the CLC 1969 and 1992, the Bunker Oil Pollution Convention 2001, the 2007 Nairobi Wreck Removal Convention, all contain mandatory insurance provisions with the requirement that a certificate evidencing this be kept on board the vessel,[37] as does EU Directive 2009/20/EC on the insurance of shipowners for maritime claims.[38] The UK's implementing

[26] S 98(1) of the Merchant Shipping Act 1995.

[27] S 142 of the Merchant Shipping Act 1995.

[28] The Merchant Shipping (Prevention of Oil Pollution) Regulations 1996 reg 36A applying penalties to breaches of regs 12, 13 and 16. The regulation gives effect to MARPOL and the stricter implementation of these regulations in EU Directive 2009.

[29] Veal, R and Tsimplis, M, 'The integration of unmanned ships into the *lex maritima*', (2017) LMCLQ 303, 318, write that 'One option would be a representative of the unmanned shipping company in each country who would be criminally liable for the ship's actions, in addition to the shore-based "master" and the owner. Such an arrangement could be effected by coastal states as a condition of entry of unmanned ships into their ports.' In effect, the employment of a hostage in every port of call.

[30] See MARPOL, Art 5.2.

[31] See generally Annex 1, regs 17, 36; Annex 2, regs 15, 16, 18.

[32] See Appendix 5 ('Certificates and documents required to be carried on board'). It would be more practical for unmanned ships to require these documents to be available in an electronic format. This would require more specific guidelines on the availability of, and access to, such documents. This matter goes beyond FAL, however, as the same issue is raised in a number of other IMO conventions. See also 'Guidelines for the use of electronic certificates', FAL.5/Circ.39/Rev.2.

[33] See para 1.3.1: 'Every ship to which this Code applies shall have on board a valid Polar Ship certificate'.

[34] See SOLAS I, regs 3–6, 3–7 and 16.

[35] See STCW Convention, reg I/11.

[36] See ISM Convention, paras 11.3, 13.6, 13.7, 13.9, 13.10.

[37] The 1992 CLC Art VII(4) requires the certificate to be carried on board, as does the Bunker Convention Art 7(4) and Art 12(4) of the Nairobi Convention.

[38] The UK has implemented this through the Merchant Shipping (Compulsory Insurance of Shipowners for Maritime Claims) Regulations 2012, SI 2012/2267, implementing EU Directive 2009/20/EC on the insurance of shipowners for maritime claims.

legislation requires the relevant certificates to be carried on board the ship and to be produced on demand by the master 'to any officer of customs and excise or of the Secretary of State and, if the ship is a United Kingdom ship, to any proper officer'. Failure to carry the certificate or to produce it as required renders the master liable on summary conviction to a fine not exceeding level 4 on the standard scale.[39] Unmanned vessels cannot comply with these regulations and provisions will need to be made to allow the provision of these certificates to be made electronically.[40]

The FAL Convention has made provision for the certificates it requires[41] to be provided in electronic form.[42] However, this does not affect the certification requirements in the IMO Civil Liability Conventions or in EU Directive 2009/20/EC on the insurance of shipowners for maritime claims. Individual contracting states may, however, conclude agreements with each other for acceptance of electronic versions of these certificates. The report of the Danish Maritime Law Association in 2017 notes that Denmark has already adapted its regulation to the issue of digital ship certificates and has, furthermore, concluded a memorandum of understanding with the Singaporean and Norwegian maritime authorities on 24 April 2017 on the spread of digital certificates internationally.[43]

D. Vessel Construction, Design and Operation: SOLAS, ISPS and Beyond

SOLAS contains a large volume of construction and design requirements. Many of these serve to protect the integrity of the vessel itself or its cargo, or that of the environment. To this extent there is no reason not to carry them over directly and apply them as such to autonomous vessels. Examples would be rules about protective coatings for ballast tanks,[44] the integrity of watertight bulkheads,[45] the robustness of propulsion machinery[46] or fire protection.[47] This is on the common sense basis

[39] S 163(6).

[40] The FAL Convention has made provision for the certificates it requires to be provided in electronic form but this does not affect the certification requirements in the IMO Civil Liability Conventions or in EU Directive 2009/20/EC on the insurance of shipowners for maritime claims.

[41] Art 2.1 provides that these are the following: general declaration; cargo declaration; ship's stores declaration; crew's effects declaration; crew list; passenger list; dangerous goods manifest; the document required under the Universal Postal Convention for mail; maritime declaration of health; security-related information as required under SOLAS reg XI-2/9.2.2; advance electronic cargo information for customs risk assessment purposes; advanced notification form for waste delivery to port reception facilities, when communicated to the IMO.

[42] See Arts 1.3bis–1.3quin.

[43] Danish Maritime Authority Report December 2017, 'Analysis of regulatory barriers to the use of autonomous ships', 3.3.3, www.dma.dk/Documents/Publikationer/Analysis%20of%20Regulatory%20Barriers%20to%20the%20Use%20of%20Autonomous%20Ships.pdf.

[44] SOLAS II-1, reg 3-2.

[45] SOLAS II-1, reg 13-1.

[46] SOLAS II-1, reg 27.

[47] See SOLAS II-2 generally.

that even if there is no risk to life because there is none on board, states have both a legal claim and a moral duty to limit marine casualties as far as possible. Again, it is increasingly the fashion to introduce so-called 'goal-based' standards that are not rigidly prescriptive, but are essentially open-ended. For example, bulk carriers and oil tankers constructed after 2016 are required to be built so as to be 'safe and environmentally friendly, when properly operated and maintained under the specified operating and environmental conditions, in intact and specified damage conditions, throughout their life'.[48] Such standards are inherently flexible; in so far as there are few or no people on board, requirements for, say, health and safety will naturally attenuate.

III. Conclusion

Many requirements in the IMO Conventions will need to be reconsidered and either disapplied or altered in the case of autonomous vessels. These fall into a number of categories.

One is redundant health and safety rules for the protection of mariners. The requirement to limit noise in engine rooms,[49] for example, makes no sense where there is no one to be deafened by it; so too, arguably, the need for fire notification and evacuation facilities for use at sea,[50] not to mention the need to carry large numbers of safety training manuals.[51] In this category also might fall the majority of the detailed rules in Chapter III of SOLAS on life-saving devices such as lifeboats, life-belts and life-rafts: there is precious little need for these where there are no souls on board to save. This is, however, subject to one caveat: were the duty to rescue those found in danger of being lost at sea to extend to requiring unmanned vessels to have facilities to take them on board, then there would be a need for at least some escape facilities as well.

Another is requirements for facilities for maintenance and human monitoring at sea: for example, rules requiring access to tanker bows in heavy weather,[52] regular inspection of watertight doors on passage,[53] and the possibility of operating ship security alert systems from the bridge and from one other location.[54] Such requirements may not fall to be eliminated, since inspections of this kind, and the monitoring of security alerts, remain desirable even in unmanned vessels; but they will have to be adjusted to allow them to be done automatically.

A third is detailed requirements for control. The existing SOLAS scheme assumes a physical 'navigation bridge' with an officer of the watch on it, from

[48] SOLAS II-1, reg 3-10.
[49] SOLAS II-1, reg 3-12.
[50] SOLAS II-2, reg 12-13. See too Polar Code, ch 7.
[51] SOLAS III, reg 35.
[52] SOLAS II-1, reg 3-3.
[53] SOLAS II-1, reg 21.
[54] SOLAS XI-2, reg 6.

which immediate control of the vessel can be carried on. A number of specific requirements are based on this. They include rules as to the details of the steering gear,[55] propulsion controls,[56] propeller pitch controls[57] and watertight compartment controls[58] to be provided on the bridge; there are also provisions for vocal communications.[59] Another category of regulations of this sort is the requirement for pilot transfers to be supervised by a qualified person with communication with the bridge.[60] Clearly these will mainly have to be modified so as to allow shore-based control (though some may become entirely redundant: for example, requirements as to voice communication devices). Away from the bridge, there are requirements for such things as emergency power and an emergency electrical switchboard near the emergency power source.[61]

Fourthly, the detailed requirements for electronic communications systems again assume a crew on board in regular communication with the shore and with other vessels. These include, for example, not only radar.[62] but a requirement for onboard radio personnel,[63] a VHF unit on the bridge,[64] continuous radio watch[65] and other matters too. These include facilities for sending distress calls by at least two separate and independent means,[66] and equipment capable of receiving shore-to-ship distress alerts, and transmitting and receiving ship-to-ship distress alerts, search and rescue co-ordinating communications, on-scene communications, maritime safety information, general radio communications to and from shore-based radio systems and bridge-to-bridge communications.[67] In addition to the requirements for hardware, there is also a requirement for the master to communicate any navigational dangers he encounters. As regards all these requirements, clearly most elements of these communications have to be maintained. No one would wish, even in the case of autonomous shipping, to remove the requirement for radio watch on distress frequencies, the ability to send distress calls, or facilities for inter-ship communication; even the facility to receive maritime safety notices on board may remain useful, if only because they will need to be relayed if the shore-based controller is outside the range of the transmitting station. But clearly the requirements will have to be adjusted, so as to refer to radio signals being transmitted to and from the shore-based controller via the vessel, rather than to someone on the vessel itself.

[55] SOLAS II-1, reg 29.
[56] SOLAS II-1, reg 49.
[57] SOLAS II-1, reg 31.
[58] SOLAS II-1, reg 13-1.
[59] SOLAS II-1, reg 50.
[60] SOLAS V, reg 23.2.
[61] SOLAS II-1, reg 42.
[62] SOLAS IV, reg 4.
[63] SOLAS IV, reg 16. 'Every ship shall carry personnel qualified for distress and safety radiocommunication purposes to the satisfaction of the Administration'.
[64] SOLAS IV, reg 6.
[65] SOLAS IV, reg 12.
[66] SOLAS IV, reg 4.
[67] SOLAS IV, reg 4.

Fifthly, clarification is needed as to numerous references in the IMO Conventions to 'the master'. The CMI has produced a spreadsheet in its submission to the IMO identifying provisions in the IMO regulations that will need clarification or amendment to deal with unmanned vessels, and identifies numerous provisions with the comment 'interpretation of the master'.[68] A working general definition could be to add to every reference to the 'master' in the IMO Conventions, and in UNCLOS, the words 'or person or persons operating and navigating the vessel'. This would, not, however deal with those provisions in the Conventions that pre-suppose the presence of an onboard crew.

Sixthly, the issue of the documentation that needs to be carried on board vessels, such as the 'blue card' evidencing that mandatory liability insurance is in place, will also need to be addressed by allowing these requirements to be satisfied by electronic certificates.

There is also the need for new standards to be developed by the IMO to deal with autonomous vessels with no crew on board. The STCW will need to be adapted to provide for training and certification standards for remote onshore controllers. These should only be located in states that are signatories to MARPOL. As an initial step, pending the development of specific STCW regulations for SBCs, the IMO could require SBCs to have 'the certifications required by national/international regulation for the ship in question', the phrase which forms part of the EU guidance on MASS testing that came out in October 2020.[69] There is also the need for the IMO to develop regulations on software security. BIMCO and the Comité International Radio Maritime, an organisation involved in the development of the marine electronics industry, have jointly prepared a proposed software maintenance standard that has been sent to the IMO for review. Its goal is to ensure software updates are secure and systematic for maintenance and to minimise hacking and malware problems.[70] The urgency of this issue was brought home by the disruption to Maersk's operation over 10 days in the summer of 2017 as a result of collateral damage from the 'nopetya' programme which probably originated as a cyber attack by Russia on Ukraine by introducing malware into a popular Ukrainian accounting package called 'M.E.Doc'. The IMO has issued MSC-FAL.1/Circ.3 Guidelines on maritime cyber risk management and the Maritime Safety Committee, at its 98th session in June 2017, also adopted Resolution MSC.428(98) – Maritime Cyber Risk Management in Safety Management Systems. The resolution encourages administrations to ensure that cyber risks are appropriately addressed

[68] Annex 2 to the CMI IWG Submission to MSC 99th Session [129–47].

[69] 'The "operators" appointed by the applicant guiding and/or supervising the specific MASS trials/tests, no matter if they are on shore or aboard, should have the certifications required by national/international regulation for the ship in question.' *EU Operational Guidelines for Safe, Secure and Sustainable Trials of Maritime Autonomous Surface Ships (Mass)* 6.1.2, see https://ec.europa.eu/transport/sites/transport/files/guidelines_for_safe_mass.pdf, accessed 25 December 2020.

[70] The IMO was due to consider the standard at the NCSR meeting in February 2018. Pilot tests for the standard were carried out in 2017, and ISO has provisionally accepted the proposal. BIMCO said it expects a working group to complete the standard in 2021, when cyber security is due to become part of ISO standards.

in existing safety management systems (as defined in the ISM Code) no later than the first annual verification of the company's Document of Compliance after 1 January 2021.

SOLAS also needs to be addressed for what it does not contain. Autonomous shipping depends entirely on the features required of the communications and remote control devices used to navigate the vessel when at sea. On these SOLAS has at present nothing to say. There will need to be what is essentially a new chapter. It will have to deal in detail with such matters as the following:

1. The reliability of propulsion and other machinery, such as steering gear, which will have to be controlled for long periods, possibly weeks, from a distance with limited possibilities of interim maintenance.[71]
2. The reliability of ancillary mechanisms such as those used for starting, stopping, controlling and reversing the propulsion machinery. This will be particularly important in manoeuvring, avoiding collisions and stopping the vessel where necessary; in any of these cases a failure could be disastrous.
3. The means of giving notice to shore controllers of dangers to the vessel or cargo, such as fire, smoke or ingress of water.
4. The means of controlling such dangers. Where there is no-one on board the use of reliable and effective automatic fire extinction and other damage control devices is crucial to the avoidance of a serious casualty. The requirements for such equipment, and for its periodic testing, will have to be very detailed and demanding.
5. Similarly, detection and avoidance devices as regards pollution. For example, there would need to be sensitive devices to detect escapes of such things as bunker oil, together with fail-safe machinery for the self-sealing of tanks or the transfer of oil from a ruptured tank to another place of storage.
6. The devices to be carried on board to 'see', 'hear' and detect other vessels and possible hazards.
7. The communications arrays and other electronics to be carried, and their capabilities.
8. The means used to transmit signals to the vessel, their efficiency and any required back-up or spare capacity.

[71] It is possible that onboard robots could be used to attend to some of the interim maintenance tasks currently undertaken by the onboard crew.

2

International Law of the Sea and Autonomous Cargo 'Vessels'

DR YOURI VAN LOGCHEM*

I. Introduction

Autonomous craft operating at sea are not a novelty. One example is their use in a military context, which goes back to the Second World War, when they were employed to clear mines and assess battle damage.[1] Since then, autonomous technology has been introduced in a variety of other offshore contexts as well, including marine scientific research (MSR), surveying activities, and exploring offshore resources.[2] Following debates about the international legal status of maritime craft using autonomous technology for military purposes, and in conducting MSR,[3] the introduction of autonomy in another maritime setting, that of merchant shipping, has put this issue on the international legal radar again.

The use of maritime autonomous craft as a means to transport cargo has yet to take flight; part of the reason for this is that they currently remain in their experimental phase.[4] Closely aligned to this is that whether using autonomous technology in international merchant shipping is poised for a future commercial breakthrough is seen differently.[5] Different views have also emerged over whether fully autonomous craft, or those that enjoy a degree of autonomy but maintain a human presence on board to intervene in their operations when necessary, will emerge as the mainstay for transporting cargo at sea. Between these extremes, there lie various variants of craft that have different levels of autonomy.[6] The level of

* Member of the Institute of International Shipping and Trade Law, Swansea University. The author would like to thank Jessica Schechinger for her invaluable comments. Any faults or omissions are, of course, the sole responsibility of the author.

[1] M Schmitt and D Goddard, 'International Law and the Military Use of Unmanned Maritime Systems' [2016] 98 *International Review of the Red Cross* 567, 570.

[2] E Van Hooydonk, 'The Law of Unmanned Merchant Shipping – An Exploration' [2014] 20 *Journal of International Maritime Law* 403, 404.

[3] Schmitt and Goddard (n 1), 568–69; Van Hooydonk (n 2), 405.

[4] Van Hooydonk (n 2), 404.

[5] ibid 405.

[6] H Ringbom, 'Regulating Autonomous Ships – Concepts, Challenges and Precedents' [2019] 50 *Ocean Development & International Law* 141, 149.

autonomy a craft possesses may well tie in with the ease with which it can be brought under the existing law of the sea framework applicable to international shipping.[7]

Autonomous craft that are currently in existence operate solely in waters that are part of one state's territory, which has allowed for its use.[8] An example is Finland, which has designated part of its internal waters as a testing area for autonomous craft.[9] The international law of the sea framework presently thus lies largely dormant, although in 2017 the UK granted its nationality pursuant to Article 91 of the 1982 Law of the Sea Convention (LOSC or Convention)[10] to an autonomous vessel through registration.[11] Most of the international law of the sea framework will be activated, however, when the voyages of autonomous cargo craft take on an international character: that is, when they travel outside of the territory (ie, internal waters, territorial sea, or archipelagic waters) of the state of nationality.

The use of autonomous technology in international shipping gives rise to various international law of the sea questions. One issue that needs to be placed in the forefront of the analysis is whether the autonomous craft used to the end of transporting goods are vessels/ships. The importance of vessel status is illustrated by the fact that this activates those parts of the international law of the sea dealing with international shipping, including their navigational rights and freedoms; see section IV. Another implication is that if a flag state attributes its nationality to an autonomous 'vessel', various obligations are incumbent on that state. Complicating matters for flag states is that some of these obligations presuppose that a master/crew is present on board a vessel (see section V.B).

At the heart of this chapter lie the public international law aspects connected to maritime autonomous cargo craft; in what follows, these will be referred to as (maritime) autonomous cargo craft, craft or 'vessels'. A discussion of certain aspects that can be considered part of the international legal framework, particularly those treaties adopted by the International Maritime Organisation (IMO), will be touched on here only incidentally. Particularly pertinent for this chapter is the international law of the sea, which divides the seas and oceans into different maritime zones and distributes a broad range of rights and obligations amongst a range of actors: coastal states, port states and flag states. In terms of treaty law, the LOSC will be the main source, as it represents the most elaborate collection of conventional rules of the law of the sea. Outside of a few states, including the UK and Norway, which allow autonomous cargo craft to be registered in their

[7] Ibid 147–48.

[8] 'Kongsberg to Test Autonomous Ship Technology' (*MarineLink*, 21 January 2020), www.marinelink.com/news/kongsberg-test-autonomous-ship-technology-474845, accessed 26 June 2020.

[9] A Felski and K Zwolak, 'The Ocean-Going Autonomous Ship – Challenges and Threats' [2020] 41 *Journal of Marine Science and Engineering* 1, 11.

[10] United Nations Convention on the Law of the Sea (adopted 10 December 1982, entered in force 16 November 1994) 1833 UNTS (LOSC, or Convention).

[11] 'First Unmanned Vessel Joins UK Ship Register', *Offshore Energy*, 14 November 2017, www.offshore-energy.biz/first-unmanned-vessel-joins-uk-ship-register/, accessed 26 June 2020.

registries,[12] state practice or *opinio iuris* is virtually absent, whereby the role of customary international law in determining the legal status of these craft is severely reduced. But this leaves untouched that parts of the LOSC have assumed customary status. Article 92(1) of the LOSC, dealing with exclusive jurisdiction for the flag state over vessels on the high seas, or Article 17 of the same Convention, laying down a right of innocent passage for vessels, are examples of provisions that can be considered customary.[13]

In terms of organisation, the chapter will begin, in section II, by sketching some background to maritime autonomous craft. It will, inter alia, lay out in broad strokes their various applications and that in connection therewith the composition of international legal rules may change. Central to the discussion that follows in section III is the issue of what constitutes a vessel/ship under international law of the sea. Tied to this determination is that vessels/ships are accorded various navigational rights and freedoms under international law of the sea, which will be examined in section IV. The central role of the flag state, with an emphasis on the jurisdiction it has over vessels flying its flag, will be analysed next in section V. Here the different flag state obligations, and the difficulties that may arise when applied to autonomous cargo craft, will be discussed. Assumptions that they qualify as vessels/ships under the LOSC are based on an evolutive/purposive interpretation of its text.[14] Whether interpreting a treaty provision in this way is in line with the rule of treaty interpretation as provided by Article 31(1)(3) of the Vienna Convention on the Law of Treaties (VCLT),[15] lies at the core of what is discussed in sections II.D and VI.A. This is followed by an assessment of what options are available for states to remedy any challenges, gaps or ambiguities that might be present in the existing international law of the sea framework concerning the use of autonomous technology in shipping. Rounding off this chapter are some concluding remarks.

II. Maritime Autonomous Craft and the Law of the Sea: An Overview

Since autonomous technology was first used at sea by navies in the Second World War, its applications have accelerated rapidly, and, beyond that, have taken root in a variety of contexts, including civil ones. Among their wide range of purposes is that autonomous craft can assist in MSR by gathering data, which can be retrieved

[12] R Veal, M Tsimplis and A Serdy, 'The Legal Status and Operation of Unmanned Maritime Vehicles' [2019] 50 *Ocean Development & International Law* 23, 29.

[13] D König, 'Flag of Ships' in R Wolfrum (ed) *The Max Planck Encyclopedia of Public International Law* (OUP, 2009), paras 25–26; RR Churchill and AV Lowe, The Law of the Sea, 3rd edn (Manchester University Press, 1988) 208–209.

[14] Veal, Tsimplis and Serdy (n 12), 27.

[15] Vienna Convention on the Law of Treaties (adopted 23 May 1969, entered into force 27 January 1980) 1115 UNTS 33 (VCLT).

upon the submergence of the autonomous craft, or in the placing of submarine cables on the seabed.[16]

In determining the international legal rules applicable to maritime autonomous craft, several elements need to be taken into consideration. First, their status; ie, are they vessels/ships from the point of view of international law of the sea? Connected to this is that those vessels meeting the requirement may in addition qualify as warships having diplomatic immunity: that is, when they can be brought under the scope of Article 29 of the LOSC. Difficulties may arise in classifying autonomous vessels as warships, however: Article 29 is framed in terms presupposing that a warship must be manned; it inter alia requires that its onboard crew must be under naval discipline.[17] This has led to the suggestion that being manned is an intractable part of a warship,[18] because the text is seemingly clear on this point.[19] Yet the opposite has been argued as well: autonomous (military) craft *simpliciter* can be accorded vessel status.[20] Underlying this view is that the LOSC must be able to keep pace with technological advancements, otherwise it is susceptible to losing its relevance.[21] However that may be, reducing the importance of the warship designation, at least when speaking about autonomous cargo craft, is that when on government service they would enjoy similar privileges to warships, including immunity (see also section IV).[22] Any entitlements of autonomous craft to immunity is connected to two considerations: first, they have to be vessels/ships; and, second, they need to be marked in a way making it clear that they are on government service.[23] If both are met, these autonomous vessels would be immune from the exercise of any jurisdiction by a state different than their flag state, unless, of course, the latter agrees thereto.

Two further variables are relevant in determining the legal rules applicable to autonomous craft: that is, their location and the activity they are engaged in. Depending on the maritime zone involved, coastal states and third states have different rights, freedoms and obligations under international law of the sea. A general rule of thumb is the closer the maritime zone is to a coastal state's coast, the more expansive its jurisdictional reach (see section V).

Consideration must also be given to the possibility of autonomous cargo craft *not* being vessels/ships in the sense of the law of the sea. Even then, however, they

[16] Van Hooydonk (n 2), 404.

[17] Art 29 of the LOSC reads in full: 'For the purposes of this Convention, "warship" means a ship belonging to the armed forces of a State bearing the external marks distinguishing such ships of its nationality, under the command of an officer duly commissioned by the government of the State and whose name appears in the appropriate service list or its equivalent, and manned by a crew which is under regular armed forces discipline.'

[18] D Vallejo, 'Electric Currents: Programming Legal Status in Autonomous Unmanned Maritime Vehicles' [2015] 47 *Case Western Reserve Journal of International Law* 405, 413.

[19] Schmitt and Goddard (n 1), 579.

[20] J Kraska, 'The Law of Unmanned Naval Systems in War and Peace' [2010] 5 *The Journal of Ocean Technology* 44, 50–53.

[21] ibid 50–52.

[22] N Klein, 'Maritime Autonomous Vehicles within the International Law Framework to Enhance Maritime Security' [2019] 95 *International Law Studies* 244, 253.

[23] Schmitt and Goddard (n 1), 579.

would still be governed by the law of the sea. The main difference is that craft not meeting the definition of a vessel/ship do not enjoy navigational rights or freedoms under the LOSC, or general international law. But this does not imply that autonomous craft would not be able to operate at sea.

Within maritime zones that lie beyond the outer limit of the territorial sea, the high seas freedoms would exist, which would encompass the freedom for craft different than vessels to operate as well. To focus on the exclusive economic zone (EEZ), where most of the high seas freedoms would apply (Article 58(2) of the LOSC), this would mean that as long as the operation of craft does not interfere with a coastal state's sovereign rights over natural resources, or any of its other jurisdictional rights, including concerning MSR, they can operate there more freely. Difficulties in terms of their operation are likely to centre around those maritime zones that are under the sovereignty of the coastal state, including territorial sea areas and archipelagic waters. Here only vessels enjoy passage rights.

The crux of the matter lies in the fact that with regard to craft that are not vessels in the sense of the law of the sea, conflicts may arise between the interests of the coastal states and those of other states, who might take different positions on whether operating them outside the limits of a coastal state's territory is acceptable. These conflicts will have to be resolved by falling back on the generic formula provided in Article 59 of the LOSC. Conflicts that emerge pursuant to this provision have be resolved on the 'basis of equity and in the light of all the relevant circumstances, taking into account the respective importance of the interests involved to the parties as well as to the international community as a whole'.

Another element that is relevant is the type of activity the autonomous craft is engaged in, as the applicable legal rules might shift according to the purpose to which it is being used. To illustrate this point, employing autonomous craft to conduct MSR within another coastal state's EEZ would require the latter's previous consent (Article 246 of the LOSC); whether these craft meet the vessel definition is irrelevant in this context. Despite their various uses, in what follows, the focus will be overwhelmingly on the use of autonomous technology in the activity of shipping goods at sea internationally.

A further relevant aspect is the level of autonomy a maritime craft is imbued with. From the technological point of view, there are various ways to distinguish between different types of maritime craft, carrying either a reduced crew or where it is fully absent. A binary division is as follows: there are those craft where the link with human control is cut completely, in that its operation is based on algorithms performed by computer systems, and craft that remain reliant on humans in some capacity; for example, where there is an onshore controller or a skeleton crew on board, who can take over the craft's operation if necessary.[24] More complicated distinctions, distinguishing multiple levels of autonomy, are also made. Here a wide spectrum of stages of autonomy is normally recognised, and with each further step on the spectrum the element of human control lessens, to

[24] Klein (n 22), 249.

culminate in the final step to where it has disappeared completely.[25] In this chapter, much of the focus will be on those autonomous craft where a master and/or crew are not physically present on board. The key factor underlying this emphasis is that these will be the types of autonomous cargo 'vessels' which will present most international law of the sea questions. To the contrary, if some seafarers and the master remain *on board*, fewer challenges seem to be presented by the international law of the sea framework. Only in some instances, however, is a distinction drawn between autonomous vessels that operate independently of human intervention, and those that are remote-controlled.

III. The Threshold Question of Defining Autonomous Cargo Craft as Ships/Vessels

On the receiving end of navigational rights and freedoms under international law are vessels/ships.[26] A first hurdle is that not all autonomous cargo craft currently in existence necessarily comply with the 'normal' appearance of a merchant ship/vessel; they are much smaller – for example, most of them do not exceed 20 metres in length.[27] An implication of their smaller measurements, and if *arguendo* assumed to be a vessel/ship, is that they may well fail to meet the tonnage requirements to be bound by certain international shipping regulations – for example, the majority of annexes to the International Convention for the Safety of Life at Sea (SOLAS)[28] would not apply to them.[29]

However, this would leave untouched the fact that those smaller-sized vessels that go to sea need to have a nationality. Through the granting of its nationality to a vessel, a flag state takes on several obligations in connection therewith. If it fails to implement a flag state duty, a violation of international law occurs (see section V).

As time progresses, however, differences in the general design of autonomous cargo craft are expected to disappear, by them taking on features that are comparable to the merchant vessels plying the seas and oceans presently.[30]

To now focus on the issue of vessel status, and the key factor that has led to questions arising around whether autonomous cargo craft meet the required definition: that is, their operation without a master, officers or crew on board.

[25] Danish Study 'Analysis of Regulatory Barriers to the Use of Autonomous Ships' by Ramboll & Core, 2017, attached to IMO Doc. MSC 99/INF.3, p 7.

[26] R Veal and H Ringbom, 'Unmanned Ships and the International Regulatory Framework' [2017] 23 *The Journal of International Maritime Law* 100, 102.

[27] 'CMI Questionnaire on Unmanned Ships – Response by Maritime Law Association of South Africa' 1, https://comitemaritime.org/wp-content/uploads/2018/05/South-africa.pdf, accessed 26 June 2020 (Response of South Africa); R Veal and M Tsimplis, 'The Integration of Unmanned Ships into the *Lex Maritima*' [2017] *Lloyd's Maritime and Commercial Law Quarterly* 303, 306–07.

[28] International Convention for the Safety of Life at Sea (adopted 1 November 1974, entered into force 25 May 1980) 1184 UNTS (SOLAS).

[29] Veal, Tsimplis and Serdy (n 12), 25.

[30] Veal and Tsimplis (n 27), 307.

A. Reviewing the State of the Art

Aside from limited exceptions,[31] the question of whether, based on the disappearance of an onboard human presence, these maritime craft shall be denied ship/vessel status, has been answered in the negative in literature.[32] On the whole, there seems to be a trend towards bringing autonomous cargo craft under the scope of those parts of the framework of the LOSC whose activation is preconditioned on them being vessels/ships. One difficulty is that the reasons underpinning these positions are not always explained on paper, or are given short thrift.[33] An argument that has surfaced, however, concentrates on the similarities between manned vessels and their unmanned counterparts: that is, they are virtually identical in terms of function, and, although currently not the case, in the future will also be in terms of size.[34] By the same logic, a 'peculiar' dichotomy would be introduced if concluding differently: whereas manned vessels are subject to international shipping regulations, their autonomous counterparts would not be.[35]

Some conclusions that autonomous cargo craft have vessel status under international law of the sea are accompanied by wording that suggests there are difficulties with accepting this view. Illustrating this is the conclusion reached by Veal and Ringbom: autonomous cargo craft 'probably' have to be considered as vessels under international law. The word 'probably' is repeated in the Comité Maritime International report, where at the root of the conclusion that autonomous cargo craft meet the qualification of a vessel/ship lies the aspect of their apparent similarity in terms of 'size, features and functions'.[36]

At the other end of the spectrum, and arguably countermanding the more tentative conclusions, are authors claiming that autonomous craft are clearly vessels/ships under international law.[37] Along these lines, Kraska presented a more sweeping argument, which can be placed at the extreme end of the spectrum: maritime autonomous craft *simpliciter* are ships/vessels. To conclude differently would be tantamount to excessive lawyering, in his view.[38] After reflecting on the existing literature, which at the time was rather limited, Van Hooydonk stated in broad terms that 'Most commentators undoubtedly rightly assume that for the purposes of the law of the sea unmanned vessels must be regarded as ships.'[39] Interestingly, the same

[31] Schmitt and Goddard (n 1), 579.

[32] Kraska (n 20), 50–53; O Daum and T Stellpflug 'The Implications of International Law on Unmanned Merchant Vessels' [2017] 23 *The Journal of International Maritime Law* 363, 365–69.

[33] Veal and Ringbom (n 26), 103, 116.

[34] 'CMI International Working Group Position Paper on Unmanned Ships and the International Regulation Framework' 3, https://comitemaritime.org/wp-content/uploads/2018/05/CMI-Position-Paper-on-Unmanned-Ships.pdf, accessed 26 June 2020 (CMI International Working Group Position Paper); Veal and Ringbom (n 26), 102.

[35] Veal and Ringbom (n 26), 103.

[36] CMI International Working Group Position Paper (n 34), 3.

[37] Kraska (n 20), 50–53.

[38] ibid 64.

[39] Van Hooydonk (n 2), 402.

author proceeds to seemingly undermine his own argument, by concluding, utilising the same caveat as some of the previously mentioned authors, that autonomous cargo craft 'probably will have to be regarded as vessels/ships'.[40]

To put matters into their proper perspective, although the majority opinion considers autonomous craft as ships/vessels under international law of the sea, or at least 'probably' or 'most likely',[41] the appropriateness of this conclusion has been doubted by a few authors. In this vein, Schmitt and Goddard, writing primarily on the status of unmanned systems for military purposes under international law, formulate a broader argument applicable across the broad spectrum of autonomous craft: in light of there being no crew, the LOSC 'is inapplicable to them'.[42]

But what underlies the appearance of the word 'probably' in several conclusions reached about autonomous cargo craft having vessel status? Perhaps, the more cautious conclusions are indicative that something is not sitting well with bringing these autonomous craft within the scope of meaning of vessel/ship under the LOSC. Where the rub would perceivably lie under this reading of the LOSC is that this concerns a future rather than current use of the oceans, which those parts of this convention seem prima facie ill-suited to deal with. Connected to this is that the VCLT, laying down the primary rule for interpreting treaties, places emphasis on the text of a treaty: in a nutshell, that is, to establish the ordinary meaning of the wording (Article 31), supplemented by its context (Article 32). Before delving into this latter issue in section D, first it is necessary to explore what constitutes a vessel/ship under international law of the sea (section B), and more specifically the LOSC (section C). Closely aligned to this is that vessels/ships enjoy entitlements to navigational rights and freedoms (see section IV). Further, if ships are seagoing, they will need to have a nationality, whereby several obligations for the flag state concerning vessels/ships flying their flag are concurrently activated (section V).

B. What Constitutes a Ship/Vessel under International Law of the Sea?

The law of the sea addresses three aspects related to ships/vessels: first, their navigational rights and freedoms; second, when coastal states would be allowed to act against vessels navigating in their maritime zones; and, third, the obligations flag states have over vessels having their nationality.[43]

Complicating matters is that no universally accepted definition of a vessel/ship exists on the international level, neither in treaty law nor customary international law. Looking at conventional law, at the First Law of the Sea Conference (UNCLOS I),

[40] ibid.
[41] Veal and Tsimplis (n 27), 331.
[42] Schmitt and Goddard (n 1), 577.
[43] Veal and Ringbom (n 26), 102.

the special rapporteur raised doubts as to whether a definition should be made for a vessel/ship in a future treaty.[44] This was despite the introduction at some point during the negotiations of a definition of a ship as: 'Un navire est un engin apte à se mouvoir dans les espaces maritimes à l'exclusion de l'espace aérien, avec l'armement et l'équipage qui lui sont propres en vue des services que comporte l'industrie à laquelle il est employé'.[45] Here, the reference to a ship needing to be properly equipped with a crew in order to be fit to operate suggests a human presence on board.[46] The doubts voiced by the special rapporteur as to whether to attempt to define a ship/vessel were seemingly widely shared by states within UNCLOS I, as the 1958 Geneva Conventions are uniformly silent on the issue.[47] Other shipping treaties, including the 1910 Collision Convention[48] and the 1999 Arrest Convention,[49] follow a similar approach.[50]

Attention has been subsequently regularly directed towards clarifying what constitutes a vessel/ship from the view of international law of the sea generally;[51] although it has also been suggested to put this intractable matter, and the more futile exercise to provide a universal definition, to rest.[52] To blunt the impact of the absence of a universal definition as to what constitutes a ship/vessel on the international level, a common approach has been to analyse definitions in various international shipping conventions,[53] and to, subsequently, reduce these definitions to a holistic one of what can be considered a vessel/ship under international law of the sea.[54] More specifically, the approach has been to ignore the differences that are present in the various definitions of a vessel/ship found in international shipping conventions and, rather, focus on the constants contained therein. When going along this route, their overall similarity seems to lie in three features, which are recognised across the range of these conventions: a vessel/ship must be man-made; it must have the capability to navigate on water; and it must be used for transportation.[55] The conclusion that would follow is that autonomous cargo craft meet this definition.

The value of this exercise of comparing definitions, to then extract the common elements from them to provide a universal definition, has been rightly

[44] ILC, 'Summary Records of the Seventh Session' (1955), vol I, UN Doc A/CN.4/79 s II, 10.

[45] ILC, 'Documents of the Sixth Session Including the Report of the Commission to the General Assembly' (1954), vol II, UN Doc A/CN.4/79, 9.

[46] Daum and Stellpflug (n 32), 366–69.

[47] Convention on the High Seas, Geneva (adopted 29 April 1958, entered in force 30 September 1962) 450 UNTS 82; Convention on the Territorial Sea and the Contiguous Zone, Geneva, (adopted 29 April 1958, entered into force 10 September 1964) 516 UNTS 205.

[48] Convention for the Unification of Certain Rules of Law Respecting Assistance and Salvage at Sea (opened for signature 23 September 1910) UKTS 1913 No 4.

[49] International Convention on Arrest of Ships (adopted 12 March 1999) UN Doc A/CONF.188.6.

[50] Van Hooydonk (n 2), 407–08.

[51] Klein (n 22), 250; Veal and Tsimplis (n 27), 308.

[52] Klein (n 22), 250–51.

[53] Veal and Ringbom (n 26), 103.

[54] Daum and Stellpflug (n 32), 365.

[55] Y-C Chiang, C Zhang and N Wang, 'The International Legal Status of the Unmanned Maritime Vehicles' [2020] 113 *Marine Policy* 1, 2.

questioned, however.[56] One problematic aspect is that although certain international conventions contain some sort of a definition of a ship/vessel, they do not necessarily help in defining what constitutes a ship/vessel in the sense of the LOSC.

A particular difficulty underlying this approach is that these various definitions have in common that they are developed having in mind the background to which a convention is meant to apply.[57] Closely aligned to this is that if a vessel being manned is not an essential element for the sphere of operation of a convention, or implied by its context, a definition is unlikely to refer to the aspect of crewing. An example is the London Dumping Convention[58] and its subsequent 1996 Protocol,[59] having the general aim of preventing polluting activities at sea, which contain a rather broad definition of a vessel in Article III.2: they refer to 'waterborne craft' in the broadest sense. Under this definition, whether a craft operating at sea is self-propelling carries no relevance, for example. While this definition extends to maritime autonomous craft, meaning that they would be covered by the London Convention and its Protocol, it makes little sense to transplant this definition to obtain an understanding of what constitutes a vessel/ship under the LOSC. There are more examples of conventions where the definition found therein interacts directly with that convention's aim. This is visible in the definition included within the 1973 Convention for the Prevention of Pollution of Ships,[60] providing in Article 2(4) that a vessel 'operates in the marine environment', which includes 'air cushion vehicles … floating craft and fixed or floating platforms'.

The diverse picture provided in international conventions as to how a vessel is defined is mirrored in national laws. To illustrate this with some examples, whereas the national laws and regulations of Croatia, Italy and Argentina require a crew/master to be present in order for a vessel to be registered,[61] those of Ireland and the UK have no such requirement.[62]

[56] Schmitt and Goddard (n 1), 577.

[57] ibid; Van Hooydonk (n 2), 406; Veal, Tsimplis and Serdy (n 12), 26.

[58] London Dumping Convention (adopted 29 December 1972, entered into force 30 August 1975) 1046 UNTS 120.

[59] 1996 Protocol to the London Convention on Prevention of Marine Pollution by Dumping of Wastes and Other Matter (opened for signature 7 November 1996, entered into force 24 March 2006) 36 ILM 1 (London Protocol).

[60] International Convention for the Prevention of Pollution from Ships (adopted 2 November 1973/17 February 1978, entered into force 2 October 1983) 1340 UNTS 61 (MARPOL Convention).

[61] 'Argentine Maritime Law Association Response to the CMI Questionnaire on Unmanned Ships' 2-3, https://comitemaritime.org/wp-content/uploads/2018/05/CMI-IWG-Questionnaire-Unmanned-Ships-ARGENTINA.pdf, accessed 26 June 2020 (Response of Argentina); 'Italy's Response to the CMI Questionnaire on Unmanned Ships' 1–2, https://comitemaritime.org/wp-content/uploads/2018/05/CMI-IWG-Questionnaire-Unmanned-Ships-ITALY.pdf, accessed 26 June 2020 (Response of Italy); 'Croatian Maritime Law Association Response to the CMI Questionnaire on Unmanned Ships' 1, https://comitemaritime.org/wp-content/uploads/2018/05/CMI-IWG-Questionnaire-Unmanned-Ships-CROATIA.pdf, accessed 26 June 2020.

[62] 'Replies of Irish Maritime Law Association to CMI Questionnaire on Unmanned Ships' 2, https://comitemaritime.org/wp-content/uploads/2018/05/CMI-IWG-Questionnaire-Unmanned-Ships-IRELAND.pdf, accessed 26 June 2020; 'British Maritime Law Association Response to the CMI Questionnaire on Unmanned Ships' 1, https://comitemaritime.org/wp-content/uploads/2018/05/CMI-IWG-Questionnaire-Unmanned-Ships-UK.pdf, accessed 26 June 2020.

Admittedly, several definitions in treaties and national laws do not include a reference to a vessel/ship having to be manned. Yet, this does not necessarily support the conclusion that a similar broad interpretation of vessel was meant to underly the reference to a vessel/ship in the LOSC. To the contrary, it stands to reason that the international rules and obligations contained therein are underlain by the thought that vessels carry a crew, master and officers on board, which is reflected in the language of the LOSC as well.[63] This is mainly because at the time that the LOSC was negotiated, the idea of using autonomous technology to ship goods internationally could not have been reasonably entertained.[64] Daum and Stellpflug conclude differently: 'it is remarkable that none of the ocean treaties scrutinised above presupposes that a ship must be manned'.[65] A difficulty with this argument, and casting doubt on this assertion, is that when focusing on the LOSC, several provisions contain language that refers to both a master and crew, which does point in the direction of them having to be present on board. Particularly relevant in this context is, for example, Article 94(3)(b) of the LOSC (see section V.B).[66]

C. What Constitutes a Ship/Vessel Under the LOSC?

A difficulty is that neither ship nor vessel is defined under the LOSC, leaving ample ground for debate over their precise meaning. Complicating matters in establishing the meaning of a vessel/ship under the LOSC further, is the fact that the issue has not been the object of judicial comment by international courts and tribunals. Also, the negotiating history at the Third Conference on the Law of the Sea (UNCLOS III) does not offer a definition of either ship or vessel.

Before addressing these issues, another question that arises is what explains the use of the words 'ships' and 'vessels' in the text of the LOSC? Are they supposed to carry different meanings, or is there no substantive rationale behind both terms having found their way into the same framework? Based on the negotiation history of the LOSC, their concurrent use in its text does not seem to be underlain by a conscious attempt at differentiation. Important is that it is only the English text that maintains this dual use of terms.[67] All other languages in which the LOSC was concluded are uniform in this respect. At the root of the difference in the English

[63] Veal and Tsimplis (n 27), 304.

[64] Kraska (n 20), 50; Response of Argentina (n 61), 5; Response of South Africa (n 27), 6; Response of Italy (n 61), 2.

[65] Daum and Stellpflug (n 32), 368.

[66] Para 3 of Art 94 of the LOSC reads as follows: 'Every State shall take such measures for ships flying its flag as are necessary to ensure safety at sea with regard, *inter alia*, to: (a) the construction, equipment and seaworthiness of ships; (b) the manning of ships, labour conditions and the training of crews, taking into account the applicable international instruments; (c) the use of signals, the maintenance of communications and the prevention of collisions.'

[67] SN Nandan and S Rosenne (eds), *United Nations Convention of the Law of the Sea 1982: A Commentary*, Vol. II (Martinus Nijhoff, 1993) 45.

text seems to lie that at UNCLOS III, two Committees held different preferences as to the usage of the terms. Whereas the Third Committee favoured the use of the word vessel – because of it being broader in scope – the Second Committee showed a preference for the word ship.[68] Despite these preferences, neither committee was entirely consistent in their usage, however, using these terms interchangeably in certain provisions, which puts into question how critical they thought the distinction was.

Turning now to the failure of the LOSC to spell out what constitutes a vessel/ship, and how to establish the meaning of the two terms absent any definition, various inferences have been made from the fact that the LOSC does not define a ship/vessel. One argument has elevated the lack of a definition as enabling autonomous craft to be brought within the meaning of vessel/ship under the LOSC.[69] An alternative explanation for vessel/ship not being defined within the LOSC may well be that its drafters saw no need for this, because of it being clear what the object was they were making provision for: the manned type. Support for this view comes from looking at the LOSC as a whole, not least in those parts where flag state obligations are laid down, several provisions can be identified that are tailored to be applied to where a vessel is manned by a master, officers and crew (see for a further discussion section V). Also, certain provisions in the LOSC will lose their relevance, either partly or in full, if it is assumed that a vessel can be unmanned; this runs counter to the view that a treaty provision cannot be interpreted in a way rendering it meaningless, which would conflict with the principle of effectiveness.[70] Two examples are Article 27 and paragraph 1 of Article 28, which in broad strokes concern the possibility for a coastal state to exercise civil or criminal jurisdiction over persons on board when a merchant vessel passes through the territorial sea, thus without, for example, entering its internal waters.

Another suggestion has been that a ship/vessel not being defined within the LOSC, is borne out of the intention to defer the issue of its definition to individual states.[71] Tied to this is that once a state has labelled something as a vessel, by giving its nationality, all other states will have to defer to this designation.[72] Support for this argument has been drawn from Article 91 of the LOSC, which is argued to illustrate the importance of definitions found in national law for obtaining a understanding of the terms ship/vessel on the international level.[73] If the language of this provision is examined in detail, this reading seems to lose some of its force, however. Article 91 of the LOSC is concerned with the 'nationality of ships'.

[68] ibid.

[69] Chiang, Zhang and Wang (n 55) 2; 'Greece's Response to the CMI Questionnaire on Unmanned Ships' 4, https://comitemaritime.org/wp-content/uploads/2018/05/CMI-QUESTIONNAIRE-ON-UNMANNED-SHIPS-Greece.pdf, accessed 26 June 2020 (Response of Greece).

[70] *Corfu Channel Case (UK v Albania) (Merits)* [1949] ICJ Rep 4, 24.

[71] Veal and Tsimplis (n 27), 309; Chiang, Zhang and Wang (n 55), 3.

[72] Veal and Tsimplis (n 27), 309; Veal, Tsimplis and Serdy (n 12), 28; Chiang, Zhang and Wang (n 55), 2; Response of Greece (n 69), 3.

[73] Veal and Ringbom (n 26), 102; Veal and Tsimplis (n 27), 303.

To this end, a state has to lay down conditions under which a ship can obtain its nationality. The implication of the phrase 'shall' being introduced in the language of Article 91, is that states are under an obligation to set such conditions. The lack of detail contained in this provision has led to the suggestion that states have complete discretionary autonomy in setting the conditions which allow for a ship to be registered.[74] However, this autonomy does not seem absolute, because the provision does refer to 'ships', which suggests that there is a minimum threshold. This threshold has been set such that the vessel must be able to observe the international requirements in relation to 'manning, safety and protection of the marine environment', including those set out in the LOSC.[75] A first, more basic, problem with this view does arise, however; is a vessel not carrying a crew able to comply with manning requirements that have been set in these international conventions? This is not least because the reference to manning is seemingly underlain by the thought that, at a minimum, there must be someone present on board a vessel. On an ordinary reading of the words 'man/manned/manning', according to the *Merriam Webster Dictionary*, it must be understood as 'to station members of a ship's crew at' a vessel.

Looking at the language of the LOSC in Article 209, dealing with activities in the area, a distinction is drawn between vessels and 'other devices' flying a state's flag. Here it thus seems implied that if a craft flies a state's flag, it cannot be considered automatically a ship/vessel in the sense of the LOSC. Further, there seems to be something inherently unsatisfactory with the argument that the designation of what constitutes a vessel is completely subject to the discretionary autonomy of a flag state, and that all other states must fall in line by accepting this.[76] When reasoned through, this would imply that if a state designates, for example, a seaplane as a vessel, other states will have to accept that designation, including when it passes through their territorial sea.

A further difficulty is that the interests of coastal states are involved as well, which have been equally recognised in the preamble of the LOSC. Considering that foreign-flagged 'vessels' will traverse through their territorial seas, and that the Convention strikes a balance between coastal state interests and navigational rights and freedoms, that coastal states must always defer to such a categorisation seems a bridge too far.

In 2016, China removed an autonomous underwater craft that was operated by the US Navy located at a point 50 nm off Subic Bay. While the US was adamant as to it being a vessel, having it categorised thus, China felt no obligation to follow this designation, regarding it to be a craft that required its prior consent.[77] Put in its proper context, this involved a situation where China took enforcement action in what constitutes its EEZ, which is more difficult to justify, given that this

[74] Chiang, Zhang and Wang (n 55), 2, 7.
[75] Veal and Tsimplis (n 27), 309.
[76] Veal, Tsimplis and Serdy (n 12), 26.
[77] ibid 24–25, 28; Chiang, Zhang and Wang (n 55), 1.

occurred outside of China's territory and that the activity, amongst others, did not bear on the sovereign rights China has over its natural resources, nor that the craft seems to have been engaged in MSR. Yet, the example does show that disputes may arise between states as a result of a state being unwilling to accept another state's characterisation of a certain maritime craft as a vessel/ship. Contrary to the view that there are apparently no limits to this discretionary autonomy, in order to be a vessel, it has to be able to comply with the international rules and standards. To this end, the flag state carries the primary responsibility to make sure that all its vessels are in compliance with these rules and standards. Here lies a potential difficulty, however, because in the application of some flag state obligations to maritime autonomous craft, several issues may arise.

D. Applying the General Rule on Treaty Interpretation to the Terms Ship/Vessel as Contained in the LOSC

When the LOSC was negotiated by states at UNCLOS III, the possibility was not foreseen that autonomous craft would appear to transport cargo internationally. But what role does this play in determining its current applicability to autonomous cargo craft?

One answer to this question is that even though this was the case, those parts of the LOSC that are concerned with international shipping need to be read purposively – which essentially is a variant of the teleological approach to treaty interpretation[78] – so that autonomous cargo craft can be caught under its scope.[79] In that light, to distinguish autonomous vessels from their manned counterparts has also been thought misplaced when considering their common purpose: that is, transporting goods.[80] Connected to this is that the key issue in ascertaining the applicability of the LOSC would be whether such autonomous craft are able to operate in accordance with the main purpose that underlies those parts of the Convention which are geared towards ensuring safety at sea. Illustrating this latter view are Veal and Tsimplis – who after acknowledging safety at sea as being the main 'purpose' underlying 'the legal framework' applicable to international shipping, including the LOSC[81] – go on to argue that this purpose is 'potentially more important' than the text of a treaty. At the heart of this purposive reading of the language of the LOSC is to look behind the text and to unearth the goal of the provisions contained therein, and to then place these in the broader light of what would be the treaty's general object and purpose. A danger inherent in this

[78] J Crawford, *Brownlie's Principles of Public International Law* (9th edn, OUP, 2019) 365.

[79] 'Comité Maritime International Replies of French Maritime Law Association to the Questionnaire on Unmanned Ships' 3, https://comitemaritime.org/wp-content/uploads/2018/05/CMI-IWG-Questionnaire-Unmanned-Ships-FRANCE.pdf, accessed 26 June 2020 (Response of France).

[80] Response of Italy (n 61), 7.

[81] Veal and Tsimplis (n 27), 313.

approach, whereby the language of a treaty provision which can be considered as the main expression of its drafters is largely set side, is that it has a strong legislative character.

But this is where the rule of treaty interpretation, as formulated under Article 31 of the VCLT, steps in. Much ink has been spilt on the interpretation of treaties in general, and treaty interpretation continues to be an issue that prompts disagreement. Views have differed significantly over Article 31 of the VCLT and how to understand the rule of interpretation it lays down, ranging from that the textual approach lies at its core to that the language of a treaty may be set aside to produce a reading that would be in line with the underlying object and purpose of a treaty.[82]

It is important to note that Article 31 of the VCLT speaks of a singular rule of treaty interpretation being contained therein.[83] At the heart of this rule, based on the language of Article 31, is to ascertain the ordinary meaning of a treaty provision. It places emphasis on the intentions of the states concerned, as exemplified by the wording of the treaty. The following internal logic underlies Article 31 of the VCLT: 'One naturally begins with text, followed by the context, and then other matters, in particular, subsequent material.'[84] An interpretation may be supplemented by looking at the circumstances that were present upon the conclusion of the treaty (Article 32 of the VCLT). Article 32 must be read in light of Article 31, and may supplement an interpretation that is based on the latter; this is when after applying the latter, the meaning of a treaty provision either remains 'ambiguous or obscure' or can be considered 'manifestly absurd or unreasonable'.

Interpreting a treaty evolutively or purposively falls under the broad umbrella of the teleological approach to treaty interpretation (essentially being a variant thereof)[85] but is not a generally accepted mean of treaty interpretation, however. In this vein, the argument has been presented that the language of Article 31 of the VCLT does not reflect the evolutionary approach to interpreting a treaty provision,[86] but rather places emphasis on its text. For example, in *Admission of a State to the United Nations*, the International Court of Justice (ICJ) stated that 'If the relevant words in their natural and ordinary meaning make sense in their context, that is the end of the matter.'[87] Another example is *Territorial Dispute (Libya v Chad)*, where in interpreting a treaty, the main emphasis was placed on its text; other interpretive means may function as a 'supplementary measure'.[88] And, moreover, difficulties may arise in distilling a treaty's overall object and purpose, particularly when a compromise was struck between various, at times, competing interests, which also may have been recognised in its preamble, for example.

[82] Crawford (n 78), 365.
[83] A Aust, *Modern Treaty Law and Practice* (2nd edn, CUP, 2013) 208.
[84] ibid.
[85] Crawford (n 78), 365.
[86] ibid.
[87] *Admission of a State to the United Nations* (Advisory Opinion) [1948] ICJ Rep 57, 4, 8.
[88] *Territorial Dispute (Libya v Chad)* (Merits) [1994] ICJ Rep 6, 21–22 [41].

A prime example of a treaty seeking to balance between various interests is the LOSC.

Due to there being no definition of a vessel/ship, it is inevitable to fall back on the ordinary meaning of the wording, supplemented by the context, to interpret the meaning of those provisions in the LOSC that establish a link for their activation with a vessel/ship. But what is the meaning ordinarily attributed to a ship/vessel? Definitions of a vessel/ship found in dictionaries are regularly circular in nature. For example, the *Online Cambridge Dictionary* defines a vessel as a 'large boat or a ship'. The same dictionary indicates that a ship is a 'large boat for travelling on water, especially across the sea'. A more elaborate definition appears in the *Collins Dictionary*, indicating that a ship is a 'large boat which carries passengers or cargo'. While a constant in these definitions is that the focus is on the physical structure of a ship, it must be of large size; most of the current autonomous cargo craft in existence do not meet this requirement, though are meant to in the future,[89] however. Admittedly, these dictionary definitions are sufficiently broad in scope to allow autonomous cargo craft to be brought within their meaning.

However, a word of caution is warranted here: an interpretation of treaty provisions that refer to a vessel/ship cannot be isolated from their context. The context includes the treaty as a whole and its structure. When supplemented by its context, as is appropriate pursuant to Article 31 of the VCLT to establish a treaty provision's ordinary meaning, it becomes clearer, however, that a link was presupposed with a master, officers and crew when the LOSC refers to a vessel/ship (see section V).

IV. The Entitlement of Vessels to Navigational Rights and Freedoms

If an autonomous craft transporting cargo is a vessel or ship, varying with the maritime zone involved, different passage regimes exist for them under international law of the sea. This ranges, as will be surveyed below, from the non-existence of navigational rights for vessels within internal waters, to the freedom of navigation that applies in the EEZ/high seas. Now to turn to the navigational rights and freedoms that are recognised under international law.

A. Internal Waters

Internal waters, being located landward of the baselines (Article 8 of the LOSC), constitute the point from which the territorial sea is measured (see the next section). Considering that internal waters are part of a state's territory, it has sovereignty over them (Article 2 of the LOSC). Two consequences follow from this:

[89] Veal and Tsimplis (n 27), 306–07.

first, that the coastal state can set conditions for entry of vessels into its internal waters; and, second, vessels can be denied access to a state's internal waters, including any ports based within its territory.[90] However, some discussion has arisen around whether international law recognises a general right of access to ports. At the heart of this discussion is the *Aramco* arbitration, which has been argued to coin a general right of access for vessels to ports.[91] Here the Arbitral Tribunal stated that under international law there is a 'great principle' which stipulates that ports should be open for foreign-flagged vessels.[92] Only when isolated from what follows in the same sentence, where the Tribunal recognised that a port may be closed if a port state's 'vital interests' do so require,[93] can the award support the argument that this translates to a general right of access for vessels under international law. Its existence is further undermined by state practice, however.[94] Two examples are that states have frequently entered into bilateral access agreements, for which there seems little use if a general access right would already exist under general international law, and that closures of ports have met with few protests from other states.[95]

In light of this, the better view is that a coastal state has discretionary autonomy in preventing vessels from gaining access to its internal waters, including ports; albeit that refusing entry to a vessel must meet reasonability requirements under international law, in that it may not constitute an abuse of right (Article 300 of the LOSC) or be discriminatory in nature. A state that excludes autonomous vessels *simpliciter* from being allowed to enter its internal waters would not be acting in a discriminatory way, however. A right of entry can derive from another international law basis, however; for instance, a bilateral access agreement or another treaty (for example, the 1923 Convention and Statute on the International Regime of Maritime Ports).[96] When ships find themselves in distress or in a *force majeure* situation, this also may create a right of entry into internal waters: that is, when human life is in peril, but the right does not extend to when cargo or the vessel itself are merely at risk.[97]

The above will apply across the full spectrum of vessels, whereby those operating autonomously can be similarly denied access to internal waters. That autonomous cargo vessels can be denied entry into internal waters has provoked some criticism;[98] but this is simply a logical corollary of a coastal state having

[90] Arts 25(2), 211(3) and 255 of the LOSC; *Military and Paramilitary Activities in and against Nicaragua (Nicaragua v United States of America)* (Merits) [1986] ICJ Rep 14, 111.

[91] *Saudi Arabia v ARAMCO* (1963) 27 ILR 117, 212.

[92] Ibid.

[93] Churchill and Lowe (n 13), 61.

[94] L de la Fayette, 'Access to Ports in International Law' [1996] 11 *International Journal of Marine and Coastal Law* 1, 22.

[95] Churchill and Lowe (n 13), 61–67.

[96] Convention and Statute on the International Regime of Maritime Ports (adopted 9 December 1923, entered into force 26 July 1926) 58 LNTS 285.

[97] Churchill and Lowe (n 13), 63.

[98] Van Hooydonk (n 2), 410; Response of Greece (n 69), 4.

sovereignty over its territory. If a vessel flying a foreign flag has entered a state's port voluntarily, it subjects itself to the territorial jurisdiction of the port state. Because ports lie within a state's territory, prescriptive and enforcement jurisdiction over vessels located therein exists for the state. However, vessels having immunity and those that have come to port due to *force majeure* or distress are amongst those that are outside the reach of the port state's jurisdictional powers; as regards the latter, this is only in so far as violations of a state's laws and regulations are connected to the *force majeure* or distress.

B. Territorial Sea

Within territorial sea, which may extend no further than 12 nautical miles (nm) from the baselines, a right of innocent passage exists for all foreign flagged vessels that operate on the surface (Article 17 of the LOSC). Craft that cannot be considered vessels would not enjoy this right, rendering their operation within the territorial sea dependent on coastal state consent.

Two potential legal bases need to be explored if a coastal state would seek to limit or deny the right of innocent passage to an autonomous vessel, because of it not carrying a crew, master or officers on board: that is, whether Articles 19 or 21 of the LOSC could function as grounds upon which such a limitation can be based.

The main question that arises concerning the applicability of Article 19 of the LOSC to limit an autonomous vessel's right of innocent passage is whether the fact that a master, crew and officers are absent renders its passage prejudicial to the peace, good order, or security of the coastal state.[99] No reference is made in this article to a vessel losing its right of innocent passage as a result of its characteristics, however; rather, there is an emphasis on activities whereby, if they are undertaken, this right can be lost. Nonetheless, there might be a possible caveat; that is, is Article 19 of the LOSC exhaustive? Opinion is split, however, on whether additional grounds which are not enumerated in this provision can render a vessel's passage non-innocent.[100] Even if one subscribes to the view that Article 19 is non-exhaustive in its current form, considering its overwhelming emphasis on activities, it might be difficult to bring the fact that there is no onboard human presence within the reach of this provision.[101]

Now to turn to whether Article 21 of the LOSC could perhaps form a basis upon which the coastal state could successfully limit the right of innocent passage for autonomous vessels. The general thrust of Article 21 is that it allows the coastal state to adopt laws and regulations pertaining to vessels engaged in innocent passage. Its first paragraph sets out the limits within which laws and regulations can be adopted by the coastal state, by giving an exhaustive enumeration of the

[99] Chiang, Zhang and Wang (n 55), 5.
[100] Kraska (n 20), 54.
[101] Veal and Ringbom (n 26), 103.

areas to which they may apply. Several grounds are recognised here, but those that may perceivably bear on autonomous cargo vessels are found in subparagraphs (a) and (f): 'the safety of navigation and the regulation of maritime traffic' and 'the preservation of the environment of the coastal State and the prevention, reduction and control of pollution thereof'. Here, the main issue would be whether there is something unique to autonomous vessels that would set them apart from their manned counterparts, and which would allow the coastal state to intervene if an autonomous vessel is engaged in innocent passage. One can argue that autonomous vessels, in terms of threats to the marine environment or the safety of navigation, are less of a danger, because of the human element being taken out of the equation. But this is oversimplifying the matter, however, as will be discussed in section V.B.

Further, there is a possible caveat in Article 21(2) of the LOSC. Here, it is stipulated that adopted laws and regulations may only relate to 'the design, construction, manning or equipment of foreign ships' if they 'are giving effect to generally accepted international rules or standards'. So, the question would become whether the international rules and standards that pertain to seagoing vessels, being the various IMO Conventions, run into difficulties when applied to autonomous vessels as some of their provisions point in the direction of that a crew/master ought to be on board.[102] One example is the International Convention on Standards of Training Certification and Watch 1978 (STCW Convention), setting requirements regarding seafarers that serve on board of a vessel, including, amongst others, watch to be kept by officers on the bridge and the engine room (Part 4 of Section A-VIII/2).[103] The above suggests that coastal states could adopt laws and regulations, if they are based on these international conventions, with the effect that autonomous vessels, to the extent that they are unable due their characteristics to comply with these standards, would be especially susceptible to being targeted. A second limitation flows from Article 24(1)(a) of the LOSC, which starts by emphasising that innocent passage can only be limited in accordance with this Convention, to go on to inter alia set the additional requirement that laws or regulations that a coastal state has adopted may not have the 'practical effect' of a vessel's right of innocent passage being 'impaired' or 'denied'.

Vessel collisions are addressed in paragraph 4 of Article 21 of the LOSC: to prevent these from occurring, vessels engaged in innocent passage will have to comply with 'all generally accepted international regulations' existing in connection therewith. Critical in this regard are the International Regulations for Preventing Collisions at Sea 1972 (COLREGS).[104] Rules that are potentially

[102] Veal and Tsimplis (n 27), 331.

[103] International Convention on Standards of Training, Certification and Watchkeeping for Seafarers (adopted 7 July 1978, entered into force 28 April 1984) UKTS 50 Cmnd 9266. Amendments in 1995, which entered into force on 1 February 1997 (STCW Convention 78/95).

[104] Convention on the International Regulations for Preventing Collisions at Sea (adopted 20 October 1972, entered into force 15 July 1977, as amended 1981, 1987, and 1989) 1050 UNTS 16 (COLREGS).

problematic when applied to autonomous vessels, are, for example, rules 2 and 5, dealing respectively with 'good seamanship' and 'proper lookout'.[105] When applied to autonomous vessels operating in violation of one of provisions contained in the COLREGS, the coastal state would be able to act against that vessel. Looking at the language of Article 24(4) of the LOSC, where the word 'all' is used in reference to collisions regulations, this implies that by virtue of being a vessel, there is no room for cherry-picking. Hence, vessels will need to comply with all collision rules as they are written. If a vessel fails to do that, its right of innocent passage may be lost.

Article 25 of the LOSC, in its second paragraph, deals with foreign vessels having a coastal state's internal waters, or a call of port located outside thereof, as their destination. If these vessels do not meet the requirements set by a coastal state for entry into its internal waters, the latter may proactively prevent infringement thereof. Thus, for the sake of argument, if a coastal state does not allow autonomous vessels in its internal waters, which is a requirement it would be permitted to set in light of it having sovereignty over its territory, Article 25(2) of the LOSC introduces the possibility for that state to take steps against those autonomous vessels that have its internal waters as their final destination: while the vessel is still physically located in the territorial sea.

However, a separate issue is what if a coastal state does not recognise the designation by a flag state that an autonomous cargo craft is a vessel, thus operating on the understanding that it does not enjoy the right of innocent passage, but being subject to coastal state consent. This seems to tie in with a discussion of Article 91 of the LOSC, which has been read by some authors as meaning that once a flag state labels something as a vessel, all other states have to defer to this designation.[106]

C. Straits

A strait in the sense of Article 37 of the LOSC must meet two requirements. First, the geographical requirement: a strait must lie between one part of the high seas or EEZ and another part of the high seas or EEZ. And, second, the functional requirement: a strait must be used for international navigation.

If a strait can be brought under the sphere of operation of Article 37 of the LOSC, there is a right of transit passage for vessels. Compared to the right of innocent passage, the right of transit passage is more akin to the freedom of navigation. This is because the strait state has more limited options to interfere with vessels engaged in transit passage. Yet, and similar to vessels exercising their right of innocent passage through the territorial sea, those engaged in transit passage must do so expeditiously and continuously. A difference is that vessels engaged in transit passage may do so in their normal mode; for example, this would allow

[105] Chiang, Zhang and Wang (n 55), 5.
[106] See for further discussion section V.A.

submarines to transit straits submerged. For autonomous cargo vessels this would potentially mean that while traversing a strait, an onboard pilotage requirement may conflict, for example, with what can be considered their normal mode: operating autonomously.

Vessels engaged in transit passage need to act in accordance with international shipping regulations (Article 39(2)(a) of the LOSC). This paragraph singles out the COLREGS as a convention that must be complied with. This leads to the question, identical to the one that can be raised concerning Article 24(4) of the LOSC, whether its text, when applied to autonomous cargo vessels, raises difficulties in terms of compliance. One example, as already seen, is that rule 5 requires vessels to have a 'proper lookout'. Different from Article 21(2) of the LOSC, which does not allow the coastal state to impose more onerous requirements as the accepted international rules and standards in relation to vessels engaged in innocent passage, the provision dealing with laws and regulations that a state can adopt relating to transit passage does not contain a similar limitation (Article 42 of the LOSC). This difference may be less important than it may at first appear, however: Article 42, more specifically in its second paragraph, makes clear that the 'practical effect' of adopted laws and regulations may not amount to 'denying, hampering or impairing' a vessel's right of transit passage. Laws and regulations that the strait state may adopt can relate to the safety of navigation and pollution (Article 42(1)(a)(b) of the LOSC) which vessels, whatever their make-up, have to abide by when engaged in transit passage within straits.

D. EEZ/High Seas

Within the EEZ, extending at a maximum to a point located 200 nm from the baselines of the coastal state (Article 57 of the LOSC), states enjoy the high seas freedom of navigation (Article 87 of the LOSC), subject to the provisions of the LOSC (Article 58(1) of the LOSC). Navigating vessels must have due regard to the sovereign rights of coastal states that extend to natural resources and related activities in the EEZ. Generally, however, EEZ rights vested in coastal states, at their core relating to the exploration and exploitation of natural resources, should not significantly impact the ability of vessels to exercise the freedom of navigation. Viewed from the perspective of the coastal state, and considering that exercising its sovereign rights to explore the natural resources contained within its own EEZ is not tied to 'particular vehicular means',[107] the coastal state has discretionary autonomy to employ autonomous craft in the process. But this is a different matter from the use of autonomous craft to transport goods internationally.

The high seas, starting usually at the outer limit of the EEZ, are open to all states on an equal basis. Here, the freedom for vessels to navigate exists for all states (Article 87(1) of the LOSC). In exercising this freedom, a state must have due regard

[107] Veal, Tsimplis and Serdy (n 12), 28.

to the interests of other states. Activities of vessels on the high seas, thus also navigation, are primarily regulated through flag state jurisdiction, placing the burden of ensuring that vessels act in compliance with the applicable international rules and standards on the state where the vessel is registered, which will be discussed next.

V. Flag State Jurisdiction

Enforcement and prescriptive jurisdiction over a vessel on the high seas,[108] and in the EEZ,[109] resides 'exclusively' with the state of nationality, that is the 'flag state'. This principle is not absolute, however, as limited exceptions exist under international law that open up the possibility for other states than the flag state to intervene in a vessel's operation, including when it is engaged in piracy.[110] In terms of their applicability, flag state obligations are not spatially limited to the high seas, extending to wherever the vessel is located. Flag state jurisdiction can thus exist in parallel with jurisdiction for the coastal state, which is the case when a vessel is within a coastal state's territory, that is, its internal waters, territorial sea or archipelagic waters.

Difficulties may arise for the flag state to fulfil the obligations it has under the LOSC when they are applied to autonomous cargo craft, among which are those it has pursuant to Articles 94 and 98. One obligation that might create particular difficulties is Article 94(4)(b) of the LOSC, prescribing that each flag state must ensure that its vessels have a (properly qualified) master, officer(s) and (not 'or') crew; and based on an ordinary reading of the text of this provision, they ought to be based on board.[111]

A. The Genuine Link Requirement

Van Hooydonk foresees difficulties arising for unmanned vessels to satisfy the requirement of there being a genuine link between flag state and vessel.[112] Underlying this argument is the fact that due to the vessel being unmanned, or the operator being onshore – and not necessarily located in the territory of the flag state – the genuine link requirement would be difficult to meet.[113] Connected to this is the question of how the flag state would be able to effectively exercise its jurisdiction over autonomous vessels, due to them operating without a human presence on board, as is required under Article 94(1) of the LOSC.[114]

[108] Art 92(1) of the LOSC.
[109] Art 58(2) of the LOSC.
[110] Arts 101 and 105 of the LOSC.
[111] Response of Greece (n 69), 4–5.
[112] Van Hooydonk (n 2), 409–10.
[113] Daum and Stellpflug (n 32), 369.
[114] Van Hooydonk (n 2), 409–10.

The latter requires that: 'Every State shall effectively exercise its jurisdiction and control in administrative, technical and social matters over ships flying its flag.' Placed in its proper perspective, however, this seemingly is an issue that does not uniquely arise in the context of autonomous craft. Rather, it is a reformulation of an already existing problem: that is, flags of convenience and the aligned issue of sub-standard shipping. In what follows, two related aspects will be explored further: the granting of nationality to vessels, and that the state in according its nationality must ensure it bears a genuine link to that vessel.

Starting with the issue of granting nationality, Article 91(1) of the LOSC stipulates that: 'ships have the nationality of the State whose flag they are entitled to fly ….' Registration of a vessel is determinative for its nationality. How this administrative procedure is organised is subject to the discretionary autonomy of states. As a result, state practice lacks uniformity.[115] Despite registration being overwhelmingly a domestic affair, international law imposes some limits on the granting of nationality. In this vein, Article 300 of the LOSC provides that nationality must be given in good faith, for example.

Closely related to this is that granting nationality is premised on the existence of a genuine link pursuant to paragraph 1 of Article 91 of the LOSC. This requirement, and its precise meaning, has generated much debate, and continues to do so. The idea underlying the genuine link requirement seems to be that the competence of a state in giving its nationality to vessels should not be unfettered. According to the forerunner of the LOSC, under Article 5 of the 1958 Geneva Convention on the High Seas, 'there must exist a genuine link between the State and the ship; in particular, the State must effectively exercise its jurisdiction and control in administrative, technical and social matters over ships flying its flag.' The gist of this article is repeated in the LOSC, although the requirements of genuine link and exercising effective jurisdiction and control are now spread out over two separate provisions: that is, Articles 91 and 94(1). A specification of the obligation incumbent on flag states to exercise jurisdiction and control over its vessels is found in Article 94(2)(b) of the LOSC, pursuant to which it has to 'assume jurisdiction under its internal law over each ship flying its flag and its master, officers and crew in respect of administrative, technical and social matters concerning the ship'; this refers to a ship's operations in a general sense.

Some guidance on how to understand the requirement of genuine link can be found in the case law of the International Tribunal for the Law of the Sea (ITLOS). In the *M/V Saiga (No 2)* case, the requirement of a genuine link has been interpreted to mean that effective implementation of flag state duties is ensured by the state where the vessel is registered.[116] The main argument lying behind this

[115] RR Churchill, 'The Meaning of the "Genuine Link" Requirement in relation to the Nationality of Ships, A Study prepared for the International Transport Workers' Federation' (2000), https://orca.cf.ac.uk/45062/1/ITF-Oct2000.pdf, 13-14.

[116] *M/V Saiga (No 2) (Saint Vincent and the Grenadines v Guinea)* (Judgment) ITLOS Reports 1999, 10, 41-42 [81–83].

consideration was that, if a state has actual control over a ship, meaning it exercises effective jurisdiction over it, a genuine link has to be assumed to exist. In *M/V Virginia G (Panama/Guinea-Bissau)*, the ITLOS went along the same lines: a flag state must 'exercise effective jurisdiction and control over that ship in order to ensure that it operates in accordance with generally accepted international regulations, procedures and practices'.[117]

Another issue is what consequences follow from an alleged absence of a genuine link between vessel and state of nationality by another state. Would it, for example, allow the state putting this link into question to deny that vessel's nationality, rendering it effectively stateless? Some insight is offered by the *M/V Saiga (No 2)* case, where the ITLOS had to deal with a contention of Guinea formulated along similar lines. More specifically, in this case there were some irregularities concerning the registration of the *M/V Saiga (No 2)* in the St Vincent and Grenadines. This led Guinea to argue that there was an absence of a genuine link between the *M/V Saiga (No. 2)* and the St Vincent and Grenadines, which allowed Guinea to deny the nationality of the ship.[118] However, the ITLOS did not go along with this line of argument, re-emphasising the main aim behind the inclusion of the genuine link requirement in Article 91(1) of the LOSC: it is to ensure that flag state duties are effectively implemented.[119] In this light a critical question is what these flag state duties are that the ITLOS refers to, and whether autonomous cargo craft raise difficulties that prevent a flag state from effectively implementing them, as is envisaged pursuant to the genuine link requirement.

B. The Impact of a Master, Officers and Crew Not Being on Board a Ship on a Flag State's Ability to Perform its Obligations

Fundamental changes have been made to the role of the master in the last century or so, coming to bear lesser responsibilities over time.[120] Whatever changes to the extent of the master's role have occurred in ship operations, the perceivable disappearance of the master from on board the vessel, as may be the case with certain types of autonomous vessels, is fundamentally different, however.

Tension with the language of the LOSC, inter alia with Article 94,[121] particularly its third and fourth paragraphs, will inevitably arise because of the master, officers, and crew no longer being present on board a vessel. This is because these provisions refer to an officer and crew, and that the master has certain obligations which for their execution seemingly rely on an onboard presence as well, for

[117] *M/V Virginia G (Panama v Guinea-Bissau)* (Judgment) ITLOS Reports 2014, 4, 45 [113].
[118] *M/V Saiga (No 2)* (n 116), 41 [82].
[119] Ibid 42 [83].
[120] Van Hooydonk (n 2), 412.
[121] Ringbom (n 6), 161.

example under Article 98 of the LOSC. Not only are flag states required to exercise their jurisdiction over vessels flying their flag, but this, similarly, extends to the master, officers and crew of these vessels, according to paragraph 2(b) of Article 94 of the LOSC. The reference to the flag state exercising jurisdiction and control in 'administrative, technical and social matter' has been read as to effectively apply to 'the persons on board' and their activities, rather than the ship itself.[122]

Paragraph 3 of Article 94 of the LOSC begins by formulating an obligation that rests on all flag states: they have to take particular measures relating to vessels flying their flag so as to ensure their safety at sea. To that end, and pursuant to paragraph 3(b) of Article 94, a flag state has to take the appropriate measures to ensure that vessels flying its flag are manned in line with the international rules and standards, and that its crew is appropriately trained. Then, paragraph 4 continues, by circumscribing that the measures enumerated under paragraph 3 'shall' relate, to the extent necessary, to three different aspects all geared towards the aim of securing safety at sea, including the manning of ships and the training of its crews.

Paragraph 4 starts under (a) by stating that vessels need to carry on board 'charts, nautical publications and navigational equipment and instruments' that enable the vessel to navigate safely. On an ordinary reading of its language, the provision leaves no room for doubt that these publications, equipment and instruments are meant to be carried on board a vessel; although the 'caveat' in the provision that has been invoked in the context of autonomous vessels is that reference is made to 'as appropriate for the safe navigation of the ship'. And, so the argument runs, taking such measures is not necessary because autonomous vessels would be able to navigate safely without having such materials on board; holding them at an onshore facility or digitally would suffice. But this forces an unnatural reading on Article 94(4)(a) of the LOSC: as is clear from its language (Article 31 of the VCLT), these materials need to be carried on the ship.

Second, under Article 94(4)(b) of the LOSC, the flag state must ensure that each vessel is in charge of a 'master and officers' who must be appropriately qualified (subparagraph b). Further, any crew must be conversant with the applicable international legal rules, to the extent necessary. A further requirement is that the master, officers and crew have to act in accordance with 'international regulations concerning the safety of life at sea, the prevention of collisions, the prevention, reduction and control of marine pollution, and the maintenance of communications by radio' (subparagraph c).

The argument has been raised that in relation to those autonomous vessels where there is a controller onshore, the latter can be considered the 'master'.[123] A more practical difficulty with accepting this argument is that the LOSC speaks of a singular master, meaning that if this requirement is transposed to an onshore controller, there has to be one person taking overall responsibility at all times.

[122] SN Nandan and S Rosenne (eds), *United Nations Convention of the Law of the Sea 1982: A Commentary*, Vol III (Martinus Nijhoff, 1995) 146.

[123] Van Hooydonk (n 2), 409–10; Veal and Tsimplis (n 27), 317–18.

The fact that the master will not be continuously present on the bridge or be the one that is navigating the vessel during a sea voyage, which might last for months, does not detract from this.[124] At least, he or she will be present on the vessel itself, and can deal with matters when they arise, due to his or her proximity. Replicating this situation onshore is likely to run into several difficulties, also in terms of labour standards.

No definition is found within the LOSC, or within another international treaty for that matter, of a 'master' of a vessel. The fact that on conventional vessels the master is more readily identified has been adduced as the underlying reason for this.[125] On an ordinary reading of the word 'master', this in a general way refers to the person that is in command of a vessel.[126] More elaborate is the *Cambridge Online Dictionary*, providing the following definition: 'Ship's masters are in charge of a ship, its crew and any cargo it is carrying, at sea and in port.' Other dictionaries are less elaborate, referring in more general terms to the person who is in command of a ship/vessel (see for example *Merriam-Webster* and *Collins Dictionary*). Article 94 of the LOSC does not, however, exclusively refer to a master, but to officers, in the plural. It is clear from the word 'and', separating the two parts of the same sentence laying down this obligation, that each ship must carry both master *and* officers; not just one or the other. An officer, according to dictionary definitions, holds a position of authority on a ship. Officers being a part of the ship's crew, based on the language of the LOSC, have thus to be based on board.

Article 94(4)(b) goes on to say that this crew's qualifications and numbers must be appropriate in light of the characteristics of the vessel. Definitions of 'crew' clearly establish a link with them being present on board a vessel. When looking at the ordinary meaning of the word crew it refers, according to the *Cambridge Online Dictionary*, to 'a group of people who work together, especially all those who work on and operate a ship'. A similar picture emerges from *Collins Dictionary* and *Merriam-Webster*, both indicating that a crew works on a ship. So, underlying the inclusion of the word 'crew' is the thought that at a minimum, some people must be on board; to conclude differently seems to compel an unnatural reading of Article 94(4) of the LOSC.

There is a caveat, however: these obligations are premised on these measures being viewed in the light of the aspect of safety of navigation; more specifically, the measures taken must be 'necessary to ensure safety at sea'.[127] One line of argument could be that autonomous vessels would be inherently safer, as a result of the human element being taken out of the equation, whereby the safety standards that have been developed for manned vessels could be lowered concurrently. Due to the newness of the technology, it is premature to tell this with any sort of

[124] Veal and Tsimplis (n 27), 317.
[125] ibid.
[126] Nandan and Rosenne (n 122), 242.
[127] Veal and Tsimplis (n 27), 313.

certainty. Caution should be urged with the making of sweeping predictions about the overall safety of autonomous craft and the concomitant lowering of standards that would be applicable to them as compared to manned vessels.[128] A reason for this is that they are going to be introduced into an environment where there inevitably is going to be interaction with human operated vessels as well. Predictions have also been made that although the frequency of vessels colliding or grounding is less when they are autonomously operated, because of the human element being replaced by algorithms, there is a converse side to this: in the event of an accident, the outfall in terms of damage and loss might be more significant compared to when a crew would have been on board.[129]

C. Rendering Assistance at Sea

The use of autonomous technology in international shipping might lead to the core obligation to render assistance at sea being undermined.[130] The language of paragraph 1 of Article 98 of the LOSC obligates a flag state to make sure that masters of vessels flying its flag help distressed persons at sea.[131] Both regulation 33 of the SOLAS and Article 10 of the Salvage Convention, for example, repeat the gist of this obligation.[132] Rescuing distressed persons at sea is thus the duty of the master that is present on the vessel; clearly, this creates significant difficulties when vessels operate autonomously. Because autonomous vessels are either unable to render assistance or can do so only to a reduced extent, depending on their design, this has been seen as a reason for flag states to not register them; that is, as long as the international legal framework fails to provide provisions specifically tailored to account for their specificities.[133]

Even though autonomous craft seem to have inherently fewer options to render assistance, mainly due to their high level of autonomy and overall design, the argument has been made that they can nonetheless serve their function in this regard, and could fulfil the requirements under international law. Their role would consist of relaying the location of distressed people to others capable of

[128] K Wróbel, J Montewka and P Kujala, 'Towards the Assessment of Potential Impact of Unmanned Vessels on Maritime Transportation Safety' [2017] 165 *Reliability Engineering and System Safety* 155–69.

[129] B Eder, 'Unmanned Vessels: Challenges Ahead' [2019] *Lloyd's Maritime and Commercial Law Quarterly* 47, 51.

[130] M Chwedczuk 'Analysis of the Legal Status of Unmanned Commercial Vessels in U.S. Admiralty and Maritime Law' [2016] 47 *Journal of Maritime Law & Commerce* 123, 146–48.

[131] I Papanicolopulu, 'The Duty to Rescue at Sea, in Peacetime and in War: A General Overview' [2016] 98 *International Review of the Red Cross* 491, 493.

[132] L Carey, 'All Hands Off Deck? The Legal Barriers to Autonomous Ships' [2017] 23 *Journal of International Maritime Law* 202, 211.

[133] 'Malta's Response to the CMI Questionnaire on Unmanned Ships' 5, https://comitemaritime.org/wp-content/uploads/2018/05/CMI-IWG-Questionnaire-Unmanned-Ships-MALTA.pdf, accessed 26 June 2020 (Response of Malta).

offering assistance, or allowing them to take shelter on board.[134] Another suggestion has been to hold autonomous vessels to the same standard as their manned counterparts.[135] However, in light of their key characteristic – autonomy – issues are raised around feasibility, if the obligation as it is written in Article 98 of the LOSC is applied to them.

This article embodies, in conventional form, the obligation to render assistance to persons in peril at sea. Nationality, or the category of persons involved – that is, whether they are, for example, refugees, stowaways, refugee-seekers, or survivors of a maritime incident – is immaterial, as the obligation extends to all of them.[136] Flag states have to ensure that the obligation to render assistance is translated into their domestic laws.[137] In terms of its scope of application, Article 98 of the LOSC, and the obligation to render assistance included therein, extends to the 'sea'. At first glance, reinforced by its use of the generic term 'sea', the geographical reach of this obligation extends to bodies of water that meet this definition. However, considering the placement of Article 98 of the LOSC in Part VII, which deals with the high seas, its sphere of operation must be considered inherently limited. By virtue of Article 58(2) of the LOSC, indicating that 'Articles 88 to 115' apply mutatis mutandis in the EEZ, the scope of the obligation to render assistance is extended to include the EEZ as well. However, falling outside the scope of Article 98 of the LOSC, are territorial sea areas. A feature that makes this conclusion potentially problematic is that Part II of the LOSC which deals inter alia with the territorial sea, does not contain a provision developed along lines identical to those of Article 98. That this was because of an oversight on the part of states at UNCLOS III which was advanced as a possible explanation.[138] Leaving this further aside, Article 18 of the LOSC has been regarded as having filled this gap, albeit impliedly. It refers to vessels engaged in innocent passage dropping anchor to offer assistance, wherefrom it would follow that by combining Articles 18, 58(2) and 98 of the LOSC, the scope of the obligation of assistance is thus that it encompasses the seas and oceans in general.[139]

A closer reading of paragraph 1 of Article 98 of the LOSC reveals that the rendering of assistance is a qualified obligation, however: its activation is entwined with there being no 'serious danger to the ship, the crew or the passengers'. Playing a crucial role in this respect is the master, with whom the decision to render assistance lies. Regulation 33 of SOLAS circumscribes the obligation further, by adding that assistance must be rendered 'in so far as such action can be reasonably expected of the master'. A different situation is that upon receiving a call for assistance,

[134] 'Response of United States MLA to CMI Questionnaire re Unmanned Ships' 11, https://comitemaritime.org/wp-content/uploads/2018/05/CMI-IWG-Questionnaire-Unmanned-Ships-US.pdf, accessed 26 June 2020.

[135] Response of Argentina (n 61), 7.

[136] R Barnes, 'Refugee Law at Sea' [2004] 53 ICLQ 47, 50.

[137] Ibid.

[138] Ibid 52.

[139] Nandan and Rosenne (n 122), 176–77.

a vessel has to respond 'with all possible speed', albeit only if heeding this call by the master can be considered reasonable (Article 98(1)(b) of the LOSC). Paragraph 1(c) lays down another obligation for the master in case a collision occurs, when assistance must be rendered to the other ship, its crew and passengers.

In a general sense, there are two issues involved concerning autonomous 'vessels' and the issue of rendering assistance at sea: first, the providing of assistance by an autonomous vessel itself; and, second, an autonomous vessel receiving assistance, because of being in distress.

Starting with the former, the application of the obligation to render assistance by autonomous vessels can be interpreted in a variety of ways. At one end of the spectrum, there is the interpretation that when no master is present on board, the obligation would simply not arise.[140] At the other side of the spectrum is the argument that the obligation applies with equal force across the full spectrum of vessels, thus equally to autonomous ones. Another line of argument that lies between these views does not deny the applicability of the obligation to autonomous vessels, but reduces its extent by tuning it to what realistically can be expected of a vessel not carrying humans on board.[141] This might imply, however, that in their design, autonomous vessels must be given the capacity to render some assistance; for example, that lifecraft are carried, which could be remotely dispatched.[142]

The second issue is whether the obligation to render assistance is qualified in another sense as well: that is, whether receiving help is entwined with there being people present on board a vessel. Resolving this issue seems entwined with the level of autonomy a vessel has; that is, whether the vessel is unmanned or retains some crew on board. This is because under paragraph 1(a), the obligation to render assistance is confined to persons who are 'in danger of being lost'. If no such persons are present on board, the obligation to render assistance pursuant to Article 98 of the LOSC would not arise for other states.[143]

VI. Charting the Way Forward

It has been suggested that once the use of autonomous technology in merchant shipping starts to expand in practice, the international legal framework will subsequently have to fall in line, either through amendment or the creation of a new legal regime.[144] This might be oversimplifying matters, however. An aspect that seems

[140] Veal and Tsimplis (n 27), 313; Veal and Ringbom (n 26), 104; Carey (n 132), 212.

[141] 'Reply by the Nederlandse Vereniging voor Vervoersrecht (NNV) (Dutch Transport Law Association) to the CMI Questionnaire of 29 March 2017' 6, https://comitemaritime.org/wp-content/uploads/2018/05/CMI-IWG-Questionnaire-Unmanned-Ships-NETHERLANDS.pdf, accessed 26 June 2020; Response of Italy (n 61), 6; Veal and Ringbom (n 26), 105.

[142] Klein (n 22), 264–65.

[143] Carey (n 132), 212.

[144] Veal and Tsimplis (n 27), 303.

to be tied to the prospective commercial success of using autonomous craft to ship goods internationally is the current international legal architecture. Possible gaps or ambiguities contained therein might prevent the use of autonomous technology in international shipping from taking root.[145]

As discussed previously, there are, to put it mildly, rough edges in the LOSC that are difficult to argue away when it is attempted to bring autonomous cargo craft under the Convention's scope; this is unless resort is had to more creative interpretations that are, at times, difficult to reconcile with the language of the LOSC, as well as its overall context. More specifically, a common approach to bypass any difficulties is to resort to an evolutive/purposive interpretation of the language of the LOSC.[146] Some judicial support for taking this approach has been garnered from the international case law; see the section after next. The general thrust of this argument is that bringing autonomous craft under those parts of the LOSC whose activation revolves around vessel status, would be warranted in light of its objective and purpose.[147] This view is sometimes supplemented by falling back on preambular language, where the importance of facilitating international communications is underscored.[148]

There are different views over whether to bring autonomous cargo craft within the scope of application of those parts of the LOSC dealing with international shipping. These views have ranged from that they cannot, or ought not,[149] to that no difficulties would arise because of them meeting the definition of a ship/vessel.[150] No matter precisely how one values the severity of these difficulties, at a minimum, it is clear that the text of the LOSC as it stands is susceptible to different interpretations. Different views over the status of autonomous cargo craft might also be seen in the positions of states, whereby the possibility of disputes arising between states is laid bare at the same time.[151] Connected to this is that an autonomous craft can change status depending on where it is located and whether a particular coastal state recognises autonomous craft as vessels. As a corollary, its status might shift from a vessel to a craft, depending on whether it traverses through the territorial sea of a coastal state recognising them as vessels or not.

One approach going forward would be to wait and see in which direction state practice develops, and whether it comes to bear out a customary rule that autonomous cargo craft are treated by states as vessels. Although state practice is still in its infancy, a widespread practice combined with an *opinio iuris* might emerge, if states were to explicitly recognise unmanned cargo craft as vessels/ships once they

[145] Klein (n 22), 247–48.
[146] Response of France (n 79), 3; Veal and Tsimplis (n 27), 313.
[147] Veal, Tsimplis and Serdy (n 12), 27.
[148] ibid.
[149] Response of South Africa (n 27), 6–7.
[150] 'Venezuelan Maritime Law Association's Answers to the CMI questionnaire on Unmanned Ships' 3, https://comitemaritime.org/wp-content/uploads/2018/05/CMI-IWG-Questionnaire-Unmanned-Ships-VENEZUELA.pdf, accessed 26 June 2020.
[151] Response of Malta (n 133), 4.

start to operate internationally. Customary law might thus become relevant, but to invoke it currently to frame an argument in favour of autonomous cargo craft having vessel status, is inappropriate. Furthermore, the responses to the informal Comité Maritime International Survey questionnaire, which are of varying quality and detail, are difficult to treat as state practice, as they do not necessarily reflect government positions, but rather those of maritime law associations.[152]

A. International Adjudication of Disputes Concerning Autonomous Maritime Craft

Disputes between states over autonomous cargo vessels could also be adjudicated under Part XV of the LOSC. The latter provides a standing mechanism that enables disputes over the application and interpretation of LOSC provisions to be referred to an international court or tribunal for binding settlement. One element underlying its introduction is that the integrity of the LOSC and its provisions is ensured. The three forums to which parties have access, according to Article 287 of the LOSC, are the ICJ, ITLOS or an Arbitral Tribunal. Only states can bring such disputes to their attention, whereby whether the compulsory dispute settlement procedures are invoked concerning a dispute that has arisen over autonomous cargo craft is tied to the willingness of states.

B. Reading the Language of the LOSC Teleologically

Arguments formulated along the lines that autonomous cargo craft fall within the meaning of 'vessel'/'ship' under the LOSC, or that provisions referring to a 'master'/'crew'/'officer' can be read as meaning that they may be located onshore, are, when placed in their proper light, underlain by a teleological approach to treaty interpretation.[153] Central to this reading is that bringing these autonomous craft under the reach of the LOSC is in line with the latter's object and purpose. Another related argument that underlies reading the text of the LOSC in this way is that pace can thus be kept with the introduction of new technologies at sea; otherwise the risk is that the LOSC becomes redundant.[154]

These readings might create a tension on two levels: first, when the provisions related to international shipping were negotiated at UNCLOS III, using autonomous technology for transporting goods had yet to appear on the horizon; and, second, tension can be created with the rule on treaty interpretation, as laid down in Article 31 of the VCLT, placing emphasis on the intentions of its drafters,

[152] But see: C Allen, 'Determining the Legal Status of Unmanned Maritime Vehicles: Formalism vs Functionalism' [2018] 49 *Journal of Maritime Law & Commerce* 499, 511–12.

[153] See section III.D.

[154] Kraska (n 20), 50–52.

as exemplified by the wording of the treaty, which may be possibly supplemented by looking at the circumstances that were present upon its conclusion.[155]

To start with some background to the LOSC. Underlying the LOSC were two general aims: first, to design a treaty that would regulate law of the sea issues comprehensively, albeit to the extent possible; and, second, to ensure universal participation in the Convention. To create a comprehensive treaty, a compromise was unavoidable, in order to reach agreement on the final text of the LOSC.[156] Different interests had to be balanced in the process, including those of coastal states and maritime states, so that the treaty would be able to command wide agreement amongst states participating in UNCLOS III. Approaching the issue of autonomous cargo craft exclusively from the standpoint of the flag state, in that its vessel designation would be paramount, and to brush over coastal states' interests, which are similarly recognised in the preamble of the LOSC, for example, and thus run parallel to those of the flag state, might overlook this aspect.

Claims about the redundancy of the LOSC that would follow, if it is not interpreted as a living instrument are generally overblown, however. New uses of the seas and oceans can be dealt with by falling back on the formula of Article 59 of the LOSC; this is irrespective of the vagueness of this provision. That being said, the provisions in the LOSC are imbued with some adaptability, but the question is where the outer limits of this adaptability lie. The other side to this is that, because of the LOSC representing a balance of different interests, there is a tipping point where this carefully constructed balance may unravel.

Support for reading a treaty provision teleologically has been derived from the ICJ's case law. One case which has been particularly invoked in support of this approach is the *Dispute regarding Navigational and Related Rights (Costa Rica v Nicaragua)*.[157] At the heart of this dispute were Costa Rica's *perpetual* navigational rights in the San Juan River under Article VI of a historical treaty (Treaty of Limits between Costa Rica and Nicaragua 1858) concluded with Nicaragua. One of the main issues that the ICJ had to address centred around the meaning of the word 'commerce'; particularly whether falling within the meaning of this word was also 'tourism'. 'Commerce' when the treaty was concluded, had a narrower meaning than it does currently: then, it mainly referred to 'trade'. The ICJ reasoned that the meaning of the word 'commerce' had not to be interpreted by reference to its original meaning, but, rather, how it was understood at the time of application of the treaty.

Underlying the view of the ICJ in the *Dispute regarding Navigational and Related Rights* is the belief that 'where the parties have used generic terms in a treaty, the parties necessarily having been aware that the meaning of the terms was likely to evolve over time, and where the treaty has been entered into for a

[155] See also section III.D.

[156] RR Churchill, 'The 1982 United Nations Convention on the Law of the Sea' in DR Rothwell, AG Oude Elferink et al (eds), *The Oxford Handbook of International Law of the Sea* (OUP, 2015) 24, 27.

[157] Veal, Tsimplis and Serdy (n 12), 27.

very long period or is "of continuing duration", the parties must be presumed, as a general rule, to have intended those terms to have an evolving meaning.'[158] Placed in its proper perspective, the ICJ invoked the evolutionary interpretation in the context of a subsequent practice, in the sense of paragraph 3(b) of Article 31 of the VCLT.[159] A caveat was given by the ICJ in the *Dispute regarding Navigational and Related Rights* case, however: when relying on an evolutive interpretation to establish the meaning of a treaty provision, it is of key importance that the drafters of a treaty must have meant to imbue a term with the capacity to evolve.[160] Similarly, in the *Namibia* advisory opinion, the ICJ underscored 'the primary necessity of interpreting an instrument in accordance with the intentions of the parties at the time of its conclusion'.[161] What thus becomes the key issue is whether, at the time of the conclusion of the LOSC, the intention of the negotiating states was to supply the particular wording of ship/vessel with the innate ability to change without the need for amendment. One aspect of this issue is whether the word ship/vessel, to paraphrase Boyle, is a 'potentially evolutionary phrase' included in the LOSC.[162] There is no clear and definitive answer to this, however; although it has been suggested that the words ship and vessel have to be considered as such terms.[163]

C. Amending the Existing Regime, Creating a New One or Involving the IMO – Scouring the Field for a Realistic Option

Several suggestions have been made to change the language of the LOSC to pave the way for the use of autonomy in international merchant shipping.[164] Along these lines, Van Hooydonk has suggested that their prospective use offers an opportunity to 'thoroughly overhaul' the LOSC.[165] No matter how extensive the changes necessary to the text of the LOSC one would subscribe to, a separate matter is its feasibility. Tied to this is the more general issue of how straightforward amendment of its text is.

Amending the LOSC is notoriously difficult. Illustrating this is that since entering into force in 1994, no changes have been made to the text of the LOSC. Although functioning as a framework convention, the LOSC makes no provision for adopting additional protocols or annexes to tackle novel issues, or to cater for

[158] *Dispute regarding Navigational and Related Rights (Costa Rica v Nicaragua)* (Judgment) [2009] ICJ Rep 213, 243 [66].

[159] G Hernández, *International Law* (OUP, 2019) 182; M Fitzmaurice, 'The Practical Working of the Law of Treaties', in M Evans (ed) *International Law* (5th edn, OUP, 2018) 138, 155.

[160] *Dispute regarding Navigational and Related Rights* (n 158), 242, [64].

[161] *Legal Consequences for States of the Continued Presence of South Africa in Namibia (South West Africa) notwithstanding Security Council Resolution 276* (Advisory Opinion) [1971] ICJ Rep 16, 31–32 [53].

[162] A Boyle, 'Further Development of the Law of the Sea Convention: Mechanisms for Change' [2005] 5 ICLQ 563, 569.

[163] Veal and Tsimplis (n 27), 314; Veal, Tsimplis and Serdy (n 12), 27.

[164] Response of France (n 79), 3–4.

[165] Van Hooydonk (n 2), 410.

new technologies, in a way similar to other framework treaties,[166] particularly those existing in an environmental context. Article 312 of the LOSC sets out the normal procedure for amendment, which closely follows the consensus procedure used in the adoption of the LOSC at UNCLOS III. This consensus procedure may be only set aside if all efforts to that end fail to bear fruit: then, amendments may be adopted by vote. If a vote succeeds, this is not the end of the matter, however, as at least 60 state parties will need to ratify or accede to this amendment for it to become binding. Here there is a further caveat: the amendment is only binding on those states that have accepted it.

A simplified procedure is laid down in Article 313 of the LOSC, which suspends the need for organising a negotiating conference. A party to the LOSC may propose an amendment of its text in writing to the UN Secretary General, who will subsequently circulate this proposed amendment amongst all state parties. Critical for the success of the amendment is whether, within a 12-month period, a state objection is raised; if so, the amendment is rejected. The caveat that exists in the normal procedure, in that amendments are only binding on states having accepted it, applies here with equal force.

An alternative approach, one that would circumvent the difficulties associated with amending the LOSC, which may well be insurmountable, would be the creation of a new legal regime.[167] Developing a regime *de novo* has the distinct advantage that the legal framework applicable to autonomous vessels can be tailor-made. An annex to the LOSC could also be negotiated, with the aim of clarifying its existing provisions, which would have the benefit of keeping the text intact. This approach is not without precedent, having been pursued three times, including in connection with straddling fish stocks.[168] Its incidental use might point to similar difficulties underlying this approach as in developing a *de novo* regime. Tied to both these options is the question of whether the use of autonomous technology in merchant shipping is a topic that is sufficiently important for states to invest the resources to go through what may be highly complex and long-winded negotiations.[169] Considering that the benefits of automation in international shipping are not universally shared within the shipping industry,[170] a recognised urgency on the parts of governments to take steps in the direction of developing a new regime or to amend the LOSC may not necessarily be present either.

[166] Boyle (n 162), 564.

[167] 'CMI IWG Questionnaire on "Unmanned Ships" – AEDM (Spain) Response' 15, https://comitemaritime.org/wp-content/uploads/2018/05/CMI-IWG-Questionnaire-Unmanned-Ships-SPAIN.pdf, accessed 26 June 2020; Eder (n 129), 56.

[168] Agreement for the Implementation of the Provisions of the United Nations Convention on the Law of the Sea of 10 December 1982 relating to the Conservation and Management of Straddling Fish Stocks and Highly Migratory Fish Stocks (IAFS) (adopted 4 August 1995, entered into force 11 December 2001) 2167 UNTS 3.

[169] Response of Italy (n 61), 6.

[170] D Dubay, 'Why We Will Never See Fully Autonomous Commercial Ships' (Center for International Maritime Security, 25 June 2019), http://cimsec.org/why-we-will-never-see-fully-autonomous-commercial-ships/40652, accessed 26 June 2020.

Perhaps a more viable approach might be the involvement of the IMO. At the outset, there is an important limitation: the IMO cannot define a vessel/ship on its own.[171] In places within the LOSC, including Articles 21(2), 119 and 207–12, reference is made to the relevance of generally accepted international agreements and standards. A variation on this wording is found in paragraph 5 of Article 94 of the LOSC, referring to international regulations, procedures and standards. The reason lying behind these references was to ensure the LOSC's capability of evolution. If it assumed that the LOSC operates on the understanding that vessels have to carry on board a master, officers and crew, the IMO taking on this issue might well be seen as acting outside of the parameters set by the LOSC.[172] On the contrary, if it assumed that autonomous craft fall with the meaning of the words ship/vessels in the LOSC, these difficulties would be mitigated.[173]

The claim that attributing vessel status to autonomous cargo craft would pave the way for the IMO to deal with these as it sees fit,[174] seems to oversimplify matters, because the LOSC contains language that indicates a human presence is assumed. At the heart of this lies the issue of the general interaction between the LOSC and the IMO: can the IMO only implement standards set out in the LOSC, or can it determine and implement its own standards using the LOSC essentially as a springboard only? This is not an issue that is going to be resolved here. Suffice it to say that, it is likely that states which believe that the IMO is essentially acting ultra vires when it comes to this matter will raise this point in deliberations on whatever instrument is devised, be it, for example, a new treaty or something similar to the Polar Code.[175] On the contrary, if no state were to raise objections along such lines, this would point to the practice of states being such that they would deem autonomous vessels to be vessels in the sense of the LOSC – or a customary rule might emerge to that effect – from which it could be concluded that the IMO is not overstepping its bounds.

VII. Concluding Remarks

How to interpret the relevant international rules applicable to maritime craft operating autonomously remains subject to divergent views. A similar pattern can be detected concerning the introduction of autonomous technology in transporting cargo, although the debates on this issue are of more recent origin. Its introduction in this latter context prompts questions around how such craft can be accommodated under the international law of the sea framework; especially, how they

[171] ibid.
[172] 'The Canadian Maritime Law Association Response to the CMI Questionnaire on Unmanned Ships' 4, https://comitemaritime.org/wp-content/uploads/2018/05/CMI-IWG-Questionnaire-Unmanned-Ships-CANADA.pdf, accessed 26 June 2020.
[173] Ringbom (n 6), 161.
[174] Ibid.
[175] Eder (n 129), 55.

can be brought under those provisions which are preconditioned on vessel status, or presuppose the existence of an onboard master/officer/crew.[176] The difficulty is that maritime autonomous craft that are used to transport cargo challenge a preconceived understanding: that is, that a merchant vessel carries a master and a crew on board in order to be able to operate. Compounding difficulties is that this was also the guiding thought on the mind of the drafters of the LOSC at UNCLOS III, as is reinforced by its language and context.

Among the international law of the sea issues that arise, the role played by the presence of a crew/master on board in determining whether a seagoing craft is a vessel/ship, is highly significant for determining the legal rules applicable to autonomous cargo craft. Its importance is illustrated by the fact that the various navigational rights and freedoms under the LOSC are accorded to vessels/ships.[177] Accompanying these rights are certain obligations, which must be shouldered by the flag state of a vessel. When some of these obligations are applied to autonomous cargo craft, particularly those in Article 94 of the LOSC, difficulties arise because of their autonomy. In a general sense, there seems to be a correlation between autonomy, and the level thereof that these craft enjoy, and the international law of the sea framework: as the human presence element declines, the more difficult it essentially becomes to bring these craft comfortably within this framework.

On the whole, however, in the literature there is a strong leaning towards classifying autonomous cargo craft as vessels/ships.[178] Relying on definitions contained in international shipping conventions is another approach that has been pursued to justify bringing autonomous cargo craft within the reach of the LOSC.[179] However, due to these definitions having been developed against a specific background, they are regularly ill-suited to be mutatis mutandis applied to a reading of the term vessel/ship under the LOSC, or to deduce a universal definition existing under general international law. Another common argument against not bringing autonomous craft within the reach of the LOSC is that elevating the lack of a crew as the main reason for arguing its non-applicability to unmanned cargo 'vessels', would overlook their similarity to 'normal' ships in all other respects.[180] Their apparent similarity is that they are both used in international trade for the transporting of goods, and that, ultimately, the appearance of autonomous craft carrying cargo will be similar to their manned counterparts. This has led to the conclusion in literature that the LOSC, or the applicable customary rules, that pertain to vessels apply with equal force to their unmanned variants. Underlying this argument is a teleological interpretation of the LOSC and its text, which, so it assumed, must be read as being meant to apply to autonomous cargo craft too.[181]

[176] See sections III, V.
[177] See section IV.
[178] Veal and Ringbom (n 26), 103.
[179] See section III.B.
[180] Veal and Tsimplis (n 27), 313.
[181] See sections III.D, VI.B.

Giving preferential treatment to an interpretation that resolves an ambiguity, by looking at the object and purpose of a treaty (that is, a teleological approach), rather than the text, may be difficult to reconcile with the rule of treaty interpretation as given in Article 31 of the VCLT.[182] Most of the analysis on incorporating autonomous cargo craft into the international legal framework as vessels/ships has skimmed over this aspect, by claiming, for example, that there is 'evidence of an increasingly "evolutionary approach" to treaty interpretation' in international case law;[183] but this seems to overstate the matter. In building this argument, the *Dispute regarding Navigational and Related Rights* case is the sole case that is seemingly relied upon. Contrary to this conclusion, several other cases can be invoked that seem less amenable to interpreting treaties evolutively/purposively, and where international courts and tribunals have placed primary emphasis on the text of a treaty when interpreting a treaty provision.[184]

Interestingly, some of the adherents of the view to not discriminate between manned vessels and their autonomous variants, employ a caveat which invariably waters down the strength of this view: that is, autonomous maritime craft used to transport cargo are 'probably'[185] (or a variation thereof) vessels/ships.[186] There is another side to this argument, however: that is, once a craft can be considered a vessel, meaning it needs to have a nationality, the flag state accepts certain obligations. It seems clear that autonomous craft will be unable to comply with certain provisions of the LOSC as they are written. If a flag state obligation is not (properly) executed, a violation of international law of the sea occurs, however.

Further, although the equal treatment argument has often found favour, its adherents seemingly have fewer difficulties with accepting that the de facto effect of this is that favourable treatment is extended to autonomous 'vessels' in certain respects. This is visible when it comes to fulfilling their obligation to render assistance at sea or that, from a practical perspective, taking enforcement action by a coastal state against autonomous craft is severely complicated, or less effective, or that particular provisions in their current form are effectively rendered useless if vessels operate autonomously (for example, Articles 27 and 28 of the LOSC).

This chapter has sought to address these issues, albeit without resolving them. Various challenges do emerge when the law of the sea framework relating to international shipping is applied to autonomous cargo craft. This includes the extent to which coastal states have jurisdiction over these craft, and the ability of the flag state to execute its duties in relation to vessels flying its flag. Varying with the applicable provision of the LOSC, the fit might be less comfortable, whereas at other times it might be more akin to fitting a square peg into a round hole. At the root of these differing views, to paraphrase Allen, is whether one adheres

[182] See section III.D.
[183] Veal, Tsimplis and Serdy (n 12), 27.
[184] Fitzmaurice (n 159), 154; Crawford (n 78), 365.
[185] Veal and Ringbom (n 26), 103; Van Hooydonk (n 2), 402.
[186] See section II.A.

to a functionalist or textualist approach to treaty interpretation.[187] As both positions are able to garner judicial support for their respective views, as the literature illustrates, passing judgment on what is the correct approach varies depending on which camp one finds oneself in. Hence, without clarifying the LOSC or an amendment of its text, or the creation of a treaty tailored specifically to deal with autonomous cargo craft, this debate is unlikely to be laid to rest.

So, the key problem, as this chapter has sought to show, is that different interpretations can be justified. These differences may be mirrored in the practice of states, creating a legal environment that might be less amenable to a smooth introduction of the use of autonomous technology in cargo shipping; if that is indeed the direction in which the economic pendulum is going to swing. Perhaps the main driver behind arguments that autonomous cargo craft can be accommodated within the existing international law of the sea framework with little difficulty, is a willingness to facilitate a new commercial development in international shipping. That is, without having to overhaul the law of the sea framework itself –[188] be it by making changes to the language of the LOSC through amendment, negotiating an annex to it to clarify its provisions, or creating a regime *de novo*.[189] However, that some argumentative acrobatics must be performed in the process, so as to smoothe the rough edges that are present in the international law of the sea framework, seems a more secondary concern. Yet, going along the route of changing the law of the sea framework has to be considered the more legally sound approach; this is irrespective of any practical difficulties that may be faced as a result.

[187] Allen (n 152), 477–514.
[188] Ringbom (n 6), 162–63.
[189] See section VI.

3

Autonomous Ships and Private Law Issues

PROFESSORS BARIŞ SOYER* AND ANDREW TETTENBORN**

As yet there is no comprehensive academic discussion about the private law issues emerging from the operation of autonomous vessels.[1] This is important for two reasons. First, fundamental uncertainty about the underlying liability rules, if it persists once autonomous vessels enter commercial operation, will result in insurers hedging their bets and reflecting this uncertainty with an increase in premiums.[2] Rate increases could in turn potentially wipe out many of the financial benefits, such as reduction in crew wages and marginal fuel cost, associated with such craft. Second, inability to predict potential liabilities might make manufacturers and service providers less keen to invest in autonomous vessel technology or in producing the incredibly complex algorithms necessary to control it, thus hampering development, or at the very least driving up costs.

This chapter therefore deals with what we see as the changes that may have to be made to accommodate autonomous vessels. It is concerned with private law liabilities (in particular collision, salvage, arrest, limitation and wreck removal) other than those arising out of carriage of passengers or goods, or directly or indirectly out of charterparties. (These latter matters will be covered in chapter four below.)

* Director of Institute of International Shipping and Trade Law, Swansea University.
** Member of the Institute of International Shipping and Trade Law, Swansea University.

[1] See, eg, E Van Hooydonk, 'The Law of Unmanned Merchant Shipping – An Exploration' (2014) 20 *The Journal of International Maritime Law* 403; R Veal and M Tsimplis, 'The Integration of Unmanned Ships into the Lex Maritima' [2017] *LMCLQ* 303; L Carey, 'All Hands off Deck: Legal Barriers to Autonomous Shipping' (2017) 23 *The Journal of International Maritime Law* 202–19, which essentially focus on how the regulatory framework could be amended to accommodate the development of autonomous shipping.

[2] See, MG Geistfeld, 'Legal Ambiguity, Liability Insurance and Tort Reform' (2011) 60 *De Paul L Rev* 539, at 559–56. It is true that the market would almost certainly adjust, with (for example) some variety of 'cyber policy' available at a reasonable premium: but this would take time, leaving considerable uncertainty meanwhile.

I. Changes to Existing Regimes

A. Liability for Negligent Navigation (Collisions)

(i) English Law

Given that the liability regime for negligent navigation is based on the ordinary law of tort, most domestic liability rules can operate just as well with autonomous or unmanned vessels as with traditional ones. Two areas may however need to be looked at more closely. One is the definition of fault; the other, the persons whose fault are operative in order to engender liability.

(a) The Definition of Fault

Currently, liability for negligent navigation is fairly strictly tied to fault. There are qualifications, the notable ones being liability to owners of dock installations under the Harbours, Piers and Docks Clauses Act 1847 and sundry other private Acts of Parliament, and cases where collision leads to pollution by oil carried as cargo or in bunkers – not to mention resulting chemical and other spills once the HNS Convention[3] comes into force. But these are exceptional cases. As a general rule, there must be proved some element of personal negligence by a vessel's owners or those in charge of her for whose acts they are liable. Although in these days of heightened security awareness and multifarious safety codes it is often possible to associate failures of machinery with negligence on someone's part, for example in failing to improve, maintain or inspect it, failure of inanimate machinery as such is not enough even to amount to presumed fault. Moreover, this is not only a feature of English law but also, in respect of collisions between ships, a matter touched on by the Brussels Collision Convention of 1910, to which the UK is a party. This will be dealt with below.

It would be conceivable to argue that this is an antiquated attitude, and that in so far as human agency is supplanted by mechanical or electronic agency, any argument in favour of fault has disappeared and strict liability should be the order of the day.[4] Indeed, to a limited extent this is the approach of the UK's new Electric and Automated Vehicles Act 2018, which makes insurers (though not owners) strictly liable for injury and damage whenever 'an accident is caused by an automated vehicle when driving itself'.[5] However, it can also be plausibly argued that

[3] The HNS Convention, as and when in force, will create a broadly parallel regime to the CLC 1969, but instead of oil will cover damage caused by hazardous and noxious cargoes. It is covered in more detail below.

[4] A convincing case for this has been made by Barış Soyer 'Autonomous Vessels and Third-Party Liabilities – The Elephant in the Room' in B Soyer and AM Tettenborn, *New Technologies, Artificial Intelligence and Shipping Law in the 21st Century* (Informa Law, 2020) at 105–16.

[5] S 2(1).

this may not be appropriate in the case of ships. Quite apart from nice questions of when a ship 'causes' a collision if fault falls out of the equation (if two ships hit each other, have both necessarily 'caused' the resulting collision?), liability insurers (that is, P & I clubs) would one suspects not be happy about strict liability for potentially very large sums, even if they were entitled to limit their liability. Furthermore, as appears below, there would be problems with the 1910 Convention were such a drastic change to be introduced unilaterally by the UK.[6]

On the other hand, if we were to leave matters as they are, the shipping community for its part might rightly complain that costs were being unfairly shifted away from autonomous vessel owners, where any deficiency was more likely to be in things for which owners were not liable, than in persons for whose acts they were. To deal with this there is a strong argument for a less drastic solution which would partly preserve the existing balance: namely, that in so far as control by software and connected devices (such as radar or sonar) supplants that by humans, malfunctions in that equipment should be regarded as functionally equivalent to human fault, and their results should thus engender liability in so far as they would have done so had they resulted from human action. Such a rule would not only avoid complaints of unfairness: it would also make any necessary amendments to the 1910 Convention (on which, see below) less drastic.

(b) Whose Fault, and Whose Liability?

With human-caused collisions the incidence of liability is straightforward. Liability for crew negligence rests firmly on the owner: even if a crewing agency technically intervenes, there is little doubt that the crewing agency will be regarded as the real employer for the purpose of vicarious liability.[7] And a fortiori, where negligence in maintenance or supervision by the owner's shore staff or management is involved. The only exception worth the name is where there is a bareboat charter: but the result here is effectively the same, merely substituting the bareboat charterer for the registered owner in the equation.

It remains to be seen what contractual arrangements owners and others will make in the case of autonomous ships: but it is possible that the position above may become a good deal less clear. At present, determining who is in charge, and hence liable, is easy. There will always be one entity, whether owner or bareboat charterer, that physically controls the ship and puts its crew on board in order to trade it: it is simply a matter of seeing who it is. But with no crew except perhaps caretakers or watchmen possibly provided by an agency, and operational control conceivably delegated to a shore-based centre specialising in such matters, things are much more uncertain. In such a situation there is a strong case for two statutory provisions on liability. First, in order to get over problems of control it is

[6] The authors' view is that a strict liability regime, if deemed appropriate, should be implemented through an international regime.

[7] *Woodland v Swimming Teachers Association* [2013] UKSC 66; [2014] AC 537 (SC).

suggested that there should be a presumption as to who has it: simplest would be a rule that liabilities attaching to the autonomous operation of a ship should lie with the registered owner, subject to proof that someone else in fact possessed, or exercised operational control, over it. Secondly, difficulties may arise over the delegation of control to third parties, who will be independent contractors and thus people for whose acts or default owners may well not be vicariously liable at common law. This insulation of owners from liability seems undesirable: to avoid doubt, it would be as well to provide expressly that the owner (or other person in charge, as defined above) shall be liable for the acts, omissions and defaults of anyone physically in control of the vessel as though they were his own.

(ii) Convention Matters

It is often forgotten that a good many rules relating to collision are convention-based. The relevant convention is the Brussels Collision Convention 1910, applicable to all collisions between vessels wherever they happen (though not to collisions between vessels and fixed structures, such as harbours or production platforms). In particular Article 2 of this requires liability to be fault-based, though not necessarily dependent on the fault of the owner or his servants: the text reads 'If the collision is accidental, if it is caused by *force majeure*, or if the cause of the collision is left in doubt, the damages are borne by those who have suffered them'. Furthermore, Article 6 expressly prohibits presumptions of fault.

A simple amending Protocol to the 1910 Convention would appear appropriate, on the following lines or something like them:

> (1) Where a ship in the course of navigation is under the control of a device not requiring human intervention, and a collision is caused by a defect in that device, the collision shall not be regarded as accidental or caused by force majeure within Article 2 of this Convention even if no-one is proved to have been at fault in respect of the defect.
>
> (2) Any liability imposed by Articles 1-4 shall attach notwithstanding that the collision is caused by the act, neglect or default of the servants and agents not on board the vessel of a third party, other than a charterer by demise, to whom control of the vessel has been entrusted.

The first of these is necessary to get over the strict requirement of fault-based liability under Article 2 and the accompanying bar on reversals of the burden of proof. The second is not strictly necessary, in that such liability could be imposed consistently with the existing wording. But it seems highly desirable to ensure that the existing liability of owners and charterers is not diluted by the introduction of land-based controlling agents.

B. Salvage

As with collision, most of the concepts of salvage work just as well with any kind of vessel, autonomous or not; salvage, after all, is overwhelmingly about the rescue of things rather than people. Three matters, however, may necessitate slight adjustment or clarification: what counts as salvage services, the position as regards authority to request them, and the duties of those in control of the vessel.

(i) Domestic Law

(a) The Nature of Salvage Services

Traditionally, salvage services must be rendered at sea, or at least in navigable waters.[8] This does not mean they must be entirely so rendered: rescue by helicopter of valuable cargo in danger at sea clearly counts as salvage, even though the helicopter is entirely land-based and any cargo rescued by it is landed and warehoused well inland. But what of services rendered entirely on land? Previously the issue has not arisen: but it might with autonomous vessels. Imagine, for example, that careful operations behind a computer screen allow a grounded autonomous LNG carrier to be refloated and her cargo retrimmed prior to her making for the nearest port of refuge. Or suppose an autonomous vessel's control codes are hacked, leaving her wallowing in danger, whereupon expert computer consultants in some west London basement manage to remove the offending malware and re-establish control. Quite apart from nice questions as to how a maritime arbitrator should reckon reasonable remuneration for such matters, is this maritime salvage at all? The answer is probably yes, at least assuming it comes from a progressive court, but we cannot be certain.[9] Thought should be given to a simple legislative provision stating that an act or activity undertaken to assist a vessel or other property in danger in navigable waters shall not be prevented from amounting to salvage merely because the entire activity takes place on land.

(b) Authority to Request Salvage Services

Authority to make a binding contract for salvage services is governed by the ordinary law of agency. This however is supplemented by Article 6.2 of the International Convention on Salvage (Salvage Convention) 1989,[10] providing that as a matter of law the master has the authority to bind both shipowner and cargo owner, and that the shipowner has the power to bind the cargo owner. These are vital provisions in order to provide the salvor with the necessary degree of legal certainty to allow him to proceed with salvage operations in the clear knowledge that he will have a claim against both vessel and cargo. They may however need adjustment in the case of

[8] *The Goring* [1988] AC 831 (HL).

[9] Theoretically the point could arise even with ordinary vessels, for instance when the temperature control software in smart containers carried on a reefer was knocked out by a violent electrical storm and steps were taken on land over a radio or satellite connection to restore the facility to adjust temperatures and thus save their contents from spoiling. But this has not (yet) happened.

[10] The Convention has been implemented into English law by s 224(1), Sch 11, Pt 1 of the Merchant Shipping Act (MSA) 1995.

autonomous vessels, for two reasons. One is that there may be no 'master': even if not entirely unmanned, a ship sailing with merely a technician or watchman on board will have on board no one technically in command. Secondly, even if a vessel is semi-autonomous, for example sailing under real-time remote control on the open seas but retaining a master for onboard control in ports and constricted waters, there is still the problem of bifurcated command: if something goes wrong at sea, who can arrange for salvage? We need, it is suggested, two additions to the traditional list of owner and master. One is the (natural) person who at the relevant time is in actual control of the vessel. The other, to deal with the case where control is subcontracted by the owner to some other specialised agency, is that agency: if an emergency arises, it should be open to that agency, at least as far as the interests of a salvor are involved, to make a binding request for salvage services.

(c) The Duty to Co-operate

Under the present law owners, master and cargo are bound to co-operate with salvors. When a vessel is under remote control there is one other party with the ability to provide salvors with the help they need, namely the person with any relevant control codes. This may be the owner; but it may not be, in so far as control has been delegated to some other agency. Even though the owner will doubtless be liable for that party's action vis-à-vis the salvor, it would be as well to put him under a direct personal duty.

(ii) Convention Matters

Since all three of the above matters technically affect the scheme of liabilities under the Salvage Convention 1989, they should feature in any autonomous vessel-related protocol to it. The possible wording would be this:

(1) Acts or activities undertaken to assist a vessel or any other property in danger in navigable waters or in any other waters may qualify as salvage operations within Article 1 even if undertaken entirely on land or other location different from that of the vessel or property involved.

(2) Article 6.2bis shall be inserted as follows:

2bis. Where a ship in the course of navigation is, or before the events giving rise to the need for salvage services was, under the control of a device not requiring human intervention, references to the master in Article 6.2 shall include any person to whom the operational control of the vessel may from time to time have been delegated.

(3) Article 8.2bis shall be inserted as follows:

2bis. Where a ship in the course of navigation is, or before the events giving rise to the need for salvage services was, under the control of a device not requiring human intervention, references to the owner and master of the vessel shall also include any third party to whom any control codes or similar information relating to the vessel have been entrusted.

C. Arrest

As with salvage and collision, there is no reason why in principle arrest should draw any distinction between manned and unmanned vessels, or between those controlled from onboard and those not so controlled. Three small adjustments to the law of ship arrest would nevertheless be highly beneficial to deal with the special position of autonomous vessels. These deal with fees due to bodies to whom control is entrusted; with the concept of 'damage done by a ship'; and with the mechanics of arrest.

(i) Technical Points

(a) Fees Due to Bodies Entrusted with Control of a Ship

It is almost certain that, were control of a ship delegated to a third party for the sake of autonomous deployment, that body would have a right of arrest in respect of a claim for payments due, on the basis that this amounted either to a claim under an 'agreement relating to the carriage of goods in a ship or to the use or hire of a ship' within section 20(2)(h) of the Senior Courts Act 1981,[11] or possibly to 'goods or materials supplied to a ship for her operation or maintenance', a term which it is established extends to services as well as goods.[12] But the matter is not beyond all doubt, and there is a strong case for providing explicitly that there is a right of arrest here.

(b) 'Damage Done by a Ship'

The concept of 'damage done by a ship' within section 20(2)(e) of the 1981 Act is wide, and it seems likely would (as should be the case) encompass damage done by a ship under remote control in the same way as any other vessel. Nevertheless the matter ought to be put beyond doubt by a brief elucidation of the relevant sub-clause.

(c) Mechanics of Arrest

In order for the court, through the Admiralty Marshal, to have proper control of a ship under arrest, it may be necessary in the case of autonomous vessels for the authorities to be furnished with the necessary operational codes for the vessel. For that purpose it would be useful were CPR 61 to be amended as to provide that any person with these codes in his possession or control was bound, on pain

[11] Compare *The Isca* (1886) LR 12 PD 34; *The Queen of the South* [1968] P 449; *The Conoco Britannia* [1972] 2 QB 543; and *The Iran Shahamat*, unrep, 1986 Fo 312.

[12] See *The Nore Challenger* [2001] 2 Lloyd's Rep. 103 (crewing agency); see also *The Fairport (No 5)* [1967] 2 Lloyd's Rep 162 and *The Edinburgh Castle* [1999] 2 Lloyd's Rep 362, at 363.

of committal for contempt of court, to make them available to the Marshal or his substitute on written demand by the latter.

(ii) Convention Points

The first two of the above points potentially might involve issues of the meaning of the International Convention for the unification of certain rules relating to Arrest of Sea-going Ships (Arrest Convention) 1952. Accordingly there is a case for a brief protocol to that effect. It might read as follows:

> (1) Where a ship in the course of navigation is under the control of a device not requiring human intervention, the reference in Article 1(1)(a) to 'damage caused by any ship either in collision or otherwise' shall include damage caused by a ship not under the direct control of any human agency.
>
> (2) Article 1(1)(r) shall be inserted as follows:
>
> > Claims for fees or any other claims arising out of an agreement to provide facilities for control of an autonomous vessel.

D. Limitation of Liability

The Convention on Limitation of Liability for Maritime Claims 1976 as amended by 1996 Protocol (LLMC 1996), on which the English right to limit is based,[13] extends the privilege of limitation beyond the owner to the 'charterer, manager and operator' of a seagoing ship.[14] There is no doubt that it is within the spirit of the Convention that where immediate operation of a vessel is entrusted to any third party, that third party should be entitled to limit. For this reason, it is suggested that this should be put beyond doubt in a short protocol to the LLMC 1996, for example as follows:

> Where a ship in the course of navigation is under the control of a device not requiring human intervention, the reference to 'operator' in Article 1.2 shall be taken as including any person to whom the operation of the vessel using that device has been entrusted.

Another point to consider with regard to limitation is the position of a shipowner. The right of limitation is not indefinite and might be lost in some instances. Under the LLMC 1996, for example, a person liable shall not be entitled to limit his liability 'if it is proved that the loss resulted from his personal act or omission, committed with the intent to cause such loss, or recklessly and with knowledge

[13] This has been implemented into English law by ss 185–86 and Sch 7 of the MSA 1995.

[14] See Art 1 of the Convention on Limitation of Liability for Maritime Claims 1976. A similar outcome will follow under the International Convention relating to the Limitation of the Liability of Owners of Sea-Going Ships 1957.

that such loss would probably result'.[15] Unless this test is amended, it is submitted that it will be virtually impossible to break the limits if a programming or software error causes a collision between an autonomous vessel and other vessels. In that scenario, it will be rather difficult if not impossible for third parties to demonstrate the personal act or omission of the shipowner. The outcome will probably be the same even if ship managers fail to upload software updates onto the system, as in most instances such conduct will fall short of 'recklessness'[16] required to break the limits.

E. Wreck Removal

The provisions for wreck removal in English law appear in sections 252–54 of the MSA 1995 (as regards wrecks in the vicinity of harbours and hazards in the territorial sea), and overlapping this sections 255A–U of the same Act, applying the 2007 Nairobi Wreck Removal Convention generally to wrecks anywhere in the UK, the territorial sea and its EEZ.[17] The Nairobi Convention powers, which are the more extensive, oblige the master and the operator of a ship wrecked within the UK Convention area to report it to the UK government, and if a UK ship is wrecked in another Convention state's EEZ, to notify that state. They also require removal of the wreck by the owner under the supervision of the coastal state, allow the state if the owner does not remove it to do the job itself at the latter's expense, and provide for mandatory P&I cover for that expense.

With one exception there is no difficulty in slotting autonomous vessels into this scheme. The exception lies in the duty to report in cases where a vessel is being controlled from onshore. Currently the duty lies on the master and operator[18] (the latter meaning essentially the owner or bareboat charterer, as the case may be).[19] If control of the vessel is delegated to a specialist onshore controller, there is some doubt as to whether the latter would count as an 'operator'. It seems fairly clear that, being in the best position to have early knowledge of the wreck, the operator ought to be under a duty to report. This ought to be provided expressly, in the cases where (a) the shore controller is situated in the UK, (b) a UK ship in the EEZ of another contracting state is involved, or (c) the wreck is in the UK EEZ.

[15] Art 4. The same test also applies in other maritime conventions, such as International Convention for the Unification of Certain Rules of Law relating to Bills of Lading 1968 and Convention relating to the Carriage of Passengers and their Luggage by Sea 1974/2002.

[16] Recklessness is understood to be 'a state of mind stopping short of deliberate intention, and going beyond mere inadvertence'. See, *R v Lawrence (Stephen)* [1982] AC 510 (HL), at 520, per Lord Hailsham.

[17] Merchant Shipping (United Kingdom Wreck Convention Area) Order 2015, SI 2015/172. The Convention applies automatically to the EEZ outside the territorial sea and territory of the coastal state, but may under Art 3.2 be applied to the latter as well. The UK has exercised this option: see the above order.

[18] Merchant Shipping Act 1995, s 255B(4).

[19] See the Nairobi Convention, Art 1.9.

This provision seems essentially compatible with the terms of the Nairobi Convention, and no amendment to that Convention is therefore necessary.

II. Reach of Particular Regimes: Definition of the Vessels to Which they Apply

Although large numbers of liability regimes, whether national or convention-based, are limited to ships or vessels (this after all is why we refer to Admiralty law as a separate subject), there is no universal agreement on what counts as a 'ship' or 'vessel'. Indeed, this is not enormously surprising: different regimes have grown piecemeal, and there is no good reason why (for example) the class of vessels subject to the law of salvage should mirror those subject to the law of maritime arrest.

This section is not concerned with such matters, except peripherally. Instead it looks at whether existing definitions of 'ship or vessel' under particular regimes remain appropriate once autonomous or unmanned vessels are brought into the picture. The conclusion it reaches is that by and large they do, and that there is no reason to adjust them. It deals briefly with each regime in turn.

A. Negligent Navigation (Collisions)

We can begin with collisions. As regards English municipal law, no issues concerning autonomous or unmanned vessels seem to arise. In the rare cases where a different regime from the ordinary law of tort applies to maritime collisions (notably as regards the comparative fault regime in sections 187–89 of the MSA 1995, the time-bar in section 190 of the same Act and the restrictions on in personam jurisdiction in section 22 of the Senior Courts Act 1981) the definition of 'ship' is that in section 313 of the 1995 Act describing a ship as 'including every type of vessel used in navigation'. There is no shortage of case law in maritime law on the meaning of 'used in navigation'. Most recently, in the context of a charge arising under section 58(2)(a) of the MSA 1995, the Court of Appeal (Criminal) in *R v Goodwin*[20] held that the phrase is confined to vessels which are used to make ordered progression over the water from one place to another. In similar fashion, the term 'navigation' was judicially defined as the 'nautical art or science of conducting a ship from one place to another' in *Steedman v Schofield*.[21] In both cases, the courts stressed that movement must be motivated by a need to perform a precise function, and progressing on the water simply for having fun without the object of going anywhere specific could not

[20] [2005] EWCA Crim 3184; [2006] 1 Lloyd's Rep 432. More recently see *Environment Agency v Gibbs* [2016] EWHC 843 (Admin); [2016] 2 Lloyd's Rep 69.

[21] [1992] 2 Lloyd's Rep 163, at 166.

be regarded as 'navigation'.[22] There is no reason to think that these authorities draw any distinction between traditional and unmanned or autonomous vessels; one can navigate as well unmanned as manned.[23]

As regards the Brussels Collision Convention 1910, this applies to collisions either between seagoing vessels or between a seagoing vessel and a vessel of inland navigation.[24] Neither concept is defined; but again, there is no conceivable reason to limit the idea of a 'vessel' to a vessel wholly under the control of those aboard her. It follows that there is no need for any change here.

B. Salvage

Turning to salvage, at common law this applied to a 'ship, her apparel and cargo, including flotsam, jetsam, and lagan, and the wreck of these and freight', whether or not actually in use as such.[25] While this excluded other marine objects which merely aided navigation,[26] it was otherwise pretty comprehensive, and there is no indication at all that ships for these purposes had to be crewed or controlled entirely from on board.

In any case, salvage in English law is now almost entirely governed by the Salvage Convention 1989.[27] Here the definition of the subjects of salvage remains extremely broad. Article 1(a) stipulates that a salvage operation means any act or activity undertaken to assist 'a vessel or any other property in danger'. In a subsequent sub-paragraph, 'vessel' is described expansively as 'any ship or craft, or any structure capable of navigation'; further, Article 1(c) describes property as 'any property not permanently and intentionally attached to the shoreline'. It is our considered view that autonomous ships are capable of navigation,[28] and even if this view is not endorsed judicially, the definition of 'property' is so broad that autonomous vessels are very likely to come under the scope of the Convention.[29]

[22] On that basis, in both cases, a jet-ski was not held to be a ship within the meaning of s 313 of the MSA 1995 which describes a ship as including 'every description of vessel used in navigation not propelled by oars'. *Cf* the decision of the Irish Supreme Court in *The Von Rocks* [1998] 2 Lloyd's Rep 198.

[23] It might be thought that an unmanned surface vehicle was not engaged in navigation: but it has been held that 'navigation' does not require any purposeful travel from A to B (eg, *The Von Rocks* [1998] 2 Lloyd's Rep 198, at 207 (Keane J)).

[24] In other words, it excludes collisions involving purely inland craft.

[25] *The Gas Float Whitton No 2* [1896] P 42, 63–64 (Lord Esher) (approved in the House of Lords at [1997] AC 337).

[26] As in *The Gas Float Whitton* itself, involving a primitive form of lightship.

[27] S 224(1), Sch 11, Pt 1 of the MSA 1995. It is subject to contrary agreement (Art 6(1) stipulates that the terms of the Convention 'shall apply to any salvage operations save to the extent that a contract otherwise provides expressly or by implication.'

[28] Sheen J, in *Steedman v Schofield* [1992] 2 Lloyd's Rep 163, at 166, said: '"Navigation" is not synonymous with movement on water. Navigation is planned or ordered movement from one place to another.' There can be little doubt that autonomous ships are capable of making such planned or ordered moves.

[29] See *Kennedy & Rose on Salvage* (9th edn, Sweet & Maxwell, 2017) at 4-173, making the point that while *The Gas Float Whitton No 2* [1897] AC 337 would probably be decided the same way under the Convention, almost any mobile rather than static marine structure is likely to be covered.

At this stage, we do not know what the technical capabilities of autonomous vessels will be, but if it proves possible for such vessels to engage in salvage operations as a salvor, for instance by towing another vessel, there is no reason why the owner of an autonomous ship should not be able to claim a salvage reward even in the absence of contract, provided the other requirements for salvage are satisfied.

C. Pollution

Turning to pollution, theoretically there can be liability based on fault for pollution emanating from ships, either in negligence (where physical damage ensues) or alternatively in public nuisance.[30] Nothing turns here, however, on the definition of a 'vessel' or 'ship', since this is a general liability arising at common law, and affects maritime and non-maritime defendants equally.

More importantly, there are two convention regimes of strict liability. The first is the Bunkers Convention 2001,[31] implemented into English law by section 153A of the MSA[32] and creating strict liability in the registered owner, bareboat charterer, manager and operator of the ship[33] to persons who suffer damage as a result of pollution caused by the escape or discharge of bunker oil.[34] In so far as autonomous ships use electric power rather than burning diesel or fuel oil, this is clearly not very relevant;[35] but there is no reason why they should not use traditional types of fuel, in which case it will matter a good deal. But the definition of 'ship' gives rise to few if any problems; it encompasses any seagoing vessel or seaborne craft of any type whatsoever.[36] Few would argue that an object that has capability to make a planned and ordered movement at sea, with the assistance of an algorithm or a remote controller, is not capable of being classified at least as a 'seagoing craft'.

The second is the Civil Liability Convention[37] imposing strict liability for spills of persistent hydrocarbons[38] carried as cargo by the registered owner of any 'seagoing vessel, sea-borne craft of any kind whatsoever constructed or adopted for the carriage of oil in bulk as cargo'. Apart from the requirement that the vessel be

[30] See generally S Rainey, '"To The Great Damage and Common Nuisance of All Liege Subjects of Our Lady the Queen": Oil Pollution Claims and Public Nuisance' in B Soyer and A Tettenborn (eds), *Pollution at Sea: Law and Liability*, (Informa Law, 2012) ch 6.

[31] Formally the London International Convention on Civil Liability for Bunker Oil Pollution Damage 2001.

[32] Under the Merchant Shipping (Oil Pollution) (Bunkers Convention) Regulations SI 2006/1244.

[33] See s 153A(7).

[34] See s 153A(1).

[35] Though not entirely irrelevant, since the liability covers luboil as well: see s 170(1) and Art 1.10 of the Convention.

[36] See s 170(1) and Art 1.1 of the Convention.

[37] Formally the International Convention on Civil Liability for Pollution Damage 1992, incorporated into English law by ss 171–82 of the Merchant Shipping Act 1995.

[38] Meaning 'any persistent hydrocarbon mineral oil such as crude oil, fuel oil, heavy diesel oil and lubricating oil, whether carried on board a ship as cargo or in the bunkers of such a ship' (Art 1(5) of the CLC 1992; see too s 170(1) of the Merchant Shipping Act 1995).

constructed or adapted to carry oil, the definition here is essentially the same as under the Bunkers Convention, and similarly seems to imply no requirement that such a vessel or craft even be manned. Certainly the fact that the vessel may be reliant on the operation of an algorithm on some mainframe in a control centre situated miles away, is not a key factor in determining whether it comes under the Convention or not.

Similarly, too, with the HNS Convention[39] (which is not in force but may well come into effect in the not too distant future) that is aimed at imposing strict liability on the owner of a vessel carrying non-oil cargoes that are nevertheless hazardous (for example, flammable, explosive, or toxic). The definition of a 'vessel' in this Convention is the same as above,[40] and the same arguments apply. Admittedly early indications are that autonomous ships might not be suitable for carrying hazardous cargoes anyway (for example, flammable, explosive, biological), as such cargoes will continue to require special considerations.[41] But if these problems are overcome, then the point may matter.

D. Wreck Removal

Wreck removal powers exist under both domestic English law and international convention. The powers under English law are contained in section 56 of the Harbours Docks and Piers Clauses Act 1847 and sections 252–54 of the Merchant Shipping Act 1995. As regards the former, it simply refers to any 'wreck or other obstruction', without specifying that it must emanate from a ship; so no problem can conceivably arise. As regards the latter, the vessels subject to the power include 'any ship or boat, or any other description of vessel used in navigation', which essentially mirrors that under section 313 of the same Act, and for the reasons given above fairly clearly covers autonomous and unmanned ships.

The Nairobi Wreck Removal Convention 2007[42] makes shipowners liable for the cost of locating, marking and removing a wreck within a state's exclusive economic zone for safety or environmental reasons. For the purposes of the Convention, a wreck is a ship or part of one that is sunk or stranded, or in danger of so being, and any object lost from it. A 'ship' is 'a seagoing vessel of any type whatsoever operating in the marine environment'; the term also includes 'hydrofoils, hovercraft, submersibles, floating craft and floating platforms except when such platforms are on location engaged in the exploration, exploitation or production of seabed

[39] Formally the London International Convention on Liability and Compensation for Damage in Connection with the Carriage of Hazardous and Noxious Substances by Sea 2010.

[40] See Art 1.1.

[41] See the Maritime Unmanned Navigation through Intelligence Networks (MUNIN) project, www.unmanned-ship.org/munin, accessed 1 July 2020.

[42] Formally the Nairobi International Convention on the Removal of Wrecks 2007, incorporated into English law under Pt IXA of the Merchant Shipping Act 1995.

mineral resources'.[43] As elsewhere, there is no indication that it matters whether a vessel is manned or where it is controlled from.

E. Limitation of Liability

Limitation under English law is now governed entirely by the LLMC 1996. A number of heads of liability covered by it are defined by reference to a 'ship': notably liability for property damage or injury occurring on board or in direct connexion with the operation of a ship;[44] claims for raising a sunken or stranded ship;[45] and claims for removing, destroying or rendering harmless cargo on board a ship.[46] The Convention does not define a 'ship';[47] but the Merchant Shipping Act 1995 does, stating that 'ship' includes 'any structure (whether completed or in the course of completion) launched and intended for use in navigation as a ship or part of a ship'. As such the definition is similar to that in section 313 of the same Act, regarding a 'ship' as 'every description of vessel used in navigation', save that an intent to use the vessel in navigation also suffices. To that extent, in so far as section 313 includes autonomous vessels, so does Schedule 7 providing for the right to limit.

If so, operators of autonomous ships can fairly clearly limit. However, how about others involved in the manufacturing process who may well be in the firing line when something goes wrong, such as software producers and program designers? Neither under the Convention nor under the 1995 Act can they limit.

F. Arrest

The arrest jurisdiction of the English courts under English municipal law is based on the jurisdiction *in rem*, which in turn is now governed entirely by section 21 of the Senior Courts Act. Under section 21(1)–(3), *in rem* claims can be brought (a) against property against which there subsists a maritime lien; (b) against a ship in respect of a claim by a mortgagee, any claim to ownership or possession of a ship, or (c) against a ship or sister-ship in respect of any of the other claims listed in section 20(2) of the Act. As regards the definition of a 'ship', this is provided by section 24(1), which (reflecting the general definition of a 'ship' in section 313 of the Merchant Shipping Act 1995) states that 'ship' 'includes any description of

[43] See Art 1.2 of the Convention and s 255R(1) of the Merchant Shipping Act 1995.
[44] See Art 2.1(a).
[45] Art 2.1(d).
[46] Art 2.1(e).
[47] The Convention only requires states party to allow seagoing ships to limit; but Sch 7 to the 1995 Act allows all vessels to do so.

vessel used in navigation'. As argued above, this means that as regards English law, there is no difficulty as regards autonomous vessels.

The 1952 Arrest Convention, on which the 1981 Act is based, is less straightforward, since it refers fairly indiscriminately to both 'ships' and 'vessels', but defines neither. This clearly raises issues as to the reach of the Convention, in particular as to whether it should apply to vessels such as dredgers or jack-up rigs, and how far it extends to ships and boats used in inland navigation.[48] There is also an additional complication that its application is in any case only compulsory in respect of ships flagged in contracting states, which gives rise to a further de facto limitation to vessels capable of being so flagged by the relevant state law.[49] However, it is suggested that these problems need not concern us here. The fact is that, whatever difficulties there may be elsewhere with delineating the subject of arrest, there is no indication anywhere in the Convention that it matters where a vessel is controlled from, or indeed whether it is manned at all. In these circumstances, the only sensible conclusion is that the 1952 Convention applies without difficulty to autonomous vessels.[50]

G. Strict Liability under the Harbours, Docks and Piers Clauses Act 1847

In an attempt to preserve the integrity of port infrastructure at the expense of P&I interests, section 74 of the Harbours Docks and Piers Clauses Act 1847 introduces a strict liability regime for the owner of a craft which damages the harbour, dock, pier, quays, or works. Section 74 makes the owner of any vessel or float of timber liable without proof of fault for any damage done by it to any harbour installation. 'Vessel' is defined[51] as any 'ship, boat, lighter, and craft of every kind, and whether navigated by steam or otherwise.' This definition[52] is about as wide as it can get, and there is little doubt that an unmanned or autonomous vessel would be comprised in it.[53]

[48] These points are all discussed at length in *Berlingieri on The Arrest of Ships* (5th edn, Informa Law, 2016).

[49] For discussion of this whole matter, see S Rainey 'What is a "Ship" under the 1952 Arrest Convention?' [2013] *LMCLQ* 50 and *Berlingieri on The Arrest of Ships* (5th edn, Informa Law, 2016), ch 3.

[50] A point made in *Berlingieri on The Arrest of Ships* (5th edn, Informa Law, 2016), para 3.14.

[51] See s 3 of the 1847 Act.

[52] As a definition, it needs to be treated with some little caution. Particular legislation applying the 1847 Act to a given port harbour not infrequently applies a different definition, and the point should be carefully checked in each case. See eg, the Hinkley Point Harbour Empowerment Order 2012 (SI 2012/1914) art 2(1) and art 3(5)(b); and the Zetland County Council Act 1974 (1974, c viii), ss 3, 4. Each of these substitutes a different, and mutually variant, definition for that in s 3.

[53] Indeed there is already authority that it encompasses an entirely inert craft such as a dumb-barge: see *Hedges & Son v London & St Katharine Docks Co* (1885) 16 QBD 597, 600–01 (Huddleston B). If a vessel entirely without means of control is covered, a fortiori a vessel controlled from on shore should equally be included.

III. Concluding Thoughts

The analysis carried out above reveals a number of significant points. First, it is evident that international regimes dealing with private law issues that can emerge from ship operations would be largely applicable for autonomous ships. There is little doubt on that, even if in practice there might be a shift of emphasis.[54] However, it is also clear that clarification on certain issues would be needed and we attempted to make suggestions as to how those matters, that is, by making slight amendments to international regimes such as Arrest Convention 1952 and Salvage Convention 1989, can be addressed.

More difficult questions that have policy implications need to be considered. For example, it might be necessary to deliberate further whether fault based regime should continue to apply for negligent navigation or there is a need to implement a strict liability regime for autonomous ships. To stick to the current fault-based regime would undoubtedly be the preferred option of the liability insurers. We have suggested that the fault-based regime could continue to apply with some amendments. However, several plausible arguments can be developed as to why a strict liability regime will be more suitable. First, it is inevitable that algorithms that will be used by autonomous vessels will reflect the ethical values of the person who designs them. For the designer, a really difficult question is programming how the autonomous vessel should act in a situation where only really poor alternatives are left. For example, should the autonomous vessel intentionally collide with another vessel or instead sail aground in a rocky area, risking massive oil pollution damage to the environment?[55] Ultimately, it will be the man-made software which makes the system do what it does; but if the programmer opts for the former option, this will create rather difficult ethical considerations for the court in determining the degree of fault in the context of a 'fault-based' liability system. Conversely, a strict liability regime will protect the interest of third-party claimants by enabling them to recover their loss without further consideration, especially in a case where they were deemed not to be worthy of protection as a result of the ethical values adopted by the software designer. Second, it has been raised as a concern that there might be instances

[54] Notably in that finding fault with programming and data breaches involves evaluating the factors which are more remote from the accident itself, than if one is assessing the conduct of the master and crew navigating a vessel.

[55] A similar question has been posed in the context of autonomous cars, known as 'the trolley problem'. This is an ethical debate evaluated in depth by JJ Thomson, 'The Trolley Problem' (1984–85) 94 *Yale LJ* 1395. The hypothetical scenario indicates that there is a runaway trolley barrelling down the railway tracks. Ahead on the tracks, there are five people tied up and unable to move. The trolley is headed straight for them. The decision-maker in the story is standing some distance off in the train yard, next to a lever. If he pulls the lever, the trolley will switch to a different set of tracks on which one person is tied up. There is a never-ending dilemma over which is the most ethical thing to do: nothing, and the trolley kills the five people on the main track. Or, pull the lever, diverting the trolley onto the side track where it will kill one person.

where machines with artificial intelligence do not perform in a way that is consistent with their designers' intentions.[56] It is possible that truly intelligent machines will learn to adapt the instructions they initially receive from humans to circumstances not directly forecast at the time of their creation. And perhaps these machines will learn to internalise values that are not the ones their creators tried to embed.[57] If this holds true, allocating fault on a traditional basis in an instance where an autonomous vessel has acquired capacity to act in a way that is contrary to the 'rules' that it has been given by its programmer will be a very difficult, if not an impossible, task. In such instance, a system of 'strict liability' would be more appropriate to address the inadequacy of tort law to resolve questions of liability that may push beyond the frontiers of science and technology. The authors acknowledge that these are not easy questions but they need to be considered at one point before autonomous ships become a commercial reality. Last but not least, the matter should be considered from the perspective of public acceptance of autonomous ships. The manufacturers will no doubt strive to ensure that such vessels do not pose any danger to other vessels, people on board other vessels, other maritime property, and environmental resources. However, it is also an undeniable reality that regulators will not allow autonomous vessels to operate if there is a significant public resistance against the use of such vessels. Social risk acceptance is a complex issue and not necessarily related to the actual risk level posed by a piece of equipment.[58] Also, as indicated earlier, it might be difficult for humans to maintain control of machines that are programmed to act with considerable autonomy.[59] There are a number of mechanisms by which a loss of control may occur: a malfunction, such as a corrupted file or physical damage to input equipment; a security breach; or a flaw in programming. These make autonomous vessels a potential source of public risk on a scale that far exceeds the more familiar forms of public risk that are solely the result of human behaviour.[60] It is, therefore, submitted that employing a strict liability regime at times when such vessels operate autonomously might assist in gaining public support. A strict liability regime would undoubtedly endorse the assurance given to the public by manufacturers that the technology used in autonomous vessels is safe, by ensuring that an effective compensation regime is available to others who might be adversely affected in extreme cases where this technology fails.

[56] N Bostrom, 'The Superintelligent Will: Motivation and Instrumental Rationality in Advanced Artificial Agents' (2012) 22 *Minds & Machines* 71–85.

[57] U Pagallo, *The Law of Robots: Crimes, Contracts and Torts* (Springer, 2013), 115–45.

[58] Interestingly, it was stressed in the MUNIN Report that not all commercial goods will be suitable for autonomous transport by sea; hazardous cargoes (eg, flammable, explosive, biological) will continue to require special considerations and possibly not be suitable for carriage by autonomous vessels. See www.unmanned-ship.org/munin/, accessed on 31 July 2020.

[59] On this matter, see generally, N Silver, *The Signal and the Noise: Why So Many Predictions Fail – But Some Don't* (Penguin, 2013).

[60] MU Scherer, 'Regulating Artificial Intelligence Systems: Risks, Challenges, Competencies and Strategies' 29 (2016) *Harvard Journal of Law & Technology* at 366–67.

Another difficult issue will be to determine whether the limitation of liability regime should be extended to manufacturers or their sub-contractors. This will be effectively a policy decision, but if the right of limitation is kept in its current format, one should bear in mind that the liability of a manufacturer of an autonomous vessel will be greater than the liabilities that a shipowner will face by third parties, given that the former might be partially or fully responsible to the replacement cost of an autonomous vessel in addition to liabilities that he will face in a recourse action. This kind of outcome could affect the availability of insurance cover and its price.

A further difficulty will be how changes in different international and domestic liability regimes can be implemented. Amending each different legal regime could prove to be a rather difficult process, and perhaps the most straightforward way will be to devise a new convention dealing with private law issues concerning autonomous ships. This is a matter that we shall turn to later in the final chapter of the book.

4

Unmanned Vessels and International Conventions for the Carriage of Goods by Sea

PROFESSOR SIMON BAUGHEN*

The international shipping industry is responsible for the carriage of around 80–90 per cent of world trade.[1] The carriage of goods by sea involves a variety of contracts, from demise, voyage and time charterparties, to bills of lading and sea waybills. Nearly all contracts under bills of lading will be subject to the provisions of some mandatory international convention, of which the most common is the Hague Rules. Almost all contracts under waybills will be subject to the operation of one of those conventions through contractual incorporation through a 'clause paramount' as will many charterparties. In this chapter, we shall consider how the contractual forms for the carriage of goods will operate when goods are carried in an unmanned ship, operating at Maritime Autonomous Surface Ship (MASS) levels 3 or 4. To recap, the four MASS levels set out by the International Maritime Organization in its scoping exercise on autonomous ships are as follows:

MASS Level 1: Ship with automated processes and decision support: Seafarers are on board to operate and control shipboard systems and functions. Some operations may be automated and at times be unsupervised but with seafarers on board ready to take control.

MASS Level 2: Remotely controlled ship with seafarers on board: The ship is controlled and operated from another location. Seafarers are available on board to take control and to operate the shipboard systems and functions.

MASS Level 3: Remotely controlled ship without seafarers on board: The ship is controlled and operated from another location. There are no seafarers on board.

* Professor of Shipping Law, Member of the Institute of International Shipping and Trade Law, Swansea University.

[1] The International Chamber of Shipping gives a figure of 90%, www.ics-shipping.org/shipping-facts/shipping-and-world-trade#:~:text=Overview,blood%20of%20the%20global%20economy, accessed 20 July 2020. UNCTAD, however, gives a figure of 80% by volume and 70% by volume, www.linkedin.com/pulse/one-question-many-answers-how-much-worlds-trade-sea-rodas-martini/.

MASS Level 4: Fully autonomous ship: The operating system of the ship is able to make decisions and determine actions by itself.

I. International Liability Conventions for the Carriage of Goods by Sea

A. The Hague and Hague-Visby Rules

The principal convention is the 1924 Hague Rules,[2] and its amended version with the 1968 Visby Protocol.[3] The Hague Rules impose a mandatory liability regime on contracts of carriage covered by a bill of lading or any similar document of title, insofar as the document relates to the carriage of goods by sea. These contracts of carriage will come within the Hague Rules if they fall within the types of contract set out in Article 10, which provides 'The provisions of this Convention shall apply to all bills of lading issued in any of the contracting States'. With the Hague-Visby Rules, the relevant provision is Article X which provides:

> The provisions of these Rules shall apply to every bill of lading relating to the carriage of goods between ports in two different States if
>
> (a) the bill of lading is issued in a contracting State, or
> (b) the carriage is from a port in a contracting State, or
> (c) the contract contained in or evidenced by the bill of lading provides that these Rules or legislation of any State giving effect to them are to govern the contract;
>
> whatever may be the nationality of the ship, the carrier, the shipper, the consignee, or any other interested person.

It is the contract of carriage between the carrier and the shipper, the fact of carriage by sea, and the existence, or contractual contemplation, of a bill of lading that determines the applicability of the Rules. The nature of the ship in which the goods are carried is of no import. The Rules do refer to 'the ship' as a party which is liable along with the carrier in Articles IV(1) and (2), which establish the defences to liability for loss or damage, and in Article III(8), which renders void any clauses in the contract of carriage relieving the carrier or the ship of liability, or lessening liability, other than as provided in the Rules. 'Ship' is widely defined as '[a]ny vessel used for the carriage of goods by sea' and does not presuppose any particular type of ship is being used, or, indeed, that it be manned.

[2] International Convention for the Unification of Certain Rules of Law relating to Bills of Lading ('Hague Rules'), and Protocol of Signature (Brussels, 25 August 1924).

[3] Protocol to Amend the International Convention for the Unification of Certain Rules of Law Relating to Bills of Lading ('Visby Rules')(Brussels, 23 February 1968). Throughout this chapter, the Hague Rules will be referred to, save where there are references to new provisions in the Visby amendments.

(i) Seaworthiness. Article III(1) of the Hague Rules

In the substance of the Rules, three obligations are imposed on the 'carrier' which could be a shipowner or charterer. First, there is Article III(1) which imposes on the carrier, before and at the beginning of the voyage to exercise due diligence to:

(a) Make the ship seaworthy;
(b) Properly man, equip and supply the ship;
(c) Make the holds, refrigerating and cool chambers, and all other parts of the ship in which goods are carried, fit and safe for their reception, carriage and preservation.

Headings (a) and (c) would remain unchanged as they apply to the physical condition of the ship (a) and its cargo-carrying spaces. With an unmanned cargo vessel, the differences from a manned vessel would be apparent in heading (b). This does not prescribe what is necessary for proper manning, equipping and supplying of the ship. There is no requirement for any onboard manning, and this obligation would probably be satisfied through having sufficient, adequately trained, shore based controllers (SBC) monitoring, and navigating the vessel remotely as necessary, with proper software and communications systems to enable safe autonomous navigation, and essential, functioning, cameras, sensors and LIDAR for communication with the SBC. At level 4, there would be a query about whether the vessel could be said to be 'properly' manned in the absence of any human input into its navigation. However, there would likely be some form of continuing onshore monitoring, and the shipowners' arrangements for this would fall under this heading.

The issue of seaworthiness pervades discussion of unmanned vessels. In this context, seaworthiness will have to extend landward, extending to software and hardware on shore, as well as to the competence of the SBCs monitoring and, as necessary, operating the vessel. The obligation of the carrier under Article III(1) will involve the following aspects of the vessel's operation: the computer hardware on the vessel by which the software controlling the vessel will be operated; the software installed; the programming of the software for the voyage to be undertaken. The competence of the human element, the SBC who will monitor the vessel's progress and if needs be, take remote control of its operation. The human element of the crew will no longer be tied in with the vessel, and although this will have an impact on classification surveys, which will need to assess those off ship elements, it will not alter the basic legal analysis. The hardware and the software on the vessel are no different from existing navigational aids, such as SATNAV and RADAR on a vessel, while it is well established that crew incompetence will render unseaworthy.[4] The preparation of a passage plan by the master is an incident of the

[4] *The Star Sea* [1995] 1 Lloyd's Rep 651, QB. *Hong Kong Fir Shipping Co Ltd v Kawasaki Kisen Kaisha Ltd* [1962] 2 QB 26, CA. In *The Eurasian Dream* [2002] EWHC 118 (Comm); [2002] 1 Lloyd's Rep 719.

vessel's initial seaworthiness before and at the start of the voyage,[5] and the same would apply as regards the inputting of voyage instructions by an SBC under MASS levels 3 and 4. With increased web awareness in the vessel's software systems, in time it is likely that the only input will be of the place of loading and discharge with all navigational details being determined by the software on the basis of up to date virtual charts.

If anything is wrong with any of these elements 'before and at the beginning of the voyage',[6] the ship will be unseaworthy, and if that is a cause of the loss or damage to cargo then the shipowner will be in breach of Article III(1), and it will be for the shipowner to exonerate itself under Article IV(1) by showing that it took due diligence to make the ship seaworthy. The timing of the seaworthiness period will fit slightly awkwardly into the brave new world of unmanned vessels and onshore remote operators. Several SBCs will probably be employed at different stages in the voyage, and each will also be simultaneously undertaking the remote operation of other vessels. Will seaworthiness through the competence of the 'crew' attach at the time the voyage starts or will this be a moveable feast attaching each time the vessel passes into the orbit of a new set of SBCs?

It should be recalled that the duty under Article III(1) is a personal 'non-delegable' one which means that the negligence of independent contractors will be treated as a failure by the carrier to take due diligence to ensure the vessel's seaworthiness.[7] So, for example, problems caused by the hacking of the vessel's computer systems would amount to a breach of Article III(1) if the necessary anti-virus programs had not been kept up to date, no matter that this was a task undertaken by an independent contractor – nor would the shipowner be able to establish due diligence in this situation. A failure to update during the voyage would be different and would amount to a breach of Article III.2 in failing properly and carefully to carry and care for the cargo. If the software installed on the vessel is itself defective, then the issue would be whether this failure occurred while the vessel was in the orbit of the shipowner. The shipowner's duty under Article III(1) does not start until the vessel comes into its 'orbit', which term is coextensive with ownership, service or control. In *The Happy Ranger*,[8] the shipowner was not liable

[5] *Alize 1954 v Allianz Elementar Versicherungs AG (The CMA CGM Libra)* [2019] EWHC 481 (Admlty); aff'd [2020] EWCA Civ 293.

[6] A breakdown shortly after leaving port will give rise to an inference that the vessel was unseaworthy on sailing. *The Theodegmon* [1990] 1 Lloyd's Rep 52.

[7] *The Muncaster Castle* [1961] AC 807, HL where the cargo was damaged by an ingress of seawater. Immediately prior to her outward voyage to the load port at Sydney, the ship had passed through her No 2 special survey and annual load line survey. The marine superintendent employed a reputable firm of ship repairers to open up all storm valves and inspection covers. After inspection, the repairers' fitter shut and secured each cover. Due to a fitter's negligence in not securing the nuts sufficiently, they were loosened by the working of the ship in rough weather and seawater got in. The owners had still failed to exercise due diligence. If the servant of the independent contractor was negligent, then the owners were still in breach of their duty. Similarly reliance on the judgments of Classification Society surveyors will also be insufficient to discharge the burden of proving due diligence. See *The Toledo* [1995] 1 Lloyd's Rep 40.

[8] [2006] EWHC 122 (Comm); [2006] 1 Lloyd's Rep 649.

for the negligence of the shipbuilder prior to that date that had resulted in defects to the vessel's cranes. However, the shipowner had failed to exercise due diligence in relation to the period after the vessel came into its orbit by failing to proof test the hooks before loading began, aware that no such testing had been done by the shipbuilder. With the acquisition of an unmanned vessel, the owners would need to show that they had run the proper tests on the software controlling its navigation. Thereafter, they would need to show that proper tests had been run to ensure the software was still functioning correctly. With the increasing likelihood of machine-learning and adaptation of the program, there is a risk that defects in the software may be generated over time which cannot be detected by such tests. A defect in the adapted navigational software would render the ship unseaworthy, but if not detectable by proper testing prior to the start of the voyage, the carrier would be able to invoke the defence of due diligence in Article IV(1) and then be able to rely on the defence in Article IV(2)(p) of latent defect.

New navigational software fitted after the acquisition of the vessel would be another matter. If defective before and at the start of the voyage, the vessel would be unseaworthy, and the carrier would not be able to show due diligence was taken to make the vessel seaworthy as the duty is non-delegable. The fault of the software programmer would be the fault of the carrier, as the fault of the ship repairer's servants was the fault of the shipowner in *The Muncaster Castle*.

The incompetence of the crew can sometimes go beyond negligence and amount to unseaworthiness. The same would apply concerning the competence of the SBCs who are operating and monitoring the vessel on its voyage. In *Hong Kong Fir Shipping Co Ltd v Kawasaki Kisen Kaisha Ltd*,[9] the vessel's diesel engines and other machinery were in reasonably good order when the vessel was delivered to the time charterers. However, by reason of their age, the engines needed to be maintained by an experienced, competent, careful and adequate engine room staff. In fact, the engine room staff was incompetent, with a chief engineer addicted to drink, thereby rendering the vessel unseaworthy.

Moreover, an otherwise competent crew can be rendered incompetent by lack of knowledge. In *Standard Oil Co of New York v Clan Line Steamers* Ltd,[10] the shipowners failed to pass on to the master instructions from the manufacturers of the vessel that the vessel had to retain water ballast when loaded with a full homogeneous cargo. The master ordered the crew to empty the vessel's ballast tanks, with the result that she keeled over and sank in calm seas. The damage was held to be attributable to the unseaworthiness of the vessel at the start of her voyage. So too, in *The Star Sea*,[11] it was held, in the context of section 39(5) of the Marine Insurance Act 1906, that the shipowner's failure to ensure that the master was familiar with the operation of the vessel's CO_2 system for extinguishing fires amounted to unseaworthiness at the start of the voyage. In *The Eurasian Dream*,[12] severe damage was

[9] [1962] 2 QB 26.
[10] [1924] AC 100.
[11] *Manifest Shipping Co Ltd v Uni-Polaris Insurance Co Ltd (The Star Sea)* [2001] UKHL 1.
[12] [2002] EWHC 118 (Comm); [2002] 1 Lloyd's Rep 719, QB.

caused when a fire broke out on a car-carrier due to the stevedores simultaneously refuelling and jump-starting cars. The third officer should have supervised them and prevented this dangerous practice.

Furthermore, the crew's lack of training in firefighting procedures meant that they were unable to contain the fire that took over the vessel and rendered it a constructive total loss. The crew's inability in this respect was caused by many factors, including the absence of walkie-talkies to enable them to communicate during the fire fighting. In addition, there was also a clear failure on the part of the shipowners to set up a proper system to ensure that the crew were able to deal with such emergencies. The shipowners had provided voluminous safety documentation, which would have taken the master two or three weeks to digest. What was needed was information on safety procedures that were related to the specific vessel.

In the context of an unmanned vessel, the crewing component of seaworthiness would extend to the competence of the SBCs monitoring the vessel's operation. For example, lack of familiarity with the vessels navigational software, or lack of training by the servants of the SBC, lack of sufficient operators to monitor multiple vessels, lack of proper shift durations, would all render the ship unseaworthy through 'crew' incompetence.

(ii) Article III(2). Care of the Cargo

Second, there is Article III(2) which requires the carrier properly and carefully to 'load, handle, stow, carry, keep, care for and discharge the goods carried'. This is a non-delegable obligation,[13] although some operations may be contractually allocated away from the shipowner to other parties such as charterers, shippers, and receivers.[14] If cargo is lost or damaged during the carrier's period of responsibility under the Rules, which runs from the start of loading to the completion of discharge, there will be a presumed breach of Article III(2) which the carrier may rebut by showing that it took proper care of the cargo or bringing itself within one of the exceptions afforded to it under Article IV(2). Crew intervention in cargo management is already diminishing and will disappear still further at levels 3 and 4. Operations such as opening and closing hatch covers during the voyage to ventilate grain cargoes may be done remotely by the SBC, but there is no reason why these could not be done completely remotely through the programmed software with the SBC maintaining only a monitoring role. The carrier's obligation under Article III(2), which is non-delegable, would encompass the performance of the SBCs in that role. If they fail to monitor the vessel properly or to perform

[13] *Hourani v T & J Harrison* (1927) 27 Ll L Rep 415.

[14] This is the position under English law, see *The Jordan II*, but in other jurisdictions applying the Hague Rules, the shipowner is treated as having undertaken all seven of the functions listed in Art II and III(2).

remote cargo operations properly during the voyage, the carrier will be in breach of its obligation under Article III(2).

(iii) Defences under Article IV

The defences available to the carrier are set out in Article IV and also apply to 'the ship'. Paragraph one provides a due diligence defence to cover liability arising out of breach of Article III(1). The duty is personal to the carrier and is non-delegable, so there is no due diligence if the ship has been rendered unseaworthy by the negligence of the crew[15] or by that of an independent contractor.[16] This may be problematic where an undetectable fault causes problems in the software programs which navigate the vessel.

Paragraph two then contains a list of specific exceptions from (a) to (q). Of particular interest is the first of these, 'Act, neglect, or default of the master, mariner, pilot, or the servants of the carrier in the navigation or in the management of the ship'. The absence of an onboard crew might be thought to remove this exception when the goods are being carried by an unmanned vessel. However, it is possible to regard the SBC as the functional equivalent of the master and, therefore, the carrier would still be able to rely on the exception in respect of loss or damage caused by any errors of navigation on their part. If the SBC is not regarded as the 'master', then they could constitute a 'servant of the carrier'. As the duties of the carrier under both Articles III(1) and (2) are non-delegable, the servants of any independent contractor engaged to perform those duties will be treated as a servant of the carrier.[17] Accordingly, servants of the SBC will be 'servants of the carrier' for the purposes of the nautical fault defence.[18] It is doubtful whether negligence by the voyage programmer would fall within the exception as such negligence would render the vessel unseaworthy. The duty is personal to the carrier and is non-delegable, so there is no due diligence if the ship has been rendered unseaworthy by the negligence of the crew[19] or by that of an independent contractor.[20]

Human input at level 4 will probably be no more than an SBC inputting the start and finish of the voyage, and human SBCs assuming operation when the software dictates – everything else will be down to the algorithms, which dictate when to involve human operators in remote navigation. This means that the nautical fault

[15] *Alize 1954 v Allianz Elementar Versicherungs AG (The CMC CGM Libra)* [2019] EWHC 481 (Admlty).

[16] *Riverstone Meat Co Pty Ltd v Lancashire Shipping Co Ltd (The Muncaster Castle)* [1961] AC 807.

[17] As regards Art III (2) see: *The Ferro*, [1893] P 38; *Hourani v T & J Harrison: Brown & Co v Same* (1927) 28 Ll L Rep 120 (CA).

[18] This is something which would not ordinarily be possible as regards servants of other independent contractors such as stevedores. See, *Heyn and others v Ocean Steamship Co Ltd* (1927) 27 Ll L Rep 334 (KB); *Hourani v T & J Harrison: Brown & Co v Same* (1927) 28 Ll L Rep 120 (CA). More than one employer can be vicariously liable for the negligence of an employee under the direction of another. *Viasystems (Tyneside) Ltd v Thermal Transfer (Northern) Ltd* [2006] 2 WLR 428, CA.

[19] *The CMC CGM Libra.*

[20] *The Muncaster Castle.*

exception in IV(2)(a) effectively disappears in respect of goods carried on a level 4 vessel. Any defect in the software controlling the vessel's navigation will not be the fault of a legal person, and the initial creator of the software will have done so long before the commencement of the voyage. Nor would defects in the software controlling the vessel's navigation be attributable to the fault of a legal person, as a software program has no personality, and the initial human creator of the software will have created it, along with its self-learning capacity, long before the commencement of the voyage in question. However, at level 4 it is conceivable that the SBC may be summoned into action by the vessel's navigational software, and the SBC's response to that call to arms in response to a compromised algorithm may be negligent. In this case, if that negligence is causative of the loss or damage, the defence will exonerate the carrier.

Another defence that is of interest would be (f) 'Act of public enemies'. This probably covers pirates but may also be extended to cover persons who hack into the vessel's computer system, on the grounds that they are the twenty-first century's 'hostes humani generis', the old description used for pirates and slavers. The final defence is in heading (q) which provides:

> Any other cause arising without the actual fault or privity of the carrier, or without the fault or neglect of the agents or servants of the carrier, but the burden of proof shall be on the person claiming the benefit of this exception to show that neither the actual fault or privity of the carrier nor the fault or neglect of the agents or servants of the carrier contributed to the loss or damage.

This would cover the hacking of the vessel's computer system, but with the burden on the carrier of proving that there had been no fault on the part of its agents, servants or carrier. After the decision of the Supreme Court in *Volcafe Ltd and Ors v Compania Sud America de Vapores SA*,[21] the carrier will also have to show it took reasonable care of the cargo, as regards the inherent vice exception in (m) and likely as regards all the other exceptions bar (a) which is based on the fault of the vessel's servants and agents in the navigation and management of the vessel or the fire exception in (b).[22]

(iv) Documentary Obligations. Article III(3)

The carrier is subject to a third, documentary, obligation under Article III(3) which provides:

> After receiving the goods into his charge the carrier or the master or agent of the carrier shall, on demand of the shipper, issue to the shipper a bill of lading showing among other things:
>
> (a) The leading marks necessary for identification of the goods as the same are furnished in writing by the shipper before the loading of such goods starts,

[21] [2018] UKSC 61.

[22] *Glencore Energy UK Ltd v Freeport Holdings Ltd (The Lady M)* [2019] EWCA Civ 388 14 March 2019.

> provided such marks are stamped or otherwise shown clearly upon the goods if uncovered, or on the cases or coverings in which such goods are contained, in such a manner as should ordinarily remain legible until the end of the voyage.
>
> (b) Either the number of packages or pieces, or the quantity, or weight, as the case may be, as furnished in writing by the shipper.
>
> (c) The apparent order and condition of the goods.
>
> Provided that no carrier, master or agent of the carrier shall be bound to state or show in the bill of lading any marks, number, quantity or weight which he has reasonable ground for suspecting not accurately to represent the goods actually received, or which he has had no reasonable means of checking.

The obligation to issue a bill of lading which contains these three pieces of information falls on three alternative parties: the carrier; the master; the agent of the carrier. Unmanned vessels raise the question of whether there will be a master, and, if so, who that will be. SBCs are likely to be considered as fulfilling the role of the master for navigational purposes, but unless electronic bills of lading are to be issued, would be unable to fulfil the master's function of issuing bills of lading. No matter, the shipper can require either the carrier or the carrier's agent to issue a bill of lading. This is subject to Article VI which allows a carrier, master or agent of the carrier to enter an agreement with the shipper on any terms, provided that no bill of lading has been or shall be issued and the terms agreed shall be embodied in a receipt which shall be a non-negotiable document and marked as such.

This trinity of parties reappear in Article III(6) as alternative parties to whom notice of loss or damage must be given in writing 'before or at the time of the removal of the goods into the custody of the person entitled to delivery thereof under the contract of carriage, or, if the loss or damage be not apparent, within three days'. The disappearance of one of these parties, the master, is no reason for the inapplicability of the Rules. Article III(6) contains a one-year time limit for commencing suit which applies to claims against the carrier and 'the ship'. The reference to 'the ship' indicates that the time bar applies to *in rem* proceedings against the carrier's ship.

(v) Dangerous Goods. Article IV(6)

The 'master' reappears in Article IV(6) which deals with the presence of dangerous goods on the ship. It provides

> Goods of an inflammable, explosive or dangerous nature to the shipment whereof the carrier, *master or agent* of the carrier has not consented with knowledge of their nature and character, may at any time before discharge be landed at any place, or destroyed or rendered innocuous by the carrier without compensation and the shipper of such goods shall be liable for all damages and expenses directly or indirectly arising out of or resulting from such shipment. If any such goods shipped with such knowledge and consent shall become a danger to the ship or cargo, they may in like manner be landed at any place, or destroyed or rendered innocuous by the carrier without liability on the part of the carrier except to general average, if any.

Depending on whether the SBC is involved in the loading of the goods, the reference to the master could refer to them. If owners are using port agents to discharge the master's functions for loading cargo and issuing bills of lading, then they would constitute the 'agent' referred to in the first sentence of the article. Their knowledge of or consent to the dangerous characteristics of the cargo would affect the carrier's two rights provided for in Article IV(6).

(vi) Protection of Third Parties

The Hague-Visby Rules, but not the Hague Rules, contain a provision which provides protection for the servant or agent of the carrier if they are sued in respect of loss or damage to goods covered by a contract of carriage falling under the Hague-Visby Rules. Article IV(bis) (2) extends to them the benefit of the carrier's defences and limits of liability under the Rules. This protection does not cover a servant or agent who is an independent contractor.[23] If the SBC is employed by the owner, they will be protected, but if they are an independent contractor, they would have to rely on a 'Himalaya' clause in the bill of lading, whether the action is founded in contract or in tort.

B. The Hamburg Rules 1978

The Hamburg Rules attach to contracts of carriage as set out in Article 2 and impose liability on the carrier and the actual carrier. The basis of liability is established under Article 5 and is one of presumed fault. As with the Hague Rules, it is the specified contract of carriage between the carrier and the shipper, and the fact of carriage by sea, that determines the applicability of the Rules. The nature of the ship in which the goods are carried is of no import.

The Rules contain just two references to 'the master'. Article 14 deals with the issue of the bill of lading to be issued by *the carrier* on the demand of the shipper and may be signed by a person having authority from the carrier. A bill of lading signed by the master of the ship carrying the goods is deemed to have been signed on behalf of the carrier. The reference to the 'master' will be redundant with an unmanned ship. For the purposes of signing bills of lading, an SBC will be unlikely to be considered a 'master' as, absent electronic bills of lading, they will be unable to sign such documents.

Article 19 deals with notice of loss, damage or delay, and paragraph 8 provides:

> For the purpose of this article, notice given to a person *acting on the carriers or the actual carriers behalf, including the master or the officer in charge of the ship*, or to a person acting on the shippers behalf is deemed to have been given to the carrier, to the actual carrier or to the shipper, respectively.

[23] The exclusion of an 'independent contractor' was inserted at the insistence of the UK delegation as it was feared that continental definitions of 'agent' would encompass independent contractors, such as stevedores.

If notice is not given this constitutes prima facie evidence of the delivery of the cargo in sound condition, and provides an absolute bar on delay claims if notice is not given within 60 days of delivery, or the time at which delivery should have been made.

C. The Rotterdam Rules 2008

The Rotterdam Rules are the most recent convention for international carriage of goods by sea. They require twenty ratifications to come into force and to date have just four. They are based on a hybrid regime combining elements of the Hamburg Rules with those of the Hague Rules, and having a multi-modal reach provided international carriage by sea is involved.

The Rotterdam Rules contain just four references to the master and crew. Their applicability is unaffected by whether or not goods are carried in a manned or unmanned vessel. Article 4 extends the protection of the carrier's defences and limitation provisions under the Convention to:

(a) The carrier or a maritime performing party;
(b) The master, crew or any other person that performs services on board the ship; or
(c) Employees of the carrier or a maritime performing party.

The SBC if an independent contractor would not be able to avail themselves of the protection of this article under (b) but would fall under (a) as a 'maritime performing party'.[24]

As with the Hague Rules, a specific obligation of seaworthiness is imposed by Article 14 on the carrier which is extended to maintaining seaworthiness throughout the voyage.[25] Breach of this obligation appears in the complex provision on liability in Article 17, again with reference to 'improper crewing' but without any requirement

[24] Art 1.6(a) 'Performing party' means a person other than the carrier that performs or undertakes to perform any of the carrier's obligations under a contract of carriage with respect to the receipt, loading, handling, stowage, carriage, care, unloading or delivery of the goods, to the extent that such person acts, either directly or indirectly, at the carrier's request or under the carrier's supervision or control.

(b) 'Performing party' does not include any person retained, directly or indirectly, by a shipper, by a documentary shipper, by the controlling party or by the consignee instead of by the carrier.

7. 'Maritime performing party' means a performing party to the extent that it performs or undertakes to perform any of the carrier's obligations during the period between the arrival of the goods at the port of loading of a ship and their departure from the port of discharge of a ship. An inland carrier is a maritime performing party only if it performs or undertakes to perform its services exclusively within a port area.

[25] The carrier is bound before, at the beginning of, and during the voyage by sea to exercise due diligence to:

(a) Make and keep the ship seaworthy;
(b) Properly crew, equip and supply the ship and keep the ship so crewed, equipped and supplied throughout the voyage;...

of onboard crewing. Paragraph 5 provides: '5. The carrier is also liable, notwithstanding paragraph 3 of this article, for all or part of the loss, damage, or delay if: (*a*) The claimant proves that the loss, damage, or delay was or was probably caused by or contributed to by (i) the unseaworthiness of the ship; (ii) *the improper crewing, equipping, and supplying of the ship*'. Article 18 provides for the carrier's liability for the breach of its obligations under this Convention caused by the acts or omissions of:

(*a*) Any performing party;
(*b*) *The master or crew of the ship;*
(*c*) Employees of the carrier or a performing party; or
(*d*) Any other person that *performs or undertakes to perform any of the carrier's obligations under the contract of carriage, to the extent that the person acts, either directly or indirectly, at the carrier's request or under the carrier's supervision or control.*

With an unmanned vessel, the carrier would be responsible for the acts or omissions of the SBC under (a) or (d). Under Article 19, some of these parties would be directly liable under the Rules if they constituted a 'maritime performing party' – 'a performing party to the extent that it performs or undertakes to perform any of the carrier's obligations during the period between the arrival of the goods at the port of loading of a ship and their departure from the port of discharge of a ship. An inland carrier is a maritime performing party only if it performs or undertakes to perform its services exclusively within a port area'.[26] This would cover SBCs and port agents undertaking the cargo loading functions currently performed by the master. There is a proviso in paragraph 4 that 'Nothing in this Convention imposes liability on the master or crew of the ship or on an *employee of the carrier or of a maritime performing party*'. If 'master' is interpreted as covering onshore remote operators of the vessel, they will fall within this proviso.

D. Title to Sue: The Carriage of Goods by Sea Act 1992

COGSA 1992 will also operate as regards the vesting of rights and obligations under bills of lading, waybills and ships delivery orders, whether the carrying vessel is manned or unmanned. The sole reference to the master in COGSA 1992 is in s.4

> A bill of lading which—
>
> (a) represents goods to have been shipped on board a vessel or to have been received for shipment on board a vessel; and
> (b) has been signed by the master of the *vessel or by a person who was not the master but had the express, implied or apparent authority of the carrier to sign bills of lading,*
>
> shall, in favour of a person who has become the lawful holder of the bill, be conclusive evidence against the carrier of the shipment of the goods or, as the case may be, of their receipt for shipment.

[26] Art 1.7.

The italicised words show that the section will operate even when the master does not sign the bill.

E. General Average

General average is a right of contribution as between the various interests in a sea voyage: the ship; the cargo owners; and the party entitled to freight. It is imposed throughout the world as part of the law of the sea. It is a form of mutual insurance that developed before the emergence of marine insurance. The right arises whenever extraordinary sacrifices have been made or extraordinary expenses incurred by one interest for the preservation of the other interests in the common adventure. The cost of such sacrifices or expenses must be borne proportionately among all of the interests in the voyage, including the interest that made the sacrifice or bore the expense. That interest will then have a direct action against the other interests in respect of their proportionate contributions.

Most contracts of carriage will make general average subject to some version of the York-Antwerp Rules. Little will change in the operation of general average with the operation of an unmanned vessel. Two provisions would, however, become otiose with an unmanned vessel. The first is jettison, the sacrifice of cargo overboard for the common safety of the maritime adventure. The second is expenses under rule XI for the wages and maintenance of crew in, to and at a port of refuge the wages of the SBC's employees during the vessel putting into a port of refuge will not fall within this rule.

II. Charterparties

Charterparties are contracts that are not subject to any mandatory international regime, and therefore, freedom of contract operates will have the full effect. Some amendment of the forms may be required when unmanned vessels are chartered, but this will be entirely up to the parties to the charter contract. There are three basic forms of charter. The demise charter, under which the charterer puts its own crew on board to operate the vessel, effectively a lease of the vessel under which possession in the vessel vests in the charterer for the duration of the contract. A time charter is a contract for the use of the vessel, under which the vessel is crewed by the owners, and the charterer obtains no possessory interest in the vessel but has the contractual right to direct the employment of the vessel within the parameters set by the terms of the charter as regards geographical limits and types of permissible cargo. A voyage charter is a contract for the carriage of the goods on a single voyage. All forms of charters involve obligations on the parts of owners and charterers. With unmanned vessels, at whatever level of autonomy in their operation, there will still be owners who will owe obligations under the contract.

What will need amendment in the standard forms for these types of contract are the references to the servants, agents or independent contractors of the owner, particularly the master, through which these obligations will be performed.

With an unmanned vessel, at MASS level 3, the navigational role of the master will be spread among two human participants, the programmer of the software for the vessel's autonomous operation on the voyage, and the SBC who will monitor the vessel's progress throughout its voyage and undertake navigation by remote operation for certain sections of the voyage. The programmer may or may not be the same person as the SBC, and programming may be performed by employees of the shipowner or an independent contractor providing navigational services to owners of the unmanned vessel.

The master also has non-navigational functions. The master supervises the loading, stowing and discharge of the cargo carried on the vessel. The master signs bills of lading. These functions will require physical presence at the ports of loading and discharge, so cannot be assigned to the SBC. Owners will need to engage port agents to fulfil these functions. In this second section, I shall consider how charter party forms need to be adapted to accommodate the diffusion of the roles of the master to various land-based personnel. I shall consider three BIMCO forms: Barecon 2001 as a bareboat charter example; NYPE 2015 as a time charter example, and GENCON 1994 as a voyage charter.

A. Demise Charters: Barecon 2001

The form contains a few references to master and crew. Each clause could be modified by replacing the italicised words with 'persons operating the vessel'.

> Cl 10(b) The *Master, officers and crew of the Vessel* shall be the servants of the Charterers for all purposes whatsoever, even if for any reason appointed by the Owners. Charterers shall comply with the regulations regarding officers and crew in force in the country of the Vessel's flag or any other applicable law.
>
> Cl 16 Non lien notice 'This Vessel is the property of (name of Owners). It is under charter to (name of Charterers) and by the terms of the Charter Party neither the Charterers *nor the Master* have any right, power or authority to create, incur or permit to be imposed on the Vessel any lien whatsoever.'
>
> Cl 26(a) War '… or against certain cargoes *or crews* or otherwise howsoever), by
>
> (b) where it reasonably appears that the Vessel, her cargo, *crew or other persons on board the Vessel*
>
> (c) or against certain cargoes *or crews*.'
>
> The references to repatriation with an unmanned vessel in the clauses below are superfluous and can be deleted.
>
> Cl 29 Repossession
>
> All arrangements and expenses relating to the settling of wages, disembarkation and repatriation of the Charterers' *Master, officers and crew* shall be the sole responsibility of the Charterers.

Part IV Hire Purchase Agreement

The Buyers undertake to pay for the repatriation of the *Master, officers and other personnel* if appointed by the Sellers to the port where the Vessel entered the Bareboat Charter as per Clause 3 (Part II) or to pay the equivalent cost for their journey to any other place.

B. Time Charters: NYPE 2015

Clause 2 imposes an obligation on owners that the vessel on delivery shall be seaworthy and in every way fit to be employed for the intended service, including the full complement of the master, officers and ratings who meet the Standards for Training, Certification and Watchkeeping for Seafarers (STCW) requirements for a vessel of her tonnage. With an unmanned vessel, these requirements will not be able to be satisfied even if the SBC could be regarded as the master, as the STCW requirements will not apply to onshore personnel. The owners' obligations as regards crew reappear in clause 6 which requires the vessel to have a full complement of a master, officer and ratings. The clause would need an amendment to refer to properly trained SBC's and the operation of appropriate software for unmanned navigation. As shown in the previous chapter, appropriate standards in both these areas will need to be developed in the IMO before international operation of unmanned vessels becomes widely accepted.

Other navigational obligations appear in clause 12(b) obliging the master to comply with the reporting procedure of the charterers' weather routing service and to follow routing recommendations from that service provided that the safety of the Vessel and/or cargo is not compromised. There is also clause 38, which gives the charterers the right to give instructions to the master as to slow steaming and ultra-slow steaming, and clause 15, which provides for the charterers to furnish the master from time to time with all requisite instructions and sailing directions, in writing, in the English language, and for the master shall keep full and correct deck and engine logs of the voyage or voyages. Clause 30, the BIMCO Hull Fouling Clause for Charterparties provides for cleaning always to be under the supervision of the master. These provisions could be amended to refer to 'the owners and/or the person or persons operating the vessel.'

Clause 8 contains three important obligations involving the master, which are fundamental to the contractual structure of a time charter. The master is to perform the voyages with due despatch. The master is to be under the orders and directions of the charterers as regards employment and agency. Charterers are to perform all cargo handling, under the supervision of the master.[27] Three distinct entities may perform these functions: the voyage programmer; the SBC; the owners' agent at the loading and discharge port. The form could be amended by replacing the reference to the master with reference to 'the owners and/or the person or persons operating the vessel'.

[27] This will make charterers responsible for these operations. The addition of the words 'and responsibility' after 'supervision' will shift responsibility back to the shipowners.

The master's involvement with cargo operations appears at various places in the form. In addition to the supervision of cargo handling by charterers referred to in clause 8, the master is entitled to refuse cargoes or, if already loaded, to unload them at the charterers' risk and expense if the charterers fail to fulfil their IMSBC Code or IMDG Code obligations as applicable.[28] The important matter of bills of lading is dealt with in clause 31, which reiterates the familiar obligation of the master to sign bills of lading or waybills for cargo as presented in conformity with mates' receipts. This is not a function that the SBC could perform, given that paper bills of lading will still be required. Alternatively, the charterers or their agents may sign bills of lading or waybills on behalf of the master, but this is subject to the owners'/master's prior written authority, always in conformity with mates' receipts. Provision of mates' receipts is probably not something that the SBC can perform remotely and will fall to owners' port agents. The clause could be amended, as with clause 8 to replace 'the master' with 'the owners and/or the person or persons operating the vessel'.

Clause 27 provides for cargo claims as between owners and charterers to be settled in accordance with the Inter-Club NYPE Agreement 1996 (as amended 1 September 2011), or any subsequent modification or replacement thereof. The agreement contains no references to an onboard crew and would function perfectly with a time charter of an unmanned vessel.

Similar amendments will also be needed to clauses giving the master discretion as regards entry into areas affected by war risks[29] and piracy[30] as well as clause 37 which requires the master to notify charterers of stevedore damage to the vessel within 24 hours. The reference in the off-hire provisions in clause 17 to 'time lost from deficiency and/or default and/or strike of officers or crew' becomes redundant unless redrafted to refer to 'servants or agents of the owners involved in the performance of the charter'. Clause 33(a) incorporates the 'both to blame collision clause' with its reference to any act, neglect or default of the Master, Mariner, Pilot or the servants of the Owners in the navigation or in the management of the vessel'.

[28] '29. Solid Bulk Cargoes/Dangerous Goods

The Master shall be entitled to refuse cargoes or, if already loaded, to unload them at the Charterers' risk and expense if the Charterers fail to fulfil their IMSBC Code or IMDG Code obligations as applicable.'

[29] '34. BIMCO War Risks Clause CONWARTIME 2013

The Vessel shall not be obliged to proceed or required to continue to or through, any port, place, area or zone, or any waterway or canal (hereinafter "Area"), where it appears that the Vessel, cargo, crew or other persons on board the Vessel, in the reasonable judgement of the Master and/or the Owners, may be exposed to War Risks whether such risk existed at the time of entering into this Charter Party or occurred thereafter.'

[30] '39. BIMCO Piracy Clause for Time Charter Parties 2013

(a) The Vessel shall not be obliged to proceed or required to continue to or through, any port, place, area or zone, or any waterway or canal (hereinafter "Area") which, in the reasonable judgement of the Master and/or the Owners, is dangerous to the Vessel, her cargo, crew or other persons on board the Vessel due to any actual, threatened or reported acts of piracy and/or violent robbery and/or capture/seizure (hereinafter "Piracy"), whether such risk existed at the time of entering into this Charter Party or occurred thereafter.'

This could still cover defaults of the SBC as the functional equivalent of the master but could be amended so that it refers to 'the servants or agents of the Owners in the performance of this charter'.

Other clauses in the form will be redundant with an unmanned vessel, such as that part of clause 13 on the space available to charterers that refers to accommodation for supercargo, and the reservation of proper and sufficient space for the vessel's master, officers, ratings, tackle, apparel, furniture, provisions, stores, clause 14 on the charterer's right to put a supercargo on board, and clause 43 on smuggling by the master, other officers and ratings.

Development of AI and the absence of an onboard crew may lead to a rise in the use of time charters in bareboat form. Owners could programme in the duration, trading limits, permitted cargoes into the charter and then leave it to the charterers to get on with the operation of the vessel and to engage SBCs and port-based personnel for cargo inspection and the issue of bills of lading.

C. Voyage Charters: GENCON 1994

The form refers to the crew or master in the following places.

Clause 2 provides owners with a general exemption 'even from the neglect or default of the Master or crew or *some other person employed by the Owners on board or ashore for whose acts they would but for this Clause*, be responsible or from unseaworthiness of the vessel … (emphasis added)'. The italicised words show that the exemption would continue to operate as regards errors by either the voyage programmer or the SBC.

Clause 5(c) provides for the master to give charterers notification of stevedore damage as soon as is reasonably possible and to endeavour to obtain stevedores' written acknowledgement of liability. This is a function that could not be performed by the SBC and would have to be performed by owners' agents at the ports of loading and discharge. As with the reference to the master in NYPE 2015 an adequate replacement would be the phrase 'the owners and/or the person or persons operating the vessel'.

Clause 6 provides for 'the vessel to give NOR if berth not available on vessel's arrival on or off the port. Master to warrant that she is ready in all respects'. The SBC could give this warranty of readiness. Alternatively, the obligation could be imposed on the owners with a specification in the rider of the particular agent of the owners from which notification will be given.

Clause 10. Bill of ladings to be signed by Master or by owners' agents. There would be no problem here with the absence of a conventional onboard master as owners' agents at the loading port could sign the bills.

Clause 11 contains the 'Both to blame collision clause' which could be amended so that it refers to 'the servants or agents of the Owners in the performance of this charter'.

There are then three clauses involving the role of the master or owners in the event of strikes, clause 16 General strike clause; war, clause 17 War Risks clause, and; ice, clause 18 General ICE clause. The latter contains a reference to the master's right to leave the loading port for fear of being frozen in, and this could be exercised by the SBC. Again the phrase 'the owners and/or the person or persons operating the vessel' would be an adequate replacement for 'the master'.

III. Conclusion

Unmanned vessels will not substantially disrupt either the international conventions for the carriage of goods by sea or existing contractual forms for charterparties. These deal with the relationship between owners and cargo interests, and owners and charterers. These relationships remain the same with an autonomous ship. References in charterparty forms to 'master' and 'crew' could simply be replaced with 'the owners and/or the person or persons operating the vessel'. However, the issue of 'fault' in relation to errors in software which is an issue in establishing liability in tort for collisions, among others, will appear in connection with the shipowner's defences to an action for cargo damages – what is due diligence to make a ship seaworthy before and at the start of the voyage when you have an unmanned vessel, what if the AI goes AWOL after the start of the voyage? This is not really a problem for fault in the remaining human operators, the onshore SBCs, but is a conceptual challenge with defective AI, particularly in a self-learning system.

Not surprisingly, no contractual clauses have yet been developed to meet the new reality of unmanned vessels, but they will likely be developed in the following areas. Compliance with any future IMO extension of STCW to onshore SBCs is likely to be a critical element of seaworthiness, and will probably be subject to express clauses, as will provisions relating to the software and hardware used for navigation of the vessel. As set out in chapter one, the development of IMO standards in these areas is going to be critical to the acceptance of unmanned vessels. Express clauses will almost certainly emerge to deal with AI defects. At the moment, there is only one such clause which is not specific to unmanned vessels – cyber security is an increasing maritime risk for conventional manned vessels. BIMCO's 2019 Cyber Security Clause Applies to Cyber Security Incident sets out a series of obligations to have proper systems, maintenance, and appropriate response plans and regular review of systems, with a default provision for a maximum liability for breach of US$100,000. However, the clause applies in relation to a Cyber Security Incident' – the loss or unauthorised destruction, alteration, disclosure of, access to, or control of a Digital Environment – and would not cover malfunctioning of the software itself.

PART II

MASS: New Legal Issues Emerging and Insurance

5

Cyber Risks, Autonomous Operations and Risk Perceptions

Is a New Liability Paradigm Required?

ASSOCIATE PROFESSOR GEORGE LELOUDAS*

I. Changing Physical World

The terrorist attacks of 9/11 demonstrated that the impact of physical risks transcends personal injuries and property damage as they gave rise to a crisis of trust in governments and organisations responsible for the security management of transport systems.

Sweeping security reforms were implemented to rebuild this trust, where the at a level travelling public could easily identify with them.[1] They attracted extensive publicity and eventually persuaded even their critics to admit that they had contributed to the restoration of public trust to the risk management capabilities of the aviation industry.[2] At the same time, the United States initiated the 'war on terror' as a way of satisfying demands for taking immediate corrective action. Controversial a decision as it was, it was a means of contributing to the restoration of trust in the security management capabilities of public institutions. Furthermore, the 'war on terror' provided a diversion from what happened in American soil by providing a dramatic development that had all the elements of a media-successful story, namely 'death, destruction, mystery, conflict, human interest, and tragedy'.[3]

The severe impact of the 9/11 events also alerted the International Maritime Organization (IMO) to the importance of managing security risks in the maritime sector and led to the swift implementation of the International Ship and Port

* Member of the Institute of International Shipping and Trade Law, Swansea University.

[1] For an analytical description of the measures, see Dempsey, 'Aviation Security: The Role of Law in the War Against Terror' (2002-2003) 41 *Columbia J Transat'l L* 649, 712ff.

[2] J Wolff, 'Risk, fear, blame, shame and the regulation of public safety' (2006) *Economics and Philosophy* 409, 416.

[3] R Cobb and D Primo, *The Plane Truth* (Brookings Institution Press, 2003), 9.

Facility Security (ISPS) Code.[4] The ISPS Code focused on physical security risks, yet it made provision that ship security assessments (SSAs) and port facility security assessments (PFSAs) should address the vulnerabilities of measures 'to protect radio and telecommunication equipment, port services and utilities, including computer systems and networks'.[5] This minimal reference to computer systems and networks reflected the low level of concern of transport regulators about non-physical risks at the beginning of the twenty-first century.

However, the regulators' focus on physical risks was not keeping pace with the technological changes that were taking place in the transport sector. Central to these changes was the increasing use of information technology (IT) systems, such as communication networks and computers, to manage operational technology (OT) systems, namely critical, physical devices and processes via 'the direct sensing, monitoring and/or control of … plant and machinery, RF communications, on and off board sensors and navigation systems'.[6] Traditionally, IT systems were involved in such physical processes in a limited manner to monitor certain components or perform selective functions, such as the operations of the vessel's autopilot. The control of operational systems was largely left to Industrial Control Systems (ICS) and Supervisory Control and Data Acquisition (SCADA) systems which required human intervention at regular intervals to collect, interpret and input the data to other devices and processes. In most cases, such intervention would require physical access to the vessel.

The attacks of 9/11 triggered a discussion about the security and safety implications of the increasing reliance on IT systems to manage critical physical infrastructures and processes in the transport sector. Dominant in this discussion were the scenarios of wrongdoers remotely seizing control of vessels to use them as weapons and threatening to remotely sabotage their machinery for financial gain. This discussion was largely academic at the time, with little interest from either regulators or the industry. Such was the lack of interest that the European Union Agency for Cybersecurity (ENISA) in its first report on the cyber security aspects in the maritime sector, concluded that 'awareness regarding cyber security aspects is either at a very low level or even non-existent in the maritime sector, this observation being applicable at all layers, including government bodies, port authorities and maritime companies'.[7] The report attributed such lack of awareness to the fact that cyber security incidents have not created 'sufficient media exposure to trigger specific and bold actions from the involved stakeholders' together with the lack of mechanisms to identify and report cyber incidents in the maritime sector.[8]

[4] T Mensah, 'The Place of the ISPS Code in the Legal International Regime. For the Security of International Shipping' (2003) 3 *WMU Journal of Maritime Affairs* 17. The text of the ISPS Code can be found in chapter XI-2 of the 1974 International Convention for the Safety of Life at Sea (SOLAS).

[5] Pt A of the ISPS Code, para 15.16.

[6] H Boyle and R Isbell, *Code of Practice. Cyber Security for Ships* (Institution of Engineering and Technology (IET), 2017), 8.

[7] European Network and Information Security Agency, 'Analysis of Cyber Security Aspects in the Maritime Sector' (2011), para 2.1.

[8] Ibid.

The conclusion was that the lack of preparedness 'could bring even more harm than in other sectors due to the probable poor coordination of the response and due to efficiency issues'.[9]

This attitude has certainly changed since the report was issued in 2011, with the issue of cyber security currently being at the top of the agenda of regulators and private transport companies. It is submitted that the following two factors have contributed to this interest.

Firstly, the convergence of IT and OT systems has been accelerated, as it provides significant gains to operators. It enables them, inter alia, to receive real-time data from their vessels to accurately predict their voyage performance in terms of fuel efficiency, emissions and waiting times at ports; to receive data about the condition of cargo in transit and use it to coordinate with intermodal participants and port authorities to reduce delays in the supply chain; schedule predictive maintenance of hull and machinery; and to reduce accidents by utilising enhanced warning systems in busy ports and shipping lanes and advanced sensing systems of the physical environment in the open seas. This convergence is expected to reach new heights with the introduction of the 'digital twin' concept in shipping where the physical performance of a vessel will be represented digitally from its construction and throughout its lifetime. Real-time performance data will be stored in cloud-based systems that can be shared with manufacturers and/or regulators and will make recommendations for optimising the vessel's performance 'digitally rather than by means of physical tests'.[10]

Secondly, the operation of transport systems witnesses a gradual move to autonomy. Transport systems increasingly become non-deterministic, 'in the sense that their behaviour depends on the input they receive from their sensors, which is combined with learning algorithms that enable modification of their current behaviour'.[11] As such, control of such systems is passed from the crew to the vehicle system depending on the automation level employed. For example, in Autonomy Level 2 of Lloyd's Registry classification, automated systems present options to the human operator who is responsible for taking the appropriate action, while in Autonomy Level 4, decisions and actions are taken by the automated system with the human operator given the opportunity to override the system only in high-impact decisions.[12]

These autonomous arrangements certainly raise liability challenges in cases of accidents caused by the malfunction of these systems that is the main topic of this edited book. Concurrently, they raise operational and liability issues arising from the remote interference with IT systems of vessels that increasingly monitor and control their navigational and operational systems. The aim of this chapter is to

[9] Ibid, para 2.1.1.

[10] DNV GL Maritime, *Digital Twins for Blue Denmark. Digital Twin Report for Danish Maritime Authority* (2018), www.dma.dk/Documents/Publikationer/Digital%20Twin%20report%20for%20DMA.PDF, last accessed 31 August 2020.

[11] M Chatzipanagiotis and G Leloudas, 'Automated Vehicles and Third-Party Liability: A European Perspective' (2020) *University of Illinois Journal of Law, Technology and Policy*, 109, 113.

[12] Lloyd's Register Group Ltd, *LR Code for Unmanned Marine Systems* (2017), s 4.1.2.

contribute to the 'cyber' debate by identifying these operational and liability issues and argue that the liability management of the IT and OT convergence in the shipping industry might require a change of paradigm. Prominent among them are passenger- and cargo-related cyber accidents as the former can have a negative effect on the social and industrial acceptability of autonomous transport systems, while the latter has the potential to expand the concept of seaworthiness.

II. The Relevance of Cyber Risks Management for Shipping Operations

Transport systems potentially have, based on their complexity, the following four layers of cyber systems:

> The first is the perceptual layer, which links cyber and physical through components like wireless sensors and GPS. The second is network systems which transmit information (e.g. satellite networks and the internet mobile communication network). The third is support systems such as cloud computing and intelligent computing, and the fourth is the application layer which links users and the physical world with cyber systems (e.g. intelligent transportation and environmental monitoring).[13]

In the context of a modern vessel, all these four layers are present. Especially in vessels with integrated bridge systems (which will become more common as we move to full autonomy of operations), power and machinery control systems, safety systems and cargo management systems are integrated with the vessel's navigation and communication systems. Such integration is not achieved by old-fashioned metal wiring, but by means of Ethernet Industrial Protocols that collect and process data via wireless and fibre-optic sensors, cameras, radars, satellite communications and cloud computing. Furthermore, passengers and crew expect that they will be able to access the internet via their personal devices while they are in transit. Such access is encouraged by operators of transport systems as it increases revenues, enhances the passengers' travelling experience by enabling them to customise their entertainment and information choices and improves the welfare of the crew as they can contact their families regularly and in a cost-effective manner.

While the combination of these systems promises to make sea transportation safer, environmentally friendlier and more entertaining while still reducing costs, it also increases the potential for disrupting the operations of a vessel. The increasing reliance on IT systems during sea transportation avoids the necessity for the perpetrator to bypass physical security measures as in the case of the 9/11 attacks. Taking control of a vessel or disrupting its operation can now potentially be achieved electronically by remotely interfering with any of these four layers.

[13] G Tonn, J Kesan, L Zhang, J Czajkowski, 'Cyber risk and insurance for transportation infrastructure' (2019) 79 *Transport Policy*, 103, 104.

Such interference can be accomplished in several ways, prominent among them being the following:

i. Implanting malicious software, such as malware, viruses, trojans, worms etc, in the IT-controlled power management system or navigational system of a vessel that might lead to "corruption of chart data held in an Electronic Chart Display and Information System (ECDIS); a failure occurring during software maintenance and patching; [and] loss of or manipulation of external sensor data, critical for the operation of a ship".[14] Such incidents have the potential to keep the vessel at port until the malicious software is cleared, new ECDIS computers are installed and a classification surveyor attends the vessel;[15]
ii. Spoofing or jamming a vessel's positioning systems, such as GPS/GNSS, or the tracking system of containers;
iii. Infecting with ransomware the main server of the ship, encrypting sensitive files and applications related to customs, passengers, crew, or scheduling and only allowing them to be released upon payment of ransom;[16]
iv. Bypassing the firewalls between the vessel's public and safety-critical network, gaining access to operationally-critical data and processes.

Until 2010, maritime-related cyber incidents 'were driven by an attempt to obtain personal or financially sensitive data'.[17] As such, the maritime companies were the targets rather than their vessels. The management of cyber risks was predominantly seen as an issue of regulatory compliance regarding the storage and processing of personal and commercial data. The Maersk-NotPetya malware and the COSCO-ransomware cyber incidents in 2017 and 2018 respectively, attracted much publicity due to the high profile of the attacked companies, yet both attacks resulted in business interruption, and the perpetrators did not specifically target offshore safety-critical infrastructures.[18]

For years, the management of cyber risks was not a priority for the shipping sector, prompting marine cyber researchers to argue that

> In comparison, even to other transportation sectors, very little has been done in the maritime sector which has been estimated to be 20 years behind cybersecurity trends based on the rate of technological integration and current state of forensic and mitigation capabilities.[19]

[14] BIMCO et al, *The Guidelines on Cyber Security Onboard Ships* (Version 3, 2018), 3, www.bimco.org/about-us-and-our-members/publications/the-guidelines-on-cyber-security-onboard-ships, last accessed 31 August 2020.

[15] Ibid, 13.

[16] Ibid, 17–8.

[17] Marsh & McLennan, *The Risk of Cyber Attack to the Maritime Sector* (2014), www.marsh.com/uk/insights/research/the-risk-of-cyber-attack-to-the-maritime-sector.html, last accessed 31 August 2020.

[18] For a detailed history of the events see Centre for Risk Studies, Judge Business School, *Cyber Risk Outlook* (2019), 25, www.jbs.cam.ac.uk/wp-content/uploads/2020/08/crs-cyber-risk-outlook-2019.pdf, last accessed 31 August 2020, and E Kovacs, 'Shipping Giant COSCO Hit by Ransomware' (26 July 2018), www.securityweek.com/shipping-giant-cosco-hit-ransomware, last accessed 31 August 2020.

[19] K Tam and K Jones, 'Situational Awareness: Examining Factors that Affect Cyber-Risks in the Maritime Sector' (2019) *International Journal on Cyber Situational Awareness*, 40, 49.

This attitude has currently changed as cyber attackers have diversified their targets attempting to 'inflict damage to property and operations by seeking to take control of industrial control systems'.[20] Such a change of approach alarmed the shipping industry as it demonstrated for the first time that cyber-perpetrators have the capabilities of targeting shipping infrastructures.

Two events in particular, made that connection obvious. The first took place on 22 June 2017, when at least 20 vessels in the Black Sea appeared in the Automatic Identification System (AIS) 20 miles inland, close to a Russian airport.[21] This was the first spoofing attack ever to be reported and was alarming for the industry because, unlike jamming of the GPS signal that triggers an alarm at the bridge as the receivers lose signal, spoofing misdirects the signal leaving operators in a state of false security.[22] Understandably, spoofing increases the risk of collisions and groundings and impedes the search for vessels that have been taken over by pirates or criminal gangs. The second event took place between 2011 and 2013 when a criminal gang infiltrated the tracking system of containers at the Port of Antwerp and stole containers in which, unbeknownst to their owners, illicit substances were hidden.[23]

These two incidents are among the first reported that highlight the potential for physical damage as a result of interference with IT systems that manage physical processes and alerted the industry. It has been recently reported that 'cyber-attacks on the maritime industry's operational technology (OT) systems have increased by 900% over the last three years'.[24] These incidents are predominantly directed towards ports as their OT systems increasingly allow remote access to manage containers.[25] It is estimated, however, that the targets will move offshore and the frequency of such interference will only increase as 'more ships trend towards autonomy'.[26]

It was in 2017 that the IMO, alarmed by this type of events, raised the need for enterprise-wide management of cyber risks by all industry-stakeholders, including public authorities and private entities. Addressing those recommendations to such a wide audience is understandable, considering that interconnectivity is the fundamental pillar of digitalised and autonomous operations. Arguably the most important part of the IMO recommendations is that a cyber risks management programme should become part of safety management systems.

[20] Marsh & McLennan (n 17).

[21] D Hambling, 'Ships Fooled in GPS Spoofing Attack Suggest Russian Cyberweapon' (10 August 2017), www.newscientist.com/article/2143499-ships-fooled-in-gps-spoofing-attack-suggest-russian-cyberweapon/#ixzz6WhFmrJOo, last accessed 31 August 2020.

[22] Ibid.

[23] Marsh & McLennan (n 17) and A Pasternack, 'To Move Drugs, Traffickers Are Hacking Shipping Containers' (21 October 2013), www.vice.com/en_us/article/bmjgk8/how-traffickers-hack-shipping-containers-to-move-drugs, last accessed 31 August 2020.

[24] Safety4Sea, 'Cyber attacks on maritime OT systems increased 900% in last three years' (20 July 2020), https://safety4sea.com/cyber-attacks-on-maritime-ot-systems-increased-900-in-last-three-years/#:~:text=Cyber%2Dattacks%20on%20the%20maritime,security%20firm%20Naval%20Dome%20reveals., last accessed 31 August 2020.

[25] Ibid.

[26] Tam and Jones (n 19), 48.

While the implementation of cyber security management plans has been compulsory under paragraphs 8.1 to 8.10 of Part B of the ISPS Code since 2004, such plans were dealing solely with unlawful interference with radio and telecommunication systems. By issuing Resolution MSC 428(98), the IMO addresses the merge of IT and OT systems.[27] The management of cyber risks is not any more the exclusive domain of security as safety-critical procedures are increasingly digitalised and controlled by IT systems. The Resolution, together with the High-Level Guidelines on Maritime Risk Management, highlights that cyber vulnerabilities equally affect the safety of operations and requires measures to be taken to secure the IT systems managing the most critical, if not all, parts of a vessel, namely 'bridge systems; cargo handling and management systems; propulsion and machinery management and power control systems; access control systems; passenger servicing and management systems; passenger facing public networks; administrative and crew welfare systems; and communication systems'.[28]

The BIMCO Cyber Guidelines, issued to assist shipowners with the implementation of the IMO mandate, also highlight this merge of safety and security management: 'the ship's security plan may need to include appropriate measures for protecting both the equipment and the connection. Due to the fast adoption of sophisticated and digitalised onboard OT systems, consideration should be given to including these procedures by reference to the SMS in order to help ensure the ship's security procedures are as up-to-date as possible'.[29] The BIMCO Cyber Guidelines require a holistic approach that reflects the interconnectivity of cyber networks. Such holistic approach is necessary as it is recognised therein for the first time that interference with the cyber component of transport systems has the potential to cause loss of life, personal injuries and property damage of a magnitude never encountered before.

As such, in the next part, we will provide some thoughts on whether the 1974 Athens Convention Relating to the Carriage of Passengers and their Luggage by Sea as amended by the 2002 Protocol (2002 Athens Convention) can deal with the liability implications of cyberattacks against cruise ships and also whether the concept of seaworthiness under the Hague-Visby Rules will eventually include elements of cyberworthiness.

This chapter aims to invite discussion on two issues that are expected to come into the spotlight for different reasons. Cyberattacks against cruise ships leading to loss of life or personal injury will undoubtedly make headlines that have the potential to amplify liability issues and put a dent in the social and industrial

[27] IMO Resolution MSC.428(98) of 16 June 2017 on Maritime Cyber Risk management in Safety Management Systems, www.imo.org/en/OurWork/Security/Guide_to_Maritime_Security/Documents/Resolution%20MSC.428(98).pdf, last accessed 31 August 2020.

[28] Guidelines on Maritime Cyber Risk Management of 5 July 2017 (MSC-FAL.1/Circ.3), para 2.1.1, www.imo.org/en/OurWork/Security/Guide_to_Maritime_Security/Documents/MSC-FAL.1-Circ.3%20-%20Guidelines%20On%20Maritime%20Cyber%20Risk%20Management%20(Secretariat).pdf, last accessed 31 August 2020.

[29] BIMCO Cyber Guidelines (n 14), 6.

acceptability of autonomous transport systems. The issue of cyberworthiness will become relevant from 2021 onwards when the deadline for operators to incorporate cyber management measures into their SMS passes and the question whether and to what extent cyberworthiness is part of the concept of seaworthiness is raised.

III. The Impact of Cyber Risks on International Conventions

A. Passenger Liability under the 2002 Athens Convention

The 2002 Athens Convention provides for two separate liability systems depending on whether the passenger's death or personal injury is caused by a shipping or non-shipping incident.[30]

A two-tier liability system is in place for death or personal injury caused by 'shipwreck, capsizing, collision or stranding of the ship, explosion or fire in the ship, or defect in the ship' (shipping incident).[31] In the first tier, the carrier is liable up to 250,000SDRs, unless it proves that the incident resulted from a) an act of war and like events or a natural phenomenon of an exceptional, inevitable and irresistible character; or b) was wholly caused by any act or omission done with the intent to cause the incident by a third party.[32] For claims between 250,000 SDRs and 400,000 SDRs (the second tier of liability), the carrier can avoid liability if it proves that the death or personal injury was not caused by its fault or neglect.[33]

When the death, personal injury or damage to cabin luggage is caused by a non-shipping incident, the burden of proof is reversed, and the passenger is required to prove that the incident which caused the loss occurred without the fault or neglect of the carrier.[34]

The first issue is whether a cyber breach that leads to personal injury of a passenger qualifies as a shipping incident. Whether it does, depends on the nature of the breach. If it affects the power management system of the cruise ship or its navigation controls it can qualify as a 'defect in a ship' which includes 'malfunction, failure … in respect of any part of the ship or its equipment when used for … the propulsion, steering, safe navigation, mooring, anchoring, arriving at or leaving berth or anchorage'.[35] Such a wide definition has the potential to cover

[30] For a comprehensive analysis of the 2002 Athens Conventions, see B Soyer and G Leloudas 'Carriage of Passengers by Sea and Air: To What Extent Can the International Regime Deliver?' (2018) *Michigan State University International Law Review* 26.

[31] Art 3(1) and Art 3(5)(a).

[32] Art 3(1).

[33] Ibid.

[34] Art 3(2).

[35] Art 3(5)(c).

most breaches affecting the ECDIS, the AIS and the GNSS systems in terms of navigation, but also the integrated bridge that brings together power and machinery control systems.

Claims for death or personal injury arising from such events could be defended by the operator on the basis that they were 'wholly caused by an act … of a third party with the intent to cause the incident'.[36] While it would be relatively straightforward to establish that the cyber breach was intentionally committed, the following two issues arise with regard to the application of the defence.

The first one is that the defence will not cover situations where the attack is orchestrated by a disgruntled employee of the carrier or the outsourced IT contractor. It will also not cover a situation where the breach is the result of a crew member inadvertently infecting the IT system by plugging into the vessel's computer system a virus-infected USB or a personal device.

The second issue relates to the requirement that the third party's action is the sole cause of the death or personal injury. Considering that perpetrators usually exploit vulnerabilities of the network system or 'trick' employees into downloading/installing infected materials into the network, it is likely that the carrier would have contributed to this incident, making this defence unusable. Having said that, interesting questions of concurrent negligence will be raised in cases of denial of service attacks where the network is effectively taken out of use by flooding it with data, as they can occur without any involvement of the operator. Considering that devices, such as cleaning and scrubbing centres, that are available to mitigate the impact of such attacks 'may not be suitable for industrial control systems onboard a ship, offshore rig or terminal',[37] it is likely that this defence can be used by the carrier in such circumstances. At the same time, similar issues will be raised, if perpetrators exploit the design vulnerabilities of systems, such as AIS which is still in the process of being encrypted.

For claims above 250,000 SDRs that arise from shipping incidents, the carrier can avoid liability if it proves that the loss occurred without its fault.[38] It is likely that this defence will be used when the perpetrators are able to manipulate an inherent vulnerability of the software for which no patch is distributed, or it will cover infections by unknown-at-the-time viruses that could not be quarantined by the anti-virus software unless the source of the virus was the personal device of a crew member that was plugged into the safety-critical network. Interesting questions of fault will also be raised if there are any software updates that could have prevented the infection of the system but were postponed for operational reasons, namely, to combine them with regular maintenance of physical systems or to reach a suitable port where such updates could be performed. It is more likely that the carrier will not be held liable in the latter case, yet the delay in the former case

[36] Art 3(1)(b).

[37] DNV GL, *Cyber security resilience management for ships and mobile offshore units in operation* (2016), 43, www.gard.no/Content/21865536/DNVGL-RP-0496.pdf, last accessed 31 August 2020.

[38] Art 3(1).

could trigger its liability on the basis that the postponement took place for reasons of convenience. It is of note that in the context of this defence 'fault or neglect of the carrier' includes the fault or neglect of its servants but not its agents.[39] In the case that a carrier outsources the maintenance and security of its IT networks, it is arguable that it bears no liability for actions or omissions enabling the infection of the network that lies within the sphere of control of the provider.

A further interesting issue arises from Article 4(6) of the Protocol which states that '[t]he burden of proving that the incident which caused the loss occurred in the course of the carriage, and the extent of the loss, shall lie with the claimant'. This provision is raising a few interesting points in terms of cyber risks: would the infection of a network system that took place prior to the departure of the cruise ship but manifested itself during carriage be considered to have occurred in the course of carriage? For example, an IT service technician, during ordinary maintenance on board a cruise ship at port, inadvertently infects its power management system with a worm via a USB device. The worm remains dormant until the cruise ship sails in full capacity and the system connects to the internet, at which point the activated worm causes it to shut down, leading to a collision.[40] It is likely that the causative incident is linked to the manifestation rather than the infection of the system, yet the cause, in fact, remains the original infestation of the network system.

B. Cyberworthiness and Contracts of Carriage of Goods

The Hague-Visby Rules raise the important issue whether the concept of seaworthiness includes elements of cyberworthiness.[41] We are currently in a transition period, as the IMO has given operators until 1 January 2021 to incorporate the management of cyber risks into their SMS and it is unlikely that, at the moment, such inclusion is expected. However, there is little doubt that as cyber incidents increase in volume, their management (or lack thereof) has the potential to affect the fitness of vessels.

The increasing control of physical devices and processes via IT systems increases the possibility that the fitness of machinery and equipment is judged by the measures that are taken to safeguard their infection from malware. As defective navigational equipment and defective safety training of the crew have all held to make a vessel unseaworthy, cyber-related deficiencies can also qualify as such. For example, cyber security training for crew would be required to prevent the plugging in of personal devices to safety-critical networks or to identify signs of spear-phishing or social engineering; vulnerabilities in the power management system controlling the propulsion system have the potential to qualify as structural

[39] Art 3(5)(b).
[40] The example is adjusted from BIMCO Cyber Guidelines (n 14), 17–18.
[41] Art III.1

deficiencies of the vessel; vulnerabilities in the ECSID have the potential to make the ship unseaworthy in a similar manner to not carrying navigational aids; and deficiencies in temperature controlling sensors might also qualify as an instance of uncargoworthiness.

Obviously, such unseaworthiness is qualified by the requirement of due diligence in the Hague-Visby Rules.[42] What could qualify as standard protections against cyber interference is expected to evolve as more investment is required to cyber-secure vessels. With IMO having provided high-level guidelines, the industrial gold standards will take some time to evolve. Moreover, in the case of cyber risks, they might not be as easy to identify as with physical risks. For example, it is suggested that remote connections to physical devices and processes on board vessels need to be strictly controlled: 'passwords alone are a weak protection method' with 'two-factor authentication systems' recommended.[43] What, however, seems to be the gold standard for onshore operations, might not translate in a marine environment as such systems are 'difficult to maintain securely in a marine environment for the lifetime of a vessel'.[44] As a result, operators are required to investigate '[m]odern approaches of two-factor authentication frameworks … such as OAuth (smartphone-based) or USB-pluggable hardware devices that appear to the computer like a regular keyboard'.[45]

At the same time, the training of crew about cyber hygiene, such as 'respecting the difference between on-board networks for operational use and recreational use' or been alerted by suspicious emails, especially identifying phishing attacks, will soon be mandatory.[46] Still, training is not sufficient by itself as carriers will be expected to restrict access to safety-critical systems to selected members of crew who would have received advanced training so that the introduction of malignant files or 'inadvertent file corruptions to bridge or engineering consoles' can be avoided.[47]

Furthermore, carriers will be required to segregate their networks on board their vessels. Yet again the standards of segregation vary as 'the minimum requirement is to have separate networks for both safety systems and critical systems for the operation of the ship'.[48] However, it is recommended that operators take a more cautious approach, and separate networks for 'administrative, entertainment and internet access' are created.[49] If data traffic is required to travel among them, 'such traffic should be controlled by a firewall or a networking device with firewalling functionality'.[50]

[42] Art IV(1).
[43] DNV GL (n 37), 31.
[44] Ibid.
[45] Ibid.
[46] S Einarsson, 'How Cyber Risk Fits into the ISM Code' (1 August 2019), www.dnvgl.com/expert-story/maritime-impact/How-cyber-risk-fits-into-the-ISM-Code.html, last accessed 31 August 2020.
[47] DNV GL (n 37), 31.
[48] Ibid, 30.
[49] Ibid.
[50] Ibid.

From this review, it is evident that the existing international conventions with their operator-centric approach will be able to deal with cyber-related claims. However, it is arguable, that a reconsideration of this approach will be required when cyber risks are seen from the prism of autonomous operations. The reasons for such reconsideration are analysed in the remaining chapter.

IV. Autonomous Operations and Cyber Risks

The shipping industry is currently going through a tremendous trust-building exercise in relation to the autonomy of operations. During this exercise, 'techno-scientific' rationality is no longer a panacea, or even a defence when dealing with the side-effects of new technologies. In that respect, it is arguable that a 'trial and error' period will be afforded as it did with several technologies, aviation predominantly among them, in the aftermath of the Industrial Revolution, where accidents were a means of learning about the reliability of industrial systems and were tolerated as part of the quest of making them safer.

The consumerisation of transport witnessed in the twenty-first century does not afford such tolerances, and any technological progress is required to come in a 'bloodless' manner; otherwise, the relevant technologies are isolated. In that respect, the example of nuclear energy is instructive as the benefits of producing energy in an environmentally friendly, compared to fossil fuels, and cost-effective manner was outweighed by the catastrophes experienced in Chernobyl and Fukushima.

In that respect, societal risk perceptions dictate that modern technologies develop in a proactive manner, factoring in the prevention of accidents from an early stage of development. An example of such proactive management is the evolution of autonomous cars where fatal accidents during the development phase that are currently taking place have been kept to a minimum. Yet, even the few fatal accidents and several near-misses that have been experienced have raised questions of acceptability of the new technology.[51] In this context, they are scrutinised by the media that question the science behind them and are quick to construct a dramatic version of reality by simplifying technical information and amplifying issues of liability.[52]

As any technological trust-building exercise these days inevitably goes through the lens of the mass media, there is no doubt that the operational autonomy of ships will undergo similar scrutiny. In this process, the management of cyber risks is fundamental for the acceptance of the risk of operating autonomous vessels, because, unlike autonomous cars, they have truly catastrophic potential; think, in this connection, the environmental disasters of *Deep Water Horizon*, the *Exxon*

[51] Chatzipanagiotis and Leloudas (n 11), 194.
[52] Ibid.

Valdez and the *Costa Concordia*. Also, it is likely that this potential will be exploited by taking advantage of the cyber vulnerabilities of these transport systems, either in order to acquire a financial benefit or to satisfy political, ideological or terrorist motives.

This is where the paradox of the digital society lies:

> Computer codes, software and algorithms … offer a … promise of exerting control over messy, undisciplined scenarios, including the efficient identification and management of risk. They offer the … power of automatically enforcing what they prescribe, doing away with human subjectivity and resultant inaccuracy and bias …. As a consequence, much faith and trust are invested in the authority of code, software and algorithms … However, if they go wrong or are manipulated maliciously, the situation can deteriorate very quickly by virtue of our very dependence on them.[53]

For the shipping sector, this statement is particularly acute as the cyber dimension is a *sine qua non* of the transition from automatic to autonomous operations. It has great potential to prevent accidents and near-misses, as it enables the real-time monitoring of safety-critical processes and accurate geographical positioning. In some respect, the digitalisation of operations aims to detach the human element from the critical-end of operations on the basis that the latter is susceptible to mistakes. However, for this to be achieved, the cyber systems must be designed in a manner that also keeps the human element away from unlawful interference or at least mitigate the impact of such interference.

In that respect, managing cyber risks is a means to an end, namely autonomous transport systems being socially accepted and their technology trusted by all constituent parts, namely regulators, passenger-, cargo- and ship-interests. Their operational and financial benefits, significant as they are, do not provide any more a carte blanche for failures but are seen from the prism of accident reduction. It is not surprising that the supporters of autonomous cars predominantly highlight their potential 'to make roads safer, reduce congestion and enhance environmental protection'.[54] Such a narrative is important in terms of social acceptance of the new risks and plays to the tune of modern social sensitivities.

Autonomous maritime systems will be judged via the same prism and their social acceptability will very much depend on their performance during the developmental phase. As such, cyber risks management acquires an important role as it is the link between traditional automatic or semi-autonomous transport systems and fully autonomous ones. Their success in preventing high profile accidents that involve loss of life or damage to property will have an impact on the development of fully autonomous systems.

Evidence suggests that '[i]n 2018, it took on average 140 days between time of infection of a victim's network and discovery of a cyber attack'.[55] Such long

[53] D Lupton, 'Digital Risk Society' in A Burgess, A Alemanno, J Zinn (eds), *Routledge Handbook of Risk Studies* (Routledge, 2016), 490, 496–97.

[54] Chatzipanagiotis and Leloudas (n 11), 195.

[55] BIMCO Cyber Guidelines (n 14), 11.

periods of detection provide ample time for maximising the impact of any breach. In that respect, perpetrators of cyber incidents, irrespective of their motives, resemble sleeping terrorists in that they have time to understand the strengths and vulnerabilities of the system under attack and to inflict the maximum level of damage. While for most commercial sectors such damage would be limited to the unlawful extraction of data, the transport sector has, in addition, to deal with the unlawful use of the means of transport. As such, securing the cyber dimension of a vessel becomes critical for managing the liability exposures of operators in the carriage of passengers and cargo.

At the moment, the shipping sector is not particularly in the public spotlight. Cyber incidents affecting it are commercially sensitive and have led to the loss of property, yet they have not triggered discussions outside the shipping domain. However, it is inevitable that the sector will experience glaring public exposure if and when cyber breaches result in collisions or the taking-over of vessels. Such events will inevitably expedite the development of cyber defences, as is always the case with lessons learned following accidents. Yet, they have the potential to slow down the development of autonomous transport systems with their almost exclusive reliance on cyber systems as the protective cocoon pierced and 'active trust is replaced by active mistrust', which, in turn, 'triggers a self-multiplication of risks by the de-bounding of risks perceptions and fantasies'.[56]

In the case of cyber risks, this de-bounding is likely to be more acute as the perpetrators of cyberattacks and their means are less visible and understood by the general public than physical terrorists. As a result, cyber risks are perceived as difficult to control and have the potential to create uncertainty and dread to a larger extent than physical risks. Whether the perpetrator is an activist, a disgruntled employee, a criminal, a terrorist group (state-sponsored or otherwise) or simply a geek-cum-hacker, the causative link is not obvious as in the case of physical events, where the physical evidence is available for the general public, usually via the prism of media, to construct its own version of what happened. While media would construct a dramatic version of any risk event by simplifying technical information and personalising issues of liability, the physical evidence would act as a limitation on the de-bounding of the scenarios of what went wrong.

The borderless nature of cyber risks, the difficulty in realising that a corporation is under attack and the difficulty in identifying the perpetrator contain elements of what Ulrich Beck characterises as 'uncontrollable risks', namely risks that cannot be controlled, cannot be maintained within national boundaries, cannot be delimited to a certain period, and where personal responsibility cannot be placed.[57] These characteristics of cyber risks expose the limitations of liability systems which in the transport sector focus upon hazards with discreet, easily traceable cause, and channel liability to operators of transport systems on the basis that they are in a

[56] U Beck, *World Risk Society* (Polity Press, 1999), 44.
[57] Ibid, 41.

better position to monitor the risk, manage it, and distribute the loss if the risk materialises. In that respect, cyber risks are not so different to risks of terrorism in that claimants can often experience serious difficulties in tracing the actual wrongdoers, as well as establishing a causal link between the risk of a cyberattack and the preventative measures that a private entity ought to have adopted.

Having said that, terrorists usually use transport systems as a means to an end – their ultimate target is not the operator, but they are using it to pass a message to a wide audience. In the case of cyber risks, the motives vary and more often than not the perpetrator targets transport systems either to gain financially, to get revenge of his treatment as an employee, to test the technology in infiltrating sophisticated cyber systems or to pass a political, religious or social message to the broader world.[58] What all these profiles have in common is that cyber infiltrations take place intentionally – with negligence confined to situations where an unsuspected employee connects his infected personal device in the cyber network of a transport system.

V. Time to Consider the Liability Paradigm?

These special characteristics of cyber risks inevitably give rise to discussions about the proper balance between public perceptions of acceptable levels of safety and security and the role that insurance, liability rules and government regulation should play in an automated shipping world. These discussions will intensify the moment accidents of autonomous transport systems take place. And while a move towards product liability is anticipated if the accident is caused by the design of the autonomous transport system,[59] such move is currently unlikely in cases where the accident is caused as a result of interference with a vessel's IT systems. The reason for such divergence of direction is that software manufacturers, unlike physical product manufacturers, have so far argued that it is unfeasible to develop absolutely secure code as 'it is most probably mathematically impossible to test for all combinations of code and hardware interactions'.[60] As a result, interference with software is inevitable 'so long as an incentive to detect and exploit such vulnerabilities exists', which in the shipping sector, as we examined earlier, are in abundance.[61] At the same time, it is not always obvious whether the software developer counts in law as a manufacturer or a service provider, the latter being more likely when tailor-made software is developed for a customer or cloud computing applications are used.[62] This discussion is outside the scope of this chapter but raises an issue of concern for the future design of civil liability systems for autonomous vessels.

[58] For a full list of potential motives, see BIMCO Cyber Guidelines (n 14), 9.

[59] R Bagshaw, 'Product Liability: Autonomous Ships' in B Soyer and A Tettenborn (eds) *Artificial Intelligence, Shipping and Developing International Framework* (Hart, 2021 (forthcoming)), ch 6.

[60] A Knight et al, *Encyclopedia of Information Technology Law* (Sweet & Maxwell, 2020), para 7.139.

[61] L Vihul, 'The Liability of Software Manufacturers for Defective Products', *The Tallinn Papers* (2014), 1, www.ccdcoe.org/uploads/2018/10/TP_02.pdf, last accessed 31 August 2020.

[62] Ibid, 9 and the discussion in Bagshaw (n 59), ch 6.

One possibility is to allocate the risk of death, personal injury or property damage caused by cyber risks to the operator, leaving it to sort out indemnity actions against the software manufacturer under their contractual agreements and national laws. This streamlining of risks has been the traditional way of dealing with liability risks in the transport sector so far, but in the case of cyber risks, indemnity actions are already criticised by software users as inadequate in achieving a fair allocation of risks for the reasons analysed above. Furthermore, this type of liability systems do not have the capacity to deal with risks of catastrophic potential where a communal of interests are affected and the implications go beyond the relationship between the operator and its customer, be it a passenger or a cargo-owner.

As we deal with a new category of risks that resemble terrorism risks in terms of operation and impact and as manufacturers are expected to play a dominant role in the operation of autonomous systems, it is appropriate to examine more innovative solutions. One of them might be to create an insurance system that will be supplemented by an industry-wide cyber fund where there will be contributions from both operators and software manufacturers and from which claims will be satisfied. Such a system has the potential to deal with the impact of uncontrollable risks as it socialises recovery and arguably encourages the development of new technologies as the cost of their malfunction is spread among all interested parties. A simplified version of such proposal where the insurer is at the centre of the liability system is currently in force in the form of the UK's Automated and Electric Vehicles Act 2018 that deals with liability arising out of the use of automated cars.[63]

Whatever the structure of the system is, it has been rightly suggested that mandatory standards of pre-release penetration testing should be imposed on software developers.[64] This way it is expected that software will contain less security vulnerabilities upon release which further results in less reliance on after-sale software patches to rectify them; the installation of which in most situations require immediate actions by the users that are not always forthcoming or possible, as in the case of a vessel being in transit.

The format of liability systems dealing with cyber risks is certainly an issue that will preoccupy future analyses. Yet, it is this author's view that any decisions cannot be made in isolation without considering the interrelation between cyber risks, autonomous operations and social risk perceptions.

VI. Conclusion

This chapter highlights that the technological development and social acceptability of autonomous transport systems rely on the effective protection of IT systems

[63] Chatzipanagiotis and Leloudas (n 11), 167–75.
[64] Vihul (n 61), 13–14.

that manage and control their safety- and security-functions. This is because the ripple effects of cyber breaches on board vessels go beyond the immediate financial loss and/or personal injuries and create a crisis of trust in new technologies that are currently developed. Unlike physical risks, cyber risks are borderless in nature and come with an inherent difficulty in identifying the perpetrator and the means of attack. Such characteristics have the potential to amplify social reactions in the aftermath of accidents and can arguably lead to the blacklisting of technologies that rely on them. As such, the chapter argues that a change of liability paradigm might be required to manage cyber risks in the transport sector as the traditional system of streamlining risks via operators might come under pressure, especially in cases of high-impact, orchestrated cyberattacks. In that respect, any future liability system regarding cyber risks shall not be decided in isolation but shall consider the autonomy of operations and its social acceptance.

6

Product Liability: Autonomous Ships

ASSOCIATE PROFESSOR RODERICK BAGSHAW*

In the law of England and Wales, the liability of a producer of a defective product depends on three bodies of law: contract, the tort of negligence and Part 1 of the Consumer Protection Act 1987.[1] The liability imposed under the 1987 Act, which implemented the 1985 Product Liability Directive,[2] can only provide compensation for death, personal injury and damage to non-commercial property,[3] but cannot be limited or excluded by a contract.[4] The tort of negligence can provide compensation for damage to commercial property as well as for the forms of damage covered by the statutory liability, but generally does not protect against

* Tutor and Fellow in Law at Magdalen College and Associate Professor in the Faculty of Law, Oxford University.

[1] In a contractual claim against an overseas producer of an autonomous ship, the law of England and Wales is likely to be the applicable law when and because it has been chosen by the parties. It is less easy to summarise the circumstances when a non-contractual product liability claim will be governed by the law of England and Wales. It appears that after departure from the European Union the answer in England and Wales will continue to be determined by a modified version of the Rome II Regulation (Reg (EC) 864/2007 of the European Parliament and the Council of 11 July 2007 [2007] OJ L199/40): see, The Law Applicable to Contractual Obligations and Non-Contractual Obligations (Amendment etc) (EU Exit) Regulations 2019, SI 2019/834. A tolerably simplified account of the effect of this provision is that the law of England and Wales will be the applicable law if claimant and defendant so choose, or – in the absence of any choice – if they are both habitually resident in the country. If neither of those bases yields an answer, then the applicable law will be decided by proceeding in sequence through a cascade of questions. If matters reach this cascade, then one situation when English law will be applicable is if the claimant is habitually resident in England and the product was 'marketed' in this country (unless the defendant could not foresee that), provided that the tort is not 'manifestly more closely connected' with a different country. For a full account, see A Dickinson, *The Rome II Regulation: The Law Applicable to Non-Contractual Obligations* (OUP, 2008, with supplement 2010) ch 5. (Even when it has been established that a case is governed by English law there may be a further hurdle in a claim based on the Consumer Protection Act 1987 because of uncertainties as to what Parliament's intention was with regard to that statute's territorial scope: see *Allen v Depuy International Ltd* [2014] EWHC 753 (QB); [2015] 2 WLR 442 [30]-[32]. I am grateful to Professor Tettenborn for drawing my attention to this point.)

[2] [1985] OJ L210/29 (amended, [1999] OJ L141/20) Council Directive 85/374/EEC of 25 July 1985 on the approximation of the laws, regulations and administrative provisions of the Member States concerning liability for defective products. The United Kingdom's withdrawal from the European Union brought about only minor changes to the text of the Consumer Protection Act 1987 (see the Product Safety and Metrology etc (Amendment etc) (EU Exit) Regulations 2019, SI 2019/696, Sch 3).

[3] Consumer Protection Act 1987, s 5(1) and s 5(3).

[4] Consumer Protection Act 1987, s 7.

purely economic losses, including disappointment as to the value of the defective product itself, and requires 'fault' to be proved. (The tort of negligence is also the main route for imposing liability on someone other than a 'producer' involved in some safety-critical way in the production or use of an autonomous ship, such as through being its designer or operator.[5]) Contractual provisions that seek to limit or exclude liability for negligence are regulated,[6] but can be effective in some circumstances. Contractual liability can provide compensation for a wider range of losses, including purely economic losses, but can generally only be relied on by those who are party to a contract with the producer and will depend on the terms (express and implied) of the contract. Provisions designed to exclude or limit contractual liability that would arise in their absence are regulated but can be effective in some circumstances.[7] Since the terms of most commonly-used shipbuilding contracts provide buyers with only limited rights against builders with regard to the quality of the vessel and seek to significantly limit liabilities,[8] the analysis that follows will focus on non-contractual product liability.

In order to sketch how non-contractual product liability may apply to autonomous ships, it may be helpful to construct some hypothetical fact patterns that might generate claims. I will assume that autonomous ships will operate by means of a system that combines a 'controller' who (i) obtains information using hardware components, such as sensors, and (ii) receives post-production information from *external sources*, such as weather reports or messages about new hazards, and (iii) is supported by, or perhaps even synonymous with, decision-making software. On the basis of this model, which has been simplified to avoid redundant repetition,[9]

[5] In England and Wales, the operator-of-a-product's tort liability for damage caused by a liability will usually depend on the tort of negligence. Elsewhere in Europe, however, operators are subject to stricter liabilities regarding particular types of product, such as automobiles. The advent of autonomous land vehicles has encouraged some policymakers to contemplate an extension of similar *strict* liabilities to the operators of particular types of autonomous product, perhaps underpinned by compulsory insurance: see eg, Expert Group on Liability and New Technologies – New Technologies formation, *Liability for Artificial Intelligence and Other Emerging Technologies* (Publications Office of the European Union 2019) 39–42; European Commission, *Report on the Safety and Liability Implications of Artificial Intelligence, the Internet of Things and Robotics* COM(2020)64, 16. See also European Parliament resolution of 20 October 2020 (2020/2014(INL)). If such liabilities *are* extended, then the practical effect might be to leave (i) operators seeking *contribution* and (ii) victims excluded from the strict liability regime as the parties chiefly interested in the possibility of establishing liability against a producer.

[6] See, eg, Consumer Rights Act 2015, Pt 2 and Unfair Contract Terms Act 1977, Pt 1.

[7] In this context, it is important to note the effects of Unfair Contract Terms Act 1977 s 26 and s 27.

[8] See, eg, the 'SAJ form', the contract that is most frequently used in general shipbuilding, first published by Shipbuilders' Association of Japan in 1974, which contains only a limited warranty with regard to the material used and the quality of the workmanship, and excludes all other warranties and liability for all consequential losses; Other commonly used forms of contracts (arguably) offer a broader guarantee: see eg, BIMCO, 'NEWBUILDCON (2007)', which defines 'defects' for the purposes of the builder's guarantee as covering 'any deficiencies or defects in the design, construction, material and/or workmanship on the part of the Builder or its Sub-contractors' and specifies the *quality* of the builder's performance as 'in accordance with good international shipbuilding and marine engineering practice'; see also, 'AWES Standard Shipbuilding Contract (1995 rev)', adopted by the Association of European Shipbuilders and Shiprepairers, Art 12 (guarantee) and Art 19 (limitation).

[9] The model does not, eg, mention hardware that *responds* to any decision made by the 'controller', such as hardware controlling engine speed or steering; but this omission is deliberate; the legal rules

I will consider situations where an accident is caused by (a) failure of a hardware component, such as a sensor; (b) a shortfall in design, such as a 'blind spot' between sensors; (c) a failure of software, such as a program that calculates what adjustments to speed and direction are required to achieve a particular course, and (d) inaccuracy of post-production information from an *external source*, such as an update about a new hazard. Furthermore, I will discuss claims involving (I) injury to a person, such as a mariner on a different vessel, (II) physical damage to external commercial property, such as a different vessel, (III) physical damage to the autonomous vessel itself, and (IV) losses as a result of an inability to use the autonomous vessel for a period for reasons other than because of the need to perform physical repairs. These variations, between them, generating only sixteen possible scenarios, clearly do not exhaust the possibilities.[10] However, they provide a good foundation for identifying several difficult issues. Nonetheless, because a significant proportion of the existing writing about product liability and autonomous products deals with more arcane problems, such as accidents caused by 'machine learning', my discussion will occasionally stray beyond the sixteen scenarios.

I. Personal Injuries

A person who has suffered a personal injury caused wholly or partly by a defect in a product can bring a claim for compensation against the producer of the product and various other parties using the Consumer Protection Act 1987 (CPA). Despite the name of the Act, an injured claimant can rely on it even if he or she was never a 'consumer' of the product concerned; such a claim could be brought by an employee working with the product,[11] or by a victim who has made no use of the product whatsoever, such as a mariner on a different vessel involved in a collision or kayaker run down by an autonomous vessel. Those who have suffered personal injuries are likely to rely on the CPA rather than the tort of negligence *unless* they are making a claim against a defendant who cannot be held liable under the Act, such as a designer or operator, or the producer of an element in an autonomous system that does not qualify as a 'product'.

relating to failure of an information-*obtaining* hardware component, such as a sensor, also apply to other hardware components.

[10] For example, I have not included a claim involving physical damage to non-commercial property, such as to the equipment of a recreational windsurfer or a private residence near the shore; most of the rules that apply to personal injury claims also apply to claims relating to physical damage to non-commercial property. (Moreover, the cost of compensating a recreational windsurfer for a significant personal injury will usually greatly exceed the cost of meeting a claim for any damage to his or her equipment.)

[11] Though such a claimant might also have other options: see, eg, Employer's Liability (Defective Equipment) Act 1969, s. 1, for the purposes of which 'equipment' is defined as including 'any plant and machinery, vehicle, aircraft and clothing'.

A. Product

An autonomous ship will count as a 'product' for the purposes of the CPA: section 1(2) defines 'product' as including 'any goods', and section 45 defines 'goods' as including 'any ship, aircraft or vehicle', and 'ship' as including 'any boat and any other description of vessel used in navigation'. Significantly, the CPA also applies to 'a product which is comprised in another product, whether by virtue of being a component part or raw material or otherwise'.[12] This provision means that in the event of the failure of a hardware component such as a sensor (scenario (a)), if the producer of the ship did not itself manufacture the component, the CPA can be applied separately to the producers of each of the two (possibly) defective products – the producer of the ship and the producer of the component. Even if it is only the failure of a component, such as a sensor, that makes a ship defective, the producer of the ship cannot escape liability by alleging that the producer of the component should be wholly responsible: both the ship and component are 'defective'. Section 2(5) of the CPA makes both producers jointly and severally liable so far as they are liable for the same damage under the CPA. The producer of a component may avoid liability, however, if it can establish that the defect was 'wholly attributable to the design of the subsequent product', that is the design of the ship in which the component was incorporated, or to compliance 'with instructions given by the producer of the subsequent product'.[13]

Where an accident occurs because of inaccurate information supplied to an autonomous ship's controller (scenario (d)), for example, where data is supplied that purports to give the location of a hazard but misidentifies the location, then the compiler of the data is very unlikely to be classified as the producer of a product: information is not 'goods'.[14] (A producer of foreseeably dangerous misinformation may, of course, commit the tort of negligence, and may well have supplied the information pursuant to a contract which includes warranties about the quality of the information or the care that has gone into producing it.) Where inaccurate information originally incorporated in a ship makes the ship defective, however, the producer of the ship can still be held liable under the CPA;[15] the ship will be

[12] CPA, s 3(1).

[13] CPA, s 4(1)(f).

[14] I have hedged with the phrase 'very unlikely' to reflect the fact that there are (at least) two ways of arguing that inaccurate data can be a 'product': these involve arguing that when inaccurate data is provided on a physical medium, such as a memory stick, the composite (memory stick *plus* the information that is on it) amounts to 'goods', or arguing that 'electricity' is expressly defined as a 'product' and data stored or transferred in electronic form is 'defective electricity'. Personally, I would expect a competent court to reject both of these attempts to treat 'inaccurate data' as within the scope of CPA's product liability regime, on the basis that both arguments would have the effect of applying different liability regimes to a publisher of inaccurate information depending on whether it was delivered orally or by way of a 'productifying' medium (on a memory stick or as electricity). The position may be clarified when the Court of Justice of the European Union decides Case C-65/20 *Vi v Krone Verlag Gesellschaft mbH & Co KG* [2020] OJ C209/4, where the question referred by the Austrian Court involves the applicability of the directive to a (physical) newspaper containing a dangerous 'health tip'.

[15] The question whether the data was incorporated in the ship before the time of its (the ship's) supply by the producer (of the ship) to another is pivotal: CPA, s 4(1)(d) and s 4(1)(2).

a 'product' even if the information (considered independently) was not, and the inaccurate information may make it into a defective product. The producer of the ship will not be liable under the CPA, however, if the only problem with the ship is the inaccuracy of information compiled by another person *after* the supply of the ship, for example, an inaccurate weather report.

For similar reasons, a *ship's producer* will not be liable if an incident is caused by the poor decision or inappropriate instruction of a human being acting as the remote-controller of an autonomous vessel, unless it can be established that the lack of a safety feature in the product's design (for example, lack of an 'over-ride' to prevent remote-instructions being executed in particular conditions) contributed to the problem.

The significance that the legislation attaches to whether a product was defective at the time that the producer supplied it to another may cause difficulties in situations where the arrangement between 'producer' and 'operator'[16] is on-going, rather than a once-and-for-all supply, in particular where the relationship involves the 'producer' updating or modifying the product. For example, one type of autonomous system that is in development involves a 'producer' having a continuing capacity to monitor and remotely-adjust a vessel's hardware (such as a ship's engine). The existence of such ongoing relationships may challenge a producer's ability to take advantage of either the defence that the defect did not exist in the product at the time when he supplied it to another or the evidential rule that a judge is not required to infer a defect 'from the fact alone that the safety of a product which is supplied after [the producer supplied the product to another] is greater than the safety of the product in question'.[17] To spell the challenge out, an injured party might argue that the ongoing relationship should be treated as a *series* of supplyings of the product (ship) to the user, since otherwise a claimant may be unable to rely on the CPA where an updating-modification has introduced a safety problem. If this argument is accepted, however, it might reduce the protection that the evidential rule provides to producers (because there would be a *later* date of supply).[18]

What about the producer of software – code – that is incorporated in an autonomous ship,[19] but fails in a way that causes an accident resulting in personal injuries (situation (c))? This question might have practical significance because

[16] The word 'operator' is intended to cover the shipowner in the simple fact-pattern of a shipbuilder supplying a ship to a shipowner who then uses it for its own purposes, and also the party in day-to-day control of the operation of the ship in more complicated fact-patterns.

[17] The defence is in CPA, s 4(1)(d) and s 4(2), and the evidential rule in s 3(2).

[18] Consumers have become used to the idea that 'producers' of products which incorporate software periodically issue updates to that software; even the existence of *this* sort of ongoing relationship may lead to the conclusion that there has been a series of *supplyings* of the product since otherwise consumers would be in a precarious situation where a software update *introduced* a safety problem.

[19] In reality, the operation of some (perhaps all) autonomous ships will depend on both software that is on board *and* software that is elsewhere (eg, on onshore computers that are involved in communicating and processing data from the ship). This situation will potentially increase the number of products that might be involved in the causing of an accident and may encourage creative claimants to push for broader readings of the notion of one product being 'comprised in' another: CPA s 1(2) (definition of 'product').

one of the major challenges in designing autonomous ships is producing code that will make decisions using incomplete and inconsistent data. (While the software issue will be particularly visible in a fully autonomous ship[20] – when the decision-making 'controller' will be software – it will also arise when defective software *influences* a decision taken by a remote or onboard human 'controller'.) The producer of a ship which incorporates defective software will, of course, have produced a product – a ship – that may be defective.[21] But the question of whether someone whose only role was to write the software will be treated as the producer of a component 'product' is more debatable. One view is that an *author* of code is someone who performs a *service*, like a naval architect or a systems-engineer, rather than a producer of 'goods'. In this view, the author of code is subject to the tort of negligence but does not fall within the scope of any potential liability under the CPA.[22] An alternative view, however, highlights that many software programs are mass-produced, resembling 'tools' more than 'information', their safety cannot be easily assessed by users, and they are frequently marketed and consumed in ways that resemble the marketing and consumption of *physical* products.[23] Those who find this alternative view convincing may be attracted – at least in the short term, while awaiting legislative intervention to settle the point – by *artificial* arguments that classify software as 'goods' under particular conditions, such as the claim that software becomes 'goods' if supplied on a physical medium, such as a

[20] Several schemes exist for classifying the autonomy levels of unmanned marine systems and cyber-enabled ships. The International Maritime Organization developed an influential four-level division for their Regulatory Scoping Exercise (reproduced, Maritime UK, Maritime Autonomous Surface Ships (MASS) UK Industry Conduct Principles and Code of Practice, (Version 3, 2019) 19) where level 3 covered remote-controlled vessels without a human crew and level 4 a 'fully autonomous ship' operated by a system 'able to make decisions and determine actions by itself'. More nuanced schemes have incorporated variables such as whether the 'autonomous' system *makes* and *implements* decisions, rather than merely *informing* or *influencing* them, and to what extent there is human supervision and a possibility of override: see eg, the grading of 'levels of control' by the European Defence Agency's Safety and Regulations for European Unmanned Maritime Systems (SARUMS) group (reproduced, Maritime UK, Maritime Autonomous Surface Ships (MASS) UK Industry Conduct Principles and Code of Practice, (Version 3, 2019) 20). Clearly, a product as complex as a ship can involve multiple systems (eg, controlling propulsion, navigation, steering, trim, etc) with different degrees of autonomy, remote control, supervision and possible override.

[21] An analogy may help to substantiate this point: a medical device that is designed to deliver drugs intravenously over an extended time will be a defective medical device (product) if it delivers twice as much of each drug as its user expects, and this assertion remains true even if the problem with the device is that the incorporated software doubles the dose that the user 'keys-in' and it is otherwise, mechanically, perfect.

[22] F Collin, 'Maritime Product Liability at the Dawn of Unmanned Ships – the Finnish Perspective', University of Turku, Faculty of Law Research Paper Series 2/2018, at 4–5, adopts this view of software with regard to the Finnish product liability law that implements the same directive.

[23] Reform to clarify the applicability of the Product Liability Directive to software has been widely recommended: eg, Expert Group on Liability and New Technologies – New Technologies formation, *Liability for Artificial Intelligence and Other Emerging Technologies* (Publications Office of the European Union, 2019), at 6 and 42, '[s]trict liability of the producer should play a key role in indemnifying damage caused by defective products and their components, irrespective of whether they take a tangible or a digital form'. See also, European Parliament resolution of 20 October 2020 with recommendations to the Commission on a civil liability regime for artificial intelligence (2020/2014(INL)) 8.

chip, or qualifies as a product because it is defective electricity.[24] If the software is not treated as 'goods', then the effect will be to leave the producer of an autonomous ship, which incorporates it, potentially the only defendant, which is liable under the CPA, and, unless the author of the software is proved to have been negligent, the ship's producer will need to turn to the contract under which it acquired the software to recoup a share of any damages payable to injured parties.

The question of whether 'software' can be a product will also be significant when considering the position of the producer of a software 'update', and the producer of a replacement software system.

B. Producer

CPA section 1(1)(a) defines the person who 'manufactured' a product as its 'producer'. The CPA will not apply to parties who played a different role in the production of a ship, for instance, as the designer of the vessel or some sub-system, or a professional supervising the manufacturing process. A defendant who repairs a ship is unlikely to be held to have 'manufactured' it, but the position may be different where a defendant substantially rebuilds a ship; repairers and refurbishers may, of course, have produced (or supplied) 'goods' that they incorporate into a ship, such as a replacement part, and may potentially be liable if *those* '*goods*' are defective.

C. Defendants Other than the Producer

As well as imposing liability on the 'producer' of a defective product, CPA section 2(2) imposes liability on anyone who has held himself out as a producer by using a trademark or other distinguishing mark in relation to the product, and anyone who has imported the product into the United Kingdom 'in order, in the course of any business of his, to supply it to another'.[25] The final condition quoted in the previous sentence means that a defendant who imports autonomous vessels into the United Kingdom in order to supply them in the course of a business, for instance by selling them, will be treated by the CPA as if it produced the vessels. However, a defendant

[24] CPA, s. 1(2) expressly defines 'electricity' as a product. The argument that software is 'electricity' when it is supplied as a flow of electrons is ingenious. But the logical extension of the argument might similarly make an email or a telephone call containing dangerously misleading advice into a defective 'product'.

[25] Clearly, the discussion under the previous subheading of whether software can ever be a product may also be important here: if, eg, software *is* treated as a product when it is on a chip, then an *importer* of such chips into the United Kingdom will be treated as if it was their producer. Until it was amended by the Product Safety and Metrology etc (Amendment etc) (EU Exit) Regulations 2019, SI 2019/696, Sch 3, CPA s 2(2)(c) extended liability to those who imported defective products into the European Union: *this* will remain the law in the Member States.

who imports autonomous vessels in order to use them itself will not be treated as a producer. Importantly, section 46(9) makes it clear that a person will not be treated as having 'supplied' a ship to a person 'by reason only that services consisting in the carriage of goods or passengers in that ship … , or in its use for any other purpose, are provided to that person in pursuance of an agreement relating to the use of the ship … for a particular period or for particular voyages, … or journeys'. So a person who imports an autonomous vessel into the United Kingdom in order to carry goods, or passengers, or to fulfil a time charter or voyage charter,[26] will not be treated as if it were a 'producer' as a result of doing so.

Even a defendant who is not a 'producer' of the defective product, or treated as its producer, can be held liable if it supplied the product and fails to comply with a request to identify the producer of the product or whoever supplied the product to it.[27] A cynical summary of the purpose behind this provision might be: to 'improve the memory' of those who have supplied defective products to others. In practice, the provision will encourage a seller of potentially safety-critical generic components, such as sensors or switches, to keep a record of who produced the components supplied to each customer.

D. Defect

Liability under the CPA depends on the 'defect' standard, which is defined in the Act as requiring a judgment as to whether 'the safety of the product is not such as persons generally are entitled to expect'.[28] What persons generally are 'entitled to expect' by way of safety need not coincide with what they expect, but the standard takes into account what information about risks has been made available to and absorbed by the public. The CPA identifies three relevant circumstances: '(a) the manner in which, and purposes for which, the product has been marketed, its get-up, the use of any mark in relation to the product and any instructions for, or warnings with respect to, doing or refraining from doing anything with or in relation to the product; (b) what might reasonably be expected to be done with or in relation to the product; and (c) the time when the product was supplied by its producer to another',[29] but provided no explicit guidance as to how these circumstances are related to the overall standard. For example, the provision does not make clear whether the effect of (a) and (b) is intended to be that bystanders are

[26] By contrast, a bareboat charter will, it seems, involve supplying a ship: see D Fairgrieve and R Goldberg, *Product Liability* (3rd edn, OUP, 2020), 8.67, where the authors draw attention to the explanation provided by Lord Lucas during the passage of the Bill: Hansard, HL (series 5) vol 487, cols 793–4 (14 May 1987). (I am grateful to Professor Tettenborn for drawing my attention to this point.)

[27] CPA, s 2(3). The conditions are more precise and detailed than the summary in the text: eg, the request must be 'made within a reasonable period after the damage occurs and at a time when it is not reasonably practicable for the person making the request to identify all those persons'.

[28] CPA, s 1(2).

[29] S 3(2).

only entitled to expect that a product will be safe when it is being used in a reasonably expected way *and* in compliance with warnings and instructions. Although there is no binding authority on the point in England, there would be good reasons for rejecting a submission in line with the previous sentence: where a producer manufactures a product that will foreseeably be a target for hijacking, persons generally may be entitled to expect that the producers' investment in safety will not be premised on *all* users of the product complying with warnings and instructions.

In practice, it seems that a 'rogue' product, that is one that is different from and less safe than the other products coming off a production line, will be defective: persons are 'entitled to expect' that their product will be as safe as others coming off the production line,[30] unless the public is aware of and has accepted the possibility of 'rogues'.[31] Such 'rogue' products are frequently referred to, following the terminology adopted by Burton J in *A v National Blood Authority*, as 'non-standard products',[32] or, under the influence of US law, as 'manufacturing defects'.[33]

Where a product is bespoke rather than mass-produced, the relevant benchmark for determining if it is a non-standard product is likely to be the blueprint or intended design. But since there is no obvious reason for expecting that autonomous ships, or their component parts, will be more frequently 'rogue' than other similar products, it is appropriate to focus attention on how the 'defect' standard will be applied to 'standard products', or 'design defects'.[34]

[30] This proposition will require modification where a production line permits a 'margin of tolerance', eg, that a safety bar should be between 1.4 cm and 1.7 cm thick, rather than requiring uniformity: although there is no explicit authority on the point, one might expect a court to rule that persons generally are entitled to expect that their product is no less safe than the product at the limit of the 'margin of tolerance' (1.4 cm).

[31] It is not easy to specify the circumstances in which a court can properly find that the public has accepted the risk to their safety of some proportion of the output of a production line being 'rogue'. Examples often given include that the public has accepted that a certain proportion of tinned peaches will contain a residual fragment of peach-stone and that some proportion of bags of lentils will contain grit. In each of these examples, we might assume that the public is generally aware of the risk *and* that at a certain point it may become more efficient for those preparing the food for consumption to manage the risk rather than for the 'producer' to invest more in seeking to eliminate it.

[32] [2001] 3 All ER 289 [36].

[33] The phrase 'manufacturing defect' is helpful in suggesting a useful distinction between problems as a result of something going wrong on the 'manufacturing line' or during a 'construction phase', affecting a particular product or batch, and something going wrong in the design process, or in the process of choosing what instructions and warnings to give to consumers. But the phrase does not fit with the production of all types of product equally well: eg, some natural products are 'harvested' or 'extracted' and may subsequently be 'inspected' for compliance with a standard rather than being 'designed' and then 'manufactured': in these situations Burton J's distinction between products that are unsafe because they do not match the required standard ('non-standard') and those that are unsafe because of a problem with the *standard* may be more helpful.

[34] Academic discussions of product liability frequently identify a third type of 'defect' labelled 'warning defects' or 'failures to warn': see, eg, D Fairgrieve and R Goldberg, *Product Liability* (3rd edn, OUP 2020), ch 12. While claimants can clearly establish a 'defect' by showing that a 'producer' has provided insufficient instructions on how to use a product safely or insufficient warnings as to the dangers of a product in ordinary or foreseeable use, the question of what 'persons generally' are 'entitled to expect' by way of instructions and warnings is similar to the question of what 'persons generally' are 'entitled to expect' by way of other design features that will improve safety.

Courts have found it more difficult to identify a stable test for 'legitimate expectations' where a product's safety risk is related to a designer's choice to reduce cost or to enhance utility in some other way. In *A v National Blood Authority*,[35] Burton J concluded that in deciding whether a standard product was defective, it was not relevant to ask whether it would have been possible for the producer to make the product safer, how costly or impractical it would have been to make the product safer, or how useful the product was, except when determining whether the public knew of and accepted a risk. For Burton J, the core question was simply whether the product was safe when used in foreseeable ways.[36] He suggested that where there were comparable products on the market, it would be relevant to compare the safety of the allegedly 'defective' product with these. Moreover, it would clearly be open to a producer to demonstrate that the public knew of and had accepted a risk, and in advancing such a submission it might be relevant to show that the allegedly 'defective' product was a cheaper, and hence more accessible, version of a useful product.[37]

A reasonable producer's response to Burton J's interpretation ought to have been to reduce the risks of its products so far as it was cost-justified to do so (that is, so far as the cost of the steps to reduce the risk would be less than the cost of the manifestation of the risk so reduced) *and* then to ensure that the public was aware of and had accepted any residual risk. Doing this would not be sufficient to avoid all liability; since a producer could still be held liable for a risk that it did not discover, and consequently could neither eliminate nor disclose.[38] But such an approach to liability would be consistent with an overall goal of enabling consumers to *choose* what product risks they accept, with an entitlement to compensation so far as they are nonetheless exposed to *unaccepted* risks.

Subsequent cases, however, have rejected Burton J's approach in favour of a more 'flexible' but indeterminate alternative. For example, Hickinbottom J in *Wilkes v DePuy International Ltd*,[39] favoured 'a holistic approach … involving the application of judgment to the exercise of balancing all relevant considerations'. Elaborating, he continued: 'Given the wide range of products (and their intended use) to which the Directive and Act apply, the court must maintain a flexible approach to the assessment of the appropriate level of safety, including which circumstances are relevant and the weight to be given to each, those factors being quintessentially dependent upon the particular facts of any case'. This passage suggests that the key concept of the level of safety that 'persons generally are entitled to expect' may vary depending on the type of product under consideration.

[35] [2001] 3 All ER 298, QBD.

[36] Ibid [71]: 'The sole question will be safety for the foreseeable use.'

[37] The underlying notion being that the public generally might *legitimately* accept additional risk in order to gain greater accessibility.

[38] Some undiscovered risks might be *undiscoverable*, and consequently entitle the defendant to rely on the 'development risk defence': see below at I.E. But, as is explained below, the defence will not cover *all* risks that a reasonable defendant did not discover.

[39] [2016] EWHC 3096 (QB); [2018] QB 627 [78]. Hickinbottom J's analysis was quoted by the Court of Appeal in pre-trial litigation in the *Seroxat Group Litigation* [2019] EWCA Civ 1924 [8].

Hickinbottom J's approach to the definition of 'defect' tilts the balance in favour of producers in three significant ways. First, he suggests that the balance between the risks that a product carries and the potential benefits of the use of the product for a consumer, and for society more generally, may 'lie at the heart of the question of appropriate level of safety', at least for a medical product.[40] Thus the question of the acceptability – to a judge – of the risk/utility balance in a product becomes more prominent and overtakes Burton J's simpler approach of asking whether those endangered by a product had been made aware of, and accepted the risks. Secondly, for Hickinbottom J, the 'avoidability' of the risk, in the sense of the practicability of producing a product with a superior balance of benefit to risk, is a relevant question.[41] Thirdly, where an expert regulator has addressed a risk associated with a product, and has either set a general safety standard – that the product complies with – or has licensed the product individually, the regulator's opinion as to the appropriate level of safety is likely to be granted considerable weight by a judge determining what level of safety 'persons generally are entitled to expect'.[42] In this context, however, it will be important to determine whether the regulator intended to express an opinion about the specific risk that injured the claimant and whether the regulator was unaware of what is now known about the nature and magnitude of the risk, and the options that exist for reducing it.

At this point, it may be appropriate to turn to five specific concerns that have been raised in the academic literature about the application of the 'defect' standard to autonomous systems.

The first such problem is that autonomous systems are likely to be non-transparent, and consequently an injured consumer may find it difficult to ascertain whether the malfunction of some element in a product contributed to his or her injury. To put the point in more concrete terms, how will a yachtsman injured by an autonomous ship *discover* that a malfunctioning sensor or an erroneous line of code contributed to the ship failing to change course in order to avoid a collision? An Expert Group recruited by the European Commission has proposed addressing such concerns with regard to autonomous devices in general by changes to the law so as to require producers to design their products so that they 'log' significant information, at least if certain conditions pertain,[43] and to allow *presumptions* to

[40] At [67].

[41] What Hickinbottom J writes, at [82], is that 'the practicability of producing a product of risk-benefit equivalence must therefore potentially be a relevant circumstance in the assessment of a product's safety'. It seems fair to assume that the word 'equivalence' is a slip; if a claimant seeking to establish that a product is defective must address 'avoidability', then they must surely address the practicality of making a *safer* product without a disproportionately greater reduction in its potential benefits.

[42] At [97]-[98] (compliance with general standards) and [101] (regulatory approval).

[43] Expert Group on Liability and New Technologies – New Technologies formation, *Liability for Artificial Intelligence and Other Emerging Technologies* (Publications Office of the European Union, 2019), key finding [20]. The full formulation of the group's finding as to the conditions under which logging should be mandatory helpfully illustrates the complexity of the issue: 'There should be a duty on producers to equip technology with means of recording information about the operation of the technology (logging by design), if such information is typically essential for establishing whether a risk of the technology materialised, and if logging is appropriate and proportionate, taking into account, in

be drawn about 'defect' and 'causation' in the absence of transparency.[44] While voyage data recorders (VDRs) are already mandatory for many ships,[45] issues may arise as to how far they can be expected to record the processes occurring on an autonomous ship, especially if some proportion of processing occurs 'onshore'.[46]

The second problem is that autonomous systems are unlikely to be supplied on the basis of a one-off transfer; frequently, the producer and the 'operator' will remain in some sort of a relationship, perhaps with the producer supplying periodic updates to software, or perhaps with the producer retaining the capacity to modify the physical state of the product. As has already been noted, these relationships will challenge a liability regime that attaches importance to the time when the defective product was supplied to another. The normalisation of such relationships will also, however, challenge the basic decision to apply different liability regimes to the production of 'goods' and the performance of services.

The third problem is related to the second and arises from the fact that the CPA's liability regime employs a definition of 'defect' that relates to the safety of the product at the time that it was put into circulation,[47] while the proliferation of continuing relationships between producer and operator with regard to a product, particularly relationships that involve 'updating', may mean that consumers' expectations of safety will similarly assume a continuing concern for safety. To put matters in more concrete terms, 'persons generally' may come to expect producers to provide 'updates' for products where these will enable a product to be safer (at least in some circumstances). Clearly, if the law is to track such 'new' expectations, it will be necessary to revise the legislation in order to extend the concept of 'defect' to cover failures to 'update' products to reach expected *revised* levels of safety.

The fourth problem overlaps with the second and third and flows from the likelihood that those who purchase 'autonomous products' will purchase 'systems', including elements associated with multiple parties rather than standalone tangible 'goods'. As before, a concept of defect developed to deal with safety problems

particular, the technical feasibility and the costs of logging, the availability of alternative means of gathering such information, the type and magnitude of the risks posed by the technology, and any adverse implications logging may have on the rights of others'.

[44] Ibid, key finding [22]: 'The absence of logged information or failure to give the victim reasonable access to the information should trigger a rebuttable presumption that the condition of liability to be proven by the missing information is fulfilled'. And [26] '... the burden of proving causation may be alleviated in light of the challenges of emerging digital technologies if a balancing of the following factors warrants doing so: (a) the likelihood that the technology at least contributed to the harm; (b) the likelihood that the harm was caused either by the technology or by some other cause within the same sphere; (c) the risk of a known defect within the technology, even though its actual causal impact is not self-evident; (d) the degree of ex-post traceability and intelligibility of processes within the technology that may have contributed to the cause (informational asymmetry); (e) the degree of ex-post accessibility and comprehensibility of data collected and generated by the technology; (f) the kind and degree of harm potentially and actually caused'.

[45] International Convention for the Safety of Life at Sea 1974, as amended (SOLAS), reg 20.

[46] In the related context of autonomous road vehicles, innovators are concerned about the *volume* of data they are likely to generate, though it may be the case that they will frequently be operating in significantly more complex environments than autonomous ships.

[47] See CPA s 3(2), especially s 3(2)(c), and also s 4(1)(d).

associated with such goods, and their component *parts* (again, tangibles) may require revision in order to reach satisfactory solutions when applied to 'systems'.[48]

The fifth problem stems from the possibility of self-modifying products, such as those which engage in 'machine learning'. Such products may give rise to special problems of transparency, in the sense that the 'reasoning' behind self-design choices may be opaque. Further, such products will raise the question of how far subsequent self-design choices can be attributed to an original producer.[49]

E. Development Risk

The CPA contains a specific defence for the benefit of innovative producers, which applies when 'the state of scientific and technical knowledge [at the time when the producer supplied the product to another] was not such that a producer of products of the same description as the product in question might be expected to have discovered the defect if it had existed in his products while they were under his control'.[50] This wording does not mirror the equivalent provision in the directive, but the divergences are such that they can be addressed through interpretation.[51] The Luxembourg Court has advised that in order to establish the defence 'the producer of a defective product must prove that the objective state of scientific and technical knowledge, including the most advanced level of such knowledge, at the time when the product in question was put into circulation was not such as to enable the existence of the defect to be discovered. Further, … that knowledge must have been accessible at the time when the product in question was put into circulation'.[52] The Court's interpretation seeks to maintain an uneasy, and perhaps

[48] Gerhard Wagner, in his important and much-cited 'Robot Liability' (published in S Lohsse, R Schulze, and D Staudenmayer (eds), *Liability for Artificial Intelligence and the Internet of Things* (Nomos/ Hart, 2019)), predicted that developments in robotics and the Internet of Things 'will shift control over these machines and appliances away from users and towards manufacturers' (at 37), and noted the substantial difficulties that will face claimants if what they acquire are 'bundles' of physical product and software programs (all including components) produced by a variety of actors, and if they are required to establish which element in such a 'bundle' was defective. Such difficulties are only likely to be exacerbated by continuing service and updated relationships being added to the mix.

[49] Two possibilities: (i) what a machine 'learns' is likely to depend on the 'challenging experiences' that it has, and the feedback that it receives as to the success (or failure) of its strategies for dealing with them, but previous operation in a specific environment may expose a machine to a range of experiences that are a poor guide to appropriate strategies for success in a different environment; (ii) it seems possible that machines will not 'learn' atomistically, but that 'experiences' and feedback will be shared across products, just as a human pilot may use the experience used in guiding one ship to refine his or her strategy for guiding another.

[50] CPA, s 4(1)(e).

[51] Case C-300/95, *European Commission v UK* [1997] ECR I-2649. At the time of the case, CPA, s 1(1) provided that the statute should be construed to make such provision as was required to give effect to the relevant directive. It is arguable that the new wording, mandated by the Product Safety and Metrology etc (Amendment etc) (EU Exit) Regulations 2019, SI 2019/696, Sch 3, will not bring about a change of interpretation since it states that this was the 1987 Parliament's intention.

[52] Case C-300/95, above, at [29].

unstable, compromise position between the defence being so broad that any producer can avoid liability by showing that its risk-research was reasonable in the circumstances (and did not detect the problem) and the defence being so narrow that its benefit is wholly illusory since it will usually be the case that discovering the defect would not have been *impossible*: the compromise invokes the 'most advanced level' of scientific and technical knowledge, rather than a reasonable level, but qualifies this by providing that the knowledge must have been 'accessible'.

The term 'accessible' is generally assumed to have been a response to the concern of the Advocate General about the likelihood of a European product manufacturer becoming aware of 'research carried out by an academic in Manchuria published in a local scientific journal in Chinese, which does not go outside the boundaries of the region'.[53] Although the migration of scientific research from paper to electronic repositories may have altered the context, the basic problem of 'accessibility' of material published in other languages remains, and new issues, such as material which has been obscurely indexed, may need to be confronted. Neither Advocate General nor Court, however, addressed the issue of information that is 'inaccessible' because it is held by a commercial rival with an economic incentive not to share it with others; perhaps the fact that a commercial rival *has* obtained the information is sufficient to establish that it was not *undiscoverable*, but this answer overlooks the role that *luck* regularly plays in scientific discovery.

One issue relating to the scope of the defence may be particularly important when problems are discovered with software, such as a vulnerability to hacking. In *A v National Blood Authority*,[54] Burton J expressed the view that the defence could not be relied on when a producer's difficulty was the impossibility of determining which *particular* product had a dangerous feature that was known to occur in some proportion of a type of products. This conclusion could be of significance if it were the case that knowledge of the possibility of many 'bugs' in software greatly exceeds the practical possibility of detecting them all before the software is operational. The conclusion has been criticised,[55] however, and acceptance of critics' broader reading of the defence would improve the prospects of the producers of software (or of products that incorporate software) escaping liability for glitches and vulnerabilities that were undetectable at the time that a particular program was put into circulation.

[53] Opinion of the Advocate General (G Tesauro), at [23].

[54] [2001] 3 All ER 298, QBD [74]: 'It would, in my judgment, be inconsistent with the purpose of the directive if a producer, in the case of a known risk, continues to supply products simply because, and despite the fact that, he is unable to identify in which if any of his products that defect will occur or recur … without accepting the responsibility for any injuries resulting, by insurance or otherwise'.

[55] See, eg, D Fairgrieve and R Goldberg, *Product Liability* (3rd edn, OUP, 2020) 13–116, quoting a question posed by S Whittaker, *Liability for Products: English Law, French Law, and European Harmonisation* (OUP 2005) 500: '[W]here a risk is known to the scientific community but its manifestation (the 'defect') is incapable of being detected in individual products and therefore prevented at any cost and in any way given the contemporary state of scientific knowledge, why should this not be thought to be a 'development risk' in that the imposition of liability would inhibit the production of innovative products?'

II. Physical Damage to External Commercial Property, Such as a Different Vessel

A claimant who has suffered physical damage to their commercial property as a result of a problem with an autonomous ship will not be able to rely on the Consumer Protection Act 1987 but may be able to bring a claim using the tort of negligence. This tort may also be relied on by any victim of an autonomous ship who wishes to bring a claim against a party *other than* the producer, such as an operator or designer.

A. Duty of Care

The primary condition for a claim in the tort of negligence is for the claimant to establish that the defendant owed it a duty of care. Such a duty will not be owed unless a reasonable person in the shoes of the defendant ought to have foreseen that there was a real possibility of someone in the claimant's position suffering the type of harm that the claimant has suffered if the defendant failed to take reasonable care. In situations where the defendant's act of producing a dangerous product causes the damage to the claimant, the foreseeability of the risk will generally be enough to establish the defendant's duty.[56]

One exception to the sufficiency of foreseeability as a foundation for a duty, that may be significant in practice, is where a defendant's activities will only cause problems for the claimant if a third party intervenes in events in a particular way. For example, producing or operating an autonomous ship with an insecure remote-control system may only be foreseeably dangerous to owners of other ships or waterside property if a third party seeks to exploit that insecurity and take control of the vessel. In such a situation, Lord Goff, in the leading case of *Smith v Littlewoods Organisation Ltd*,[57] suggested that a defendant may owe a duty not to create a 'source of danger' that a third party will foreseeably interfere with and 'spark off'.[58] Similarly, as Robert Goff LJ he had previously suggested that a defendant might be under a duty not to 'present' a wrongdoer 'with the means to commit the wrong, in circumstances where it is obvious or very likely that he will do so – as, for example, where he hands over a car to be driven by a person

[56] See, eg, *Marsden and Gault on Collisions at Sea* (15th edn, Sweet & Maxwell, 2020) 4-033: 'It is trite law that the manufacturer of any article owes a duty of care to anyone reasonably foreseeable as likely to be injured by defects in it: and this principle clearly applies to shipbuilders'. (In the original, the sentence includes a citation to *Donoghue v Stevenson* [1932] AC 562.)

[57] [1987] AC 241 (HL).

[58] This formulation of the duty echoes the discussion at pp 272–73, where Lord Goff identified *Haynes v Harwood* [1935] 1 KB 146 as a 'classic example' of the relevant principle: in *Haynes*' case, the defendant's carter left a horse-drawn van unattended in a crowded street, the horses bolted when a boy threw a stone at them, and a policeman was injured when stopping them.

who is drunk, or plainly incompetent, who then runs over the plaintiff'.[59] Thus the *exceptional* basis for the duty seems to depend on the inherent dangerousness of the 'source of danger', or the likelihood of the third party *employing* it in an unreasonably dangerous manner. The Court of Appeal has twice ruled that there is no general duty on the owner of a bus to take reasonable care to prevent it from being driven away by an unauthorised driver.[60] However, there may be some prospect of autonomous vessels, or at least some sub-group of them, being sufficiently dangerous and tempting to ground a duty on their producers to take reasonable steps to reduce the likelihood of them being hijacked.[61]

B. Fault

The duty imposed in the tort of negligence is a duty to take reasonable care of the claimant's protected interest, with the appropriate level of care being set by asking what a reasonable person would have done in the defendant's position. It is generally accepted that a reasonable person would not take any steps to deal with a risk that was not reasonably foreseeable as a real possibility at the time of the alleged breach. Where a risk is foreseeable, however, then the steps that a reasonable person would take would be related to the reasonably foreseeable scale of the risk, the severity of injury that might occur if the risk eventuated, and the cost of reducing the risk either through an investment in precautions or the benefits foregone as a result of a modification in behaviour.[62]

Those who suggest that the function of the tort of negligence is to deter *inefficient* dangerous behaviour frequently suggest that a reasonable person would invest in

[59] *P Perl (Exporters) Ltd v Camden London Borough Council* [1984] QB 342 at 359. As an illustration of this proposition, Robert Goff LJ cited a first instance decision from Ontario, Canada: *Ontario Hospital Services Commission v Borsoski* (1975) 54 DLR 3d 339. In this case, however, the defendant had instructed the claimant, whom he knew to be incompetent (having failed his driver's test three times) and intoxicated, to drive his (the defendant's) car.

[60] The better-known authority is *Topp v London Country Bus (South West) Ltd* [1993] 1 WLR 976 CA, though both Dillon and Rose LLJ thought that the decision in *Denton v United Counties Omnibus Co*, The Times, 6 May 1986; Court of Appeal (Civil Division) Transcript No 421 of 1986, CA, was indistinguishable. The claimant had succeeded in the similar, earlier case of *Hayman v London Transport Executive* (unreported), 4 March 1982; Court of Appeal (Civil Division) Transcript No 74 of 1982, CA, but in *Denton* the Court of Appeal suggested that the issue of whether a duty was owed had probably been conceded in *Hayman*. In *Hayman*, the defendants had been made aware of unauthorised youths entering and driving off buses that were left unmanned in a particular roadside bay, and in *Denton*, Nourse LJ expressly left open the question whether a duty might have been owed if there had been a large number of similar incidents of unauthorised driving away of buses from the depot concerned.

[61] Attentive readers will have noticed that the cases put forward as supporting the suggestion that *producers* may owe such a duty of care actually involved defendants more comfortably classed as *operators*: it is certainly likely that *operators* of autonomous ships will *also* owe duties to take care to prevent them from becoming a source of danger to third parties, but this will not preclude the possibility that in some circumstances a *producer* ought to have done more to prevent their products become a source of danger when used in a predictable way.

[62] See D Fairgrieve and R Goldberg, *Product Liability* (3rd edn, OUP, 2020) 14-10.

precautions if their cost is lower than the cost of the accidents that such precautions would avoid. This may be true, except in the case where more than one person could take steps to prevent an accident, and one such person's steps would be cheaper than the others; here efficiency might favour only the *cheapest* cost avoider being subject to a duty to take steps. A more difficult question is whether the converse is true: is it true that a reasonable person would not feel obliged to invest in precautions where their cost is greater than the cost of the accidents that such precautions would avoid? There is little doubt that *real* people investing in precautions frequently incur costs that are substantially in excess of the cost of the accidents that they are likely to avoid. More pertinently, in real situations, particularly those involving innovative products, reliable information about the frequency and severity of particular types of accidents, and even about the real costs of particular precautions, is frequently unavailable, so courts are likely to resort to heuristics when determining whether a defendant has met a reasonable standard of care. Common heuristics may include, whether the problem with the product was a result of a misstep on the production line, whether the product's design complied with compulsory and voluntary regulatory standards, and, whether a human being would have been likely to out-perform the autonomous product in the same situation.[63]

III. Physical Damage to the Autonomous Vessel Itself

We have already noted that the CPA 1987 cannot be used to claim compensation for damage to commercial property, and also contains a provision preventing claims for 'damage to the product itself or for the loss of or any damage to the whole or any part of any product which has been supplied with the product in question comprised in it'.[64] As a result, if a defective sensor incorporated in an autonomous ship causes the loss of the ship, the *owner* will not be able to use the CPA to obtain compensation from either the producer of the ship or the producer of the sensor (even if the ship was non-commercial). It may also be difficult for the owner to sue either of these parties in the tort of negligence since English law regards the loss suffered by the owner as purely economic loss;[65] assuming that the owner purchased the ship, the loss is conceptualised as the owner having paid far too much for a low-quality vessel, rather than the scenario being analysed as an instance of the producer's act physically damaging the owner's property.[66]

[63] J-S Boghetti, 'How Can Artificial Intelligence be Defective?' in S Lohsse, R Schulze, and D Staudenmayer (eds), *Liability for Artificial Intelligence and the Internet of Things* (Nomos / Hart 2019) 68–69 treats it as straightforward that a producer should not 'put into circulation an algorithm which creates more dangers than the human actions it is intended to replace'.

[64] CPA, s 5(2).

[65] *Murphy v Brentwood LBC* [1991] 1 AC 398, HL.

[66] To put the same point another way: the producer is treated as having produced property with a self-destructive defect inherent in it, and *this* is what the owner *purchased*; the producer never inflicted physical damage on the owner's property.

Generally, a defendant will only be held to have been subject to a duty (enforced by the tort of negligence) to take care to protect the owner against such (purely economic) loss if the defendant has 'assumed responsibility' for doing so. Merely *producing* a physical product, such as a ship, is unlikely to be treated as involving any such 'assumption of responsibility'. But if a producer has also agreed to perform a service for the owner, such as *advising* him on what sort of vessel will meet his needs, or *servicing* the ship to ensure that it remains seaworthy, the producer may have 'assumed responsibility' for performing these tasks competently so as to avoid causing economic loss to the owner. This said, agreements to perform such services will frequently be contractual so that the possibility of a claim in tort will frequently become significant only in unusual circumstances where there is some procedural reason why it is advantageous to describe the claim as based on a tort.[67]

The distinction between the producer's general duty to take reasonable care not to produce a product that will cause physical damage to *other* property (which is governed by the law presented under subheading II) and the lack of any general duty to protect the purely financial interests of a potential purchaser of defective property, means that the question what counts as *other* property becomes significant in negligence cases. For example, where a producer manufactured both an autonomous ship *and* an onshore remote-control device, it is possible to imagine situations where an owner might want to claim that the negligently-produced remote-control device had caused physical damage to *other* property, that is the ship. Similarly, where one producer manufactured a defective sensor, which a second producer incorporated in an autonomous ship, and the failure of the sensor caused the loss of the ship, the owner might want to claim that the negligently-produced sensor had caused physical damage to *other* property, that is the ship-minus-sensor. An owner's submission that a producer's negligence has caused physical damage to *other* property is likely to be strongest when the owner has acquired the items of property separately, with the case becoming even stronger if they were acquired at different times, most frequently where the product causing the problems was acquired after acquisition of the *other* property that it is alleged that it damaged. Thus if a producer manufactured an onshore remote-control device, which was acquired by the owner, who had also previously acquired a ship that could be controlled by this device, it would be relatively straightforward to treat the ship as *other* property and to treat the producer of the remote-control device as under a duty to take care not to manufacture it in such a way that it might damage the ship. In contrast, where there appears to be a single acquisition it is likely to be more difficult to treat what was acquired as more than one piece of property, particularly if the scenario is one where one 'part' would be treated as having acceded to another.[68]

[67] In the leading case of *Henderson v Merrett Syndicates Ltd* [1995] 2 AC 145, HL, it was advantageous to frame a claim as based on the tort of negligence in order to circumvent the fact that the limitation period for bringing a contractual claim had expired.

[68] The issue is discussed in detail by Robert Stevens in *Tort and Rights*, at pp 26–30. See also *Clerk and Lindsell on Torts* (23rd edn, Sweet & Maxwell, 2020) 10-22–10-25, where the author recommends attaching less significance to whether a replacement component was fitted *before* the claimant acquired it.

IV. Losses as a Result of an Inability to Use the Autonomous Vessel for a Period for Reasons Other than the Need to Perform Physical Repairs

Where a problem with an autonomous ship means that it cannot be used for a period of time (or can only be used in a less efficient way, for example, at a slower speed or with a reduced capacity) English law will classify this loss of use[69] as 'purely economic' loss, a phrase that means that it is a form of loss that is not *consequential* on damage to the claimant's person or physical property.[70] As a general rule, the tort of negligence only imposes a duty on someone to take reasonable care of the purely economic interests of another if the potential duty-holder has 'assumed responsibility' for looking after those interests, and the general position is that the producer of a product does not, by merely manufacturing the product, 'assume responsibility' for protecting the economic interests of future purchasers.[71] In most situations where one person has taken on the task of looking after the economic interests of another, there will be a contract, since the parties will want to be clear about exactly what has been undertaken, and provide for such things as payment, dispute resolution procedures and limitations on liability. The tort of negligence, however, supplements contractual liability where the parties find themselves in a relationship 'akin to contract' because the defendant has 'indicated' to the claimant, expressly or implicitly, that he or she is willing to act in a particular way so as to take care of the claimant's interests. A common example of such a situation is where a defendant has undertaken to provide a claimant with advice about a matter that calls for a degree of expertise. In the context of autonomous maritime systems, it seems likely that operators will be significantly dependent on expert advice from producers and others, though much of this is likely to be delivered either under contract or in contexts where special pre-contractual liability schemes are applied.

[69] The position will be governed by the law discussed under the previous subheading where the loss of use also *causes* physical damage to *other* property, eg, where an owner's inability to use a particular autonomous ship to carry its goods promptly means that these goods deteriorate physically.

[70] Where the loss of use *is* consequential on damage to physical property, eg, loss of use during a period when physical damage is being repaired, an owner who is entitled to claim for the physical damage will also be able to claim for this *consequential loss*, subject to the question of remoteness.

[71] In a marine context, see *Hamble Fisheries Ltd v L Gardner and Sons Ltd (The 'Rebecca Elaine')* [1999] 2 Lloyd's Rep 1 (CA), following Lord Bridge in *Murphy v Brentwood LBC* [1991] 1 AC 398, 475: '[I]f a manufacturer produces and sells a chattel which is merely defective in quality, even to the extent that it is valueless for the purpose for which it is intended, the manufacturer's liability at common law arises only under and by reference to the terms of any contract to which he is a party in relation to the chattel, the common law does not impose on him any liability in tort to persons to whom he owes no duty in contract but who, having acquired the chattel, suffer economic loss because the chattel is defective in quality.'

V. Conclusions

This chapter has outlined the main *tortious* liabilities of producers of autonomous ships under the law of England and Wales and identified some elements of those liability regimes that may be difficult to apply to such products and some ways in which the development of autonomous maritime systems may challenge the basic structure of the existing liability regimes. There is a significant prospect, however, that the law set out so far will never be applied to incidents involving autonomous ships because the law changes in one or more of the following three ways: (i) the liability under the CPA 1987 is amended so as to clarify that it can apply to the authors of software, and perhaps also the suppliers of data; (ii) a strict liability scheme is enacted, as has occurred for automated road vehicles under the Automated and Electric Vehicles Act 2018;[72] or (iii) producers will choose to undertake extensive *additional* extra-legal liabilities in order to build trust in their products.[73]

[72] The European Parliament resolution of 20 October 2020 with recommendations to the Commission on a civil liability regime for artificial intelligence (2020/2014(INL)) recommends enactment of a Regulation to impose strict liability, backed by mandatory insurance, on the 'operators' of high-risk AI-systems.

[73] In the field of automated road vehicles, Volvo's President and CEO Håkan Samuelsson has undertaken that 'Volvo will accept full liability whenever one of our cars is in autonomous mode', and rival developers have made similar statements. These undertakings have been made, however, against a background of liability regimes for traffic accidents in many European states, which effectively impose strict liability on the owner of the vehicle, underpinned by insurance.

7

Maritime Autonomous Surface Ships: Marine Insurance Response to Risks

PETER MACDONALD EGGERS QC*

I. Introduction

Imagine a cargo-carrying vessel in the midst of a voyage in international waters. There is a valuable cargo on board. The weather is deteriorating. The vessel may negotiate the ensuing storm and reach its destination without harm. Alternatively, it might all go wrong. The vessel may founder in a surging sea. The result could be the exposure of the owner of the vessel to substantial financial losses: the total loss of the vessel and the loss of the income to be earned on the voyage. It could also expose the shipowner to legal liabilities to the owner of the cargo, the charterers, the mortgagees, joint venturers, and the crew members on board the vessel, as well as to potential criminal and civil liabilities to affected states. Casualties such as this are not uncommon. Such losses and liabilities are regulated by private and public laws and regularly dealt with by the Courts, enforcing contractual terms, extra-contractual responsibilities, statutes or international conventions. The risks attendant on such a voyage are very often protected by a range of insurance policies: policies on the hull, cargo, liability and financial loss, as well as protection and indemnity club cover.[1]

Imagine, however, if there is no human being on board the vessel during the voyage. The vessel is autonomous, meaning that it is controlled remotely by the operator on shore or controlled by the artificial intelligence in computers on board the vessel or on shore. Alternatively, imagine that the vessel is wholly or partly operated from shore or by artificial intelligence, but there are crew members on board who can assume control over the vessel. Are the usual range of insurance products sufficient for this purpose? Would insurers be content to insure such

* Barrister, 7 King's Bench Walk; Honorary Fellow of the Institute of International Shipping and Trade Law, University of Swansea.

[1] See generally L Zhu and R Xing, 'A Pioneering Study of Third-party Liability Insurance for Unmanned/autonomous commercial ships' [2019] JBL 442.

risks by using traditional insurance policies? What additional considerations arise in the risk presentation and the placing of insurance? How should marine insurance deal with the risks arising from instances of cyberattacks, cyber ransoms and cyber terrorism upon such information and operational technological systems?

The autonomous operation of sea-going vessels (Maritime Autonomous Surface Ships or 'MASS') will inevitably employ complex computer systems regulating their operation, including navigation, bridge operations, propulsion systems, communications, maintenance, cargo operations, cargo care, access and security systems, safety management, and environmental protection. All of these will be networked with other computer systems via the internet and satellite communications. Vessels already have complex computer systems, but this will increase substantially as the autonomous operations of such systems become more sophisticated. Such systems are plainly exposed to various risks, including defective design, erroneous operation and deliberate attack by cyber-pirates and cyber-terrorists. Such cyber risks will become heightened as more individuals and organisations have (cabled or remote) access to such systems.[2]

Accordingly, in order to review the issues arising for marine insurance from the use of autonomous vessels, the management and insurance of cyber risks is a critical consideration. Lloyd's has defined cyber risks as 'any risk where the losses are cyber-related, arising from either malicious acts (e.g. cyber-attack, infection of an IT system with malicious code) or non-malicious acts (e.g. loss of data, accidental acts or omissions) involving either tangible or intangible assets'.[3] Cyber risks have been defined generally by the International Maritime Organisation ('IMO') to refer to 'a measure of the extent to which a technology asset is threatened by a potential circumstance or event, which may result in shipping-related operational, safety or security failures as a consequence of information or systems being corrupted, lost or compromised'.[4]

This chapter addresses these questions by considering the following topics:

i. Developments in the maritime industry both as to the growth of information and operational technologies and the response to cyber risks.
ii. The presentation of the risk by the assured to the marine insurer.
iii. The effect of the insurer's knowledge on the assured's risk presentation.
iv. The risks insured by traditional marine insurance policies.
v. The provisions developed by the insurance industry to affirm the existence or absence of cover for relevant risks.
vi. The potential statutory liability of insurers for incidents affecting autonomous vessels.
vii. Issues with respect to the presentation, investigation and handling of claims.

[2] See N Newman, 'Cyber Pirates Terrorising the High Seas', Engineering and Technology, 18 April 2019.

[3] *Lloyd's Market Bulletin* Y5258 dated 4 July 2019.

[4] IMO Guidelines on Maritime Cyber Risk Management, MSC-FAL.1/Circ 3, 5 July 2017.

The review of these topics will assist in deciding upon the first steps which should be taken to render marine insurance products suitable to deal with the new world of autonomous vessels.

II. Developments in the Maritime Industry

The IMO is currently undertaking a review, or 'scoping exercise', of marine autonomous surface ships (MASS) having regard to questions of safety, security and environmental protection, and how issues arising in connection with MASS should be addressed in IMO instruments and international conventions (including pollution and limitation of liability conventions). This review is being undertaken as part of its larger Strategic Plan to 'Integrate new and advancing technologies in the regulatory framework', and expected to be completed by the end of 2020.[5] As part of this review, the IMO will consider the differing degrees of automation: (1) the use of automated processes and decision on board a vessel which is operated and controlled by mariners; (2) the use of remotely controlled vessels with mariners on board the vessel who can take control and operate systems on board; (3) the use of remotely controlled vessels without mariners on board; and (4) the use of fully autonomous vessels whose operating system enables the vessel to make decisions and execute actions by itself.

Pending the completion of this scoping exercise, in June 2019, the IMO's Maritime Safety Committee approved interim guidelines for MASS trials, including guidelines that trials should be conducted in a manner that provides at least the same degree of safety, security and protection of the environment as provided by the relevant IMO instruments and that onboard or remote operators of MASS should be appropriately qualified for operating MASS subject to the trial. In addition, the Committee recommended that appropriate steps should be taken to ensure sufficient cyber risk management of the systems and infrastructure used when conducting MASS trials.

With this in mind, and in order to understand how marine insurance policies can address the risks associated with information and operational technologies such as those used in the autonomous operation of vessels, it is worthwhile examining the steps taken by the maritime industry to deal with such cyber risks. In this respect, a distinction is made between cyber security and cyber safety; the former being concerned with the protection of data from unauthorised access, manipulation and corruption; the latter being concerned with the loss of availability and integrity of data and the use and operation of the relevant technologies.[6]

On 16 June 2017, the IMO adopted resolution MSC 428(98) providing that 'an approved safety management system should take into account cyber risk

[5] www.imo.org/en/MediaCentre/HotTopics/Pages/Autonomous-shipping.aspx, accessed 1 August 2020.

[6] The Guidelines on Cyber Security Onboard Ships Version 3 (BIMCO, CLIA, ICS, Intercargo, Intermanager, Intertanko, IUMI, OCIMF and World Shipping Council) ('the Cyber Guidelines').

management in accordance with the objectives and functional requirements of the ISM Code' and recommending that states bring this to the attention of all stakeholders. On 5 July 2017, the IMO issued Guidelines on Maritime Cyber Risk Management, providing high-level recommendations on maritime cyber risk management.[7]

Soon afterwards, BIMCO, CLIA, ICS, Intercargo, Intermanager, Intertanko, IUMI, OCIMF and World Shipping Council issued Guidelines on Cyber Security Onboard Ships Version 3 ('the Cyber Guidelines'). The Cyber Guidelines identified the threats to cyber risk management, including the actions of activists, criminals, terrorists and states, by means of malware, phishing, water holing, and social engineering, as well as the intentional or unintentional actions or omissions of shipowners' personnel in operating technology and computer systems, and the absence or obsolescence of computer systems and software. These threats are exacerbated by the use of wireless networking between vessels and onshore management. The Cyber Guidelines make provision for the assessment of cyber risks, the development of protection and detection measures, including the upgrade and maintenance of software and anti-virus and anti-malware tools, and preparing a response to a cyber incident.

III. Issues Concerning Good Faith

A. The Assured's Duty of Fair Presentation of the Risk

Before an insurance contract is concluded, the risk must be fairly presented by the assured to the insurer, meaning that the assured must provide full and accurate disclosure of material information or at least sufficient information to put a prudent insurer on notice that it needs to make further enquiries for the purpose of revealing further information. Prior to the entry into force of the Insurance Act 2015, the assured's duty was to provide full disclosure of all material circumstances, but there was an exception to the duty of disclosure, whereby the assured was excused from disclosing information if the insurer waived such disclosure by having received a summary of material information, putting the insurer on notice of the existence of further material information, but failed to ask for that information.[8] However, since the entry into force of the Insurance Act 2015, the principal duty is that the assured must disclose every material circumstance which the assured knows or ought to know, but 'failing that', the assured must disclose material circumstances 'which gives the insurer sufficient information to put a

[7] IMO Guidelines on Maritime Cyber Risk Management, MSC-FAL.1/Circ 3, 5 July 2017.

[8] *Container Transport International Inc v Oceanus Mutual Underwriting Association (Bermuda) Ltd* [1984] 1 Lloyd's Rep 476, 496–98, 511–12, 529–30; *WISE (Underwriting Agency) Ltd v Grupo Nacional Provincial SA* [2004] EWCA Civ 962; [2004] 2 Lloyd's Rep 483; *Aldridge v Liberty Mutual Insurance Europe Ltd* [2016] EWHC 3037 (Comm), paras 33–38.

prudent insurer on notice that it needs to make further enquiries for the purpose of revealing those material circumstances'.[9]

There is an equivalent duty on the insurer to provide such disclosure, at least at common law.[10] However, the practical existence of that duty is in some doubt since the entry into force of the Insurance Act 2015, since (a) section 17 of the Marine Insurance Act 1906 was amended to remove the express reference to the reciprocal nature of the duty, although section 17 still states that the marine insurance contract is 'based upon the utmost good faith', which is said to have been retained as an interpretative principle,[11] (b) the universal and sole common law remedy for breach of the duty of utmost good faith – avoidance – was abolished by section 14 of the Insurance Act 2015, and (c) the Insurance Act 2015 otherwise makes no reference to the insurer's duty.

The purpose of the duty of fair presentation of the risk – in particular, the duty of disclosure – has been said to correct the imbalance of knowledge which generally exists between the assured, who knows relatively a great deal about the subject matter being insured, and the insurer who knows relatively little.[12] The essence of the duty of disclosure is that the assured must disclose material information which the assured knows or ought to know,[13] even if the assured does not appreciate the materiality of the information in question.[14]

Under the Insurance Act 2015, what constitutes the assured's knowledge for the purposes of the duty of disclosure is quite broad. A corporate assured will be taken to know what is known to one or more individuals who are part of the assured's senior management, meaning 'individuals who play significant roles in the making of decisions about how the insured's activities are to be managed or organised'.[15] Accordingly, if any one individual member of a corporate assured's senior management is aware of a relevant material circumstance, that circumstance will have to be disclosed to the insurer. The individuals included within the assured's senior management might be numerous, especially in a substantial concern.[16] The assured's activities for the purposes of such corporate knowledge are likely to include the management of the assured's information and operational technology systems and this may well entail the assured's knowledge of the cyber risks affecting those systems. If so, the assured's disclosure might well have to include information relating to the cyber security and

[9] Insurance Act 2015, s 3(4). See *Young v Royal and Sun Alliance plc* [2019] CSOH 32; [2019] Lloyd's Rep IR 482, paras 67–72.

[10] *Carter v Boehm* (1766) 3 Burr 1905; *Banque Keyser Ullmann SA v Skandia (UK) Insurance Co Ltd* [1990] 1 QB 665; [1991] 2 AC 249; *Aldrich v Norwich Union Life Insurance Co Ltd* [2000] Lloyd's Rep IR 10, 268, 281–82. See also s 17 of the Marine Insurance Act 1906.

[11] Explanatory notes, para 117.

[12] *Pan Atlantic Insurance Co Ltd v Pine Top Insurance Co Ltd* [1995] 1 AC 501, 542.

[13] Insurance Act 2015, s 3(4)(a).

[14] *Joel v Law Union and Crown Insurance Company* [1908] 2 KB 863, 884–85.

[15] Insurance Act 2015, s 4(8)(c).

[16] The Explanatory Notes, para 56, state that 'this is likely to include members of the board of directors but may extend beyond this, depending on the structure and management arrangements of the insured'.

safety management systems developed and implemented by the assured, and any failure to comply with such systems as well as any issues arising from defects in the computer hardware and software used by the assured. Any individual who plays a significant role in decision-making about the assured's vessel's cargo operations, safety, security, operation and technology systems, and the employment of mariners and information technology professionals may well be included in the assured's senior management. The implications of this definition of corporate knowledge will require the assured to assess the state of knowledge of each member of the senior management team.

Even more significantly, all assureds are also obliged to disclose material circumstances which the assured ought to know, namely what should reasonably have been revealed by a reasonable search of information available to the assured (whether the search is conducted by making enquiries or by any other means). This includes information held within the assured's organisation or information held by any other person.[17] It is unclear to what extent a reasonable search must be undertaken. The Explanatory Notes accompanying this requirement of a reasonable search suggest this replicates the law under section 18(1) of the Marine Insurance Act 1906,[18] but it seems clear that the removal of the restrictive qualification 'in the ordinary course of business',[19] and the imposition of an obligation of search have considerably broadened that which is taken to represent the assured's knowledge for the purposes of the duty of disclosure.

This definition of knowledge which informs the assured's duty of disclosure is potentially far-reaching when it comes to autonomous vessels. The operation of autonomous vessels depends on extensive computer programming and algorithms, which systems, at their height, as presently understood, discover, analyse and learn from data. Such computer programs and algorithms are invariably designed, maintained and perhaps hosted or operated by service providers, rather than the assured itself.[20] In addition, the cyber safety and cyber security issues referred to above will shape the disclosure to be provided. Accordingly, subject to the requirement of reasonableness, it may well be incumbent on the assured to make enquiries with service providers, employed with respect to the operation of the insured vessel, about the information and operations technology used in respect of the vessel, and cyber safety and security systems relating to the vessel, in order to obtain the following information for the purposes of disclosing the same to the insurer:

i. The type and nature of the computer systems, both hardware and software, external or in-house systems, operated or used by the assured.

[17] Insurance Act 2015, s 4(6)-(7).

[18] Explanatory Notes, para 56.

[19] *Australia & New Zealand Bank v Colonial & Eagle Wharves Ltd* [1960] 2 Lloyd's Rep 241, 252; *Simner v New India Assurance Co Ltd* [1995] LRLR 240, 253–5; *ERC Frankona Reinsurance v American National Insurance Co* [2005] EWHC 1381 (Comm); [2006] 1 Lloyd's Rep IR 157, para 173.

[20] Explanatory Notes, para 56: 'The scope of the phrase "information held … by any other person" in this context is intended to be flexible'.

ii. Information reflecting on the performance of the relevant computer programs and algorithms, such as consistency of performance, errors or faults in the programs, the possibility of bias in the operation of such programs and algorithms, and the limitations of such programs.
iii. Information identifying the extent to which the computer programs and algorithms cater for the relevant vessel's operations, from the trade routes it follows, the types of cargo it carries, the geopolitical risks it evaluates, or the weather patterns it monitors.
iv. Information revealing the degree with which it can interact and co-operate with external computer systems, whether operated by port authorities, cargo terminals, or other shipowners.
v. Information revealing the extent to which the computer programs and algorithms have been exposed or are likely to be exposed to security threats, such as hacking, malware, or the appropriation of the identities of persons within the assured's organisation or the organisations of commercial partners or customers.
vi. Information demonstrating the learning achieved by the assured's programs and manifested by a change in the conduct of the assured's business.

In addition to the knowledge of service providers, if any person within an assured's organisation has knowledge of such information, that may well have to be disclosed either being information treated as known to the assured, assuming that such person is a member of the company's senior management, or otherwise if such a person should be consulted for the purposes of the assured's duty of reasonable search. Further, the assured may have to consult electronic databases in order to fulfil the duty of reasonable search.

This is all in addition to the traditional searches which an insured shipowner makes for the purposes of complying with the duty of fair presentation of the risk. This might, in sum, amount to a wealth of information which the assured is obliged to provide to the insurer. It will then be necessary for the assured to evaluate this information and perhaps draw attention to the more relevant or material information, given that, under the Insurance Act 2015, the assured must disclose material circumstances in a manner which is reasonably clear and accessible to a prudent insurer.[21] This, it has been said, 'is intended to target, at one end of the scale, "data dumps", where the insurer is presented with an overwhelming amount of undigested information. At the other end, it is not expected that this requirement would be satisfied by an overly brief or cryptic presentation'.[22]

B. The Effect of the Insurer's Knowledge on the Assured's Risk Presentation

The assured's duty of fair presentation of the risk is tempered by whatever the insurer already knows or ought to know, including (i) that which an agent knows

[21] Insurance Act 2015, s 3(3)(b).
[22] Explanatory Notes, para 46.

and ought reasonably have passed on to the underwriter; (ii) 'the relevant information is held by the insurer and is readily available to' the underwriter; (iii) matters of common knowledge; and (iv) matters which an insurer in a particular market would be expected to know in the ordinary course of business.[23] If a marine insurer knows or is taken to know such information, the assured is not obliged to disclose the same to the insurer, even if the information is material.

In considering what a marine insurer should be taken as knowing, there should be concern as to how which the insurance industry is considering cyber risks as a whole. In July 2017, the Prudential Regulation Authority ('the PRA') issued Supervisory Statement SS4/17 'Cyber insurance underwriting risk', in which it was said that the PRA expected relevant firms to be able to identify, quantify and manage cyber insurance underwriting risk, having regard to (1) affirmative cyber risk, that is insurance policies that explicitly include or exclude cover for cyber risks, and (2) non-affirmative cyber risk, that is insurance policies that do not expressly include or exclude cyber risks, but which risks may *sub silentio* be covered or excluded by traditional insurance wordings. As to non-affirmative cyber risks, the PRA expected that firms give active consideration to how their insurance policies respond to cyber risks with a view to introducing cover for affirmative risks. The PRA further expected that firms would actively assess and manage their cyber risk exposures and that they 'understand the continuously evolving cyber landscape and demonstrate a commitment to developing their knowledge of cyber insurance underwriting risk'.[24]

By Market Bulletin Y5258 dated 4 July 2019, the Corporation of Lloyd's stated that Lloyd's underwriters should ensure that their policies affirm or exclude cyber cover from 1 January 2020, in respect of first party property damage policies, and during 2020–21, in respect of liability policies and treaty reinsurance policies. Cyber risks policies are now commonly issued. Further, a number of insurers, including protection and indemnity clubs, have identified the forms of cover which might be available to insure the operation of autonomous vessels.

Inevitably, marine insurers will become more and more knowledgeable of the risks attending the use of autonomous vessels specifically and cyber risks generally. To this end, what an insurer knows or ought to know will restrict the scope of the duty of disclosure upon the assured in this context. The information available to the insurer may well include information held by any person or an electronic database maintained within the insurer's organisation.[25] In *Sea Glory Maritime Co v Al Sagr National Insurance Co (The Nancy)*,[26] one of the issues which arose was whether the assured should have disclosed to the insurer Port State Control inspections and detentions of the insured vessel prior to the conclusion of the

[23] Insurance Act 2015, s 5(2)–(3). See also Marine Insurance Act 1906, s 18(3)(b).

[24] PRA SS4/17, para 4.2.

[25] Explanatory Notes, para 54: s 5(2)(b) of the Insurance Act 2015 'is intended to require the relevant underwriter to make a reasonable effort to search such information as is available to them within the insurer's organisation, such as in the insurer's electronic records'.

[26] [2013] EWHC 2116 (Comm); [2014] 1 Lloyd's Rep 14.

marine policy. In the event, the Court held that the non-disclosure of such information (even if it had been material) did not induce the relevant underwriter to enter into the contract of insurance. There was a further issue as to whether the assured was relieved of the duty to disclose such information by reason of the fact that the underwriter could have accessed the information via certain electronic databases. Blair, J said:[27]

> 170. The claimants' contentions on the MIA 1906 sections 18(3)(b) (presumed knowledge) and 18(3)(c) (waiver) raise essentially the same point, which is that the information about the detentions, though not disclosed, was available online, and that the expert evidence is that it is market practice for insurers to access such information on renewal. As stated above, by the ITC terms, the insurance was subject to English law and practice. It has not been suggested that Al Sagr, which is one of the largest insurers in the UAE, lacks any means of access, and it plainly does not.
>
> 171. The claimants say that it should have accessed information subscription services such as Sea-web or Lloyd's MIU. Had it done so, it would have seen at least the summary of detentions on Sea-web (to which it subscribed at the time of renewal) and could have raised enquiries on any detentions which had occurred since the last renewal. In response, the claimants would have provided the information I have described above as to the deficiencies at Suez. Hence, it is submitted, the defendant is presumed to have knowledge of them, alternatively a waiver arises because the online information was such as to prompt a reasonably careful insurer to make further inquiries.
>
> 172. The defendant submitted however that as a matter of law, there is no presumption of knowledge of the facts concerning particular ships merely on the ground that they have been published in Lloyd's List or any other newspaper (it cited Arnould, ibid, at para 16–194). It submitted that electronic databases such as Lloyd's MIU and Sea-web are to be treated in the same way as newspapers.
>
> 173. I do not think that it is correct to say that electronic databases should be treated as equivalent[2014] Lloyds Rep. IR 136to information in hard copy such as newspapers. The rationale for taking a restrictive view as to the latter is to be found in Morrison v Universal Marine Insurance Co (1872) LR 8 Ex 40. At page 54, Baron Bramwell said that to hold that the underwriter is bound to carry in his head all that is contained in Lloyd's List relating to a ship in which he has no interest, rather than to hold the owner of the ship bound to disclose it, would be to put a difficult and needless burden on the underwriter.
>
> 174. That reflected the commercial realities of the day. However, an underwriter does not have to carry the information in an electronic database in his head. Online information is available to be called up when required, and the evidence of the expert underwriters in the present case is that the usual practice in the market is to do so.
>
> 175. A reasonable underwriter is presumed to know matters which he should have known from the facts in his possession or matters which he had means of learning from the sources available to him (see Garnat, ibid, at para 135(f)).

[27] Ibid, at [170]–[175].

> However, I agree with the defendant that the fact that information is available to an underwriter online does not necessarily give rise to a presumption of knowledge. As the editors of Arnould put it in their discussion of this subject, the question ultimately reduces to whether there has been a fair presentation of the risk in all the circumstances (ibid at para 16–181). Whilst the circumstances may include the availability of online information, whether the insurer should be treated as having knowledge of it is something which has to be judged on the particular facts (ibid at para 16–194).

It is therefore entirely possible that information which is available to an insurer via an electronic database will be known or deemed to be known to the insurer for the purposes of defining the breadth of the assured's duty of disclosure. Under the Insurance Act 2015, it is less clear whether this extends to information held in subscription or public electronic databases held and maintained externally, but which the underwriter has access to from his or her computer screen within the insurer's organisation, and whether such accessible information would fall within the scope of the insurer's knowledge, given that under section 5(2)(b), the relevant information must be 'held by the insurer and is readily available' to the underwriter. It seems likely, although the point remains untested, that information will be treated as being held by an insurer, if it is accessible by the underwriter within the insurer's organisation, even if the information is held outside the insurer's premises. Otherwise, the insurer's knowledge would be very narrowly circumscribed in setting the boundaries of the assured's disclosure obligations.

This means that any information relating to the risks attendant upon the operation of autonomous vessels and cyber risks generally may well be accessible to an underwriter and therefore may relieve the assured of the obligation to disclose such information. This is especially the case given the industry's and regulators' encouragement or requirement to ensure that insurers become better informed about such risks.

With the information presented by the assured,] and available to the insurer, the insurer will have to take into account that information to evaluate the risk. It is, of course, not for the assured to advise the insurer as to how the risk is to be evaluated.[28] Traditionally, marine insurers have to exercise greater discretionary judgment in evaluating risk, given that a marine insurer does not have the volume of data which is available to the underwriters of mass insurance products, such as life, health and motor insurance. However, with the generation of data by and for the use of artificial intelligence systems, Usage Based Insurance (UBI) which relies on the analysis, often powered by telematics, of a large volume of data from the performance of the relevant insured adventures may become more common.[29]

[28] *Iron Trades Mutual Insurance Co Ltd v Companhia de Seguros Imperio* (1991) 1 Re LR 213; *Decorum Investments Ltd v Atkin (The Elena G)* [2001] 2 Lloyd's Rep 378, para 25; *Glencore International AG v Alpina Insurance Co Ltd* [2003] EWHC 2792 (Comm); [2004] 1 Lloyd's Rep 111, para 122.

[29] S Cooper, 'Insurance and artificial intelligence: Underwriting, claims and litigation', ch 13 of Soyer and Tettenborn (eds), *New Technologies, Artificial Intelligence and Shipping law in the 21st Century*, (Informa, 2019), 179.

With the growing economic exploitation of such systems, there will be greater access available to insurers to an increasing amount of information, depending on the type of artificial intelligence being used.

IV. The Cover Afforded by Traditional Marine Policies: Non-affirmative Cover and Exclusions

In section 1 of the Marine Insurance Act 1906, a contract of marine insurance is an indemnity insurance contract. That means that marine insurance policies are intended to compensate the assured for relevant losses caused by the identified insured perils. The types of losses ordinarily insured against under marine insurance policies are reflected by the types of marine adventure referred to by section 3 of the 1906 Act, namely property losses (that is physical damage giving rise to a partial or total loss or the deprivation of possession giving rise to a total loss),[30] financial losses (for example, loss of revenue or income or additional expenditure), and third party liabilities.

The insured perils very often insured against in the hull marine insurance market include marine navigation risks of perils of the seas, fire, explosion, piracy, and the Inchmaree perils (including latent defect, crew negligence, repairer's negligence, barratry), and war and strikes risks such as the perils of war, strikes, lockout, political risks (for example, capture, seizure, detainment, arrest, restraint), and malicious acts and terrorism.[31] This is in contrast to cargo insurance, where 'all risks' are commonly insured against,[32] meaning any cause of loss will be covered, provided that such cause is accidental or fortuitous,[33] as well as specified war and strikes risks. A shipowner will also characteristically have protection and indemnity insurance which traditionally insures against liabilities in respect of seafarers and passengers, life salvage, collision, property damage, cargo, pollution, quarantine risks, life salvage, environmental damage and removal of wrecks.

If this were the limit of insurance coverage available to shipowners, the question arises as to what scope for cover would exist in the event of a defect or fault in the computer or artificial intelligence systems operated or used by the shipowner, whether introduced in error or deliberately, or present in the systems from their creation. For this purpose, regard must be had to both the perils insured against in a traditional marine insurance policy and the perils excluded. It should be emphasised, however, that the fact that the subject matter of the insurance is an autonomous vessel (known as a MASS), that will be a relevant consideration to be

[30] Marine Insurance Act 1906, ss 56, 57, 58, 60, 69.

[31] See, eg, Institute Time Clauses – Hulls (1995), cl 6; International Hull Clauses 2003, cl 2; Institute War and Strikes Clauses Hull – Time (1995).

[32] Institute Cargo Clauses (A) 1982 and 2009.

[33] *Schloss Brothers v Stevens* [1906] 2 KB 665, 673; *British & Foreign Marine Insurance Co v Gaunt* [1921] AC 41, 47, 51–52, 57–58.

taken into account in construing the extent of cover afforded by a marine policy. This will also be a relevant consideration in the construction of cargo policies at least where it is readily apparent that the cargo is being or will be carried on an autonomous vessel.

Cover may be provided for defects in a vessel's computer, software and network systems in that the Inchmaree Clause in many marine hull policies also insures against loss or damage caused by 'latent defect in the machinery or hull',[34] provided that there has been no want of due diligence on the part of the shipowner or the vessel's manager.[35] In order to be an insured peril, such defect must be unknown to the assured and must not be discoverable upon an examination which a reasonably careful skilled person would make.[36] It is important to emphasise, however, that the cover afforded by the Inchmaree Clause is for loss or damage caused by the latent defect, and not the latent defect itself. That means that the insured vessel must be physically lost or damaged by reason of the latent defect (for example, where the computer program defect causes the vessel to ground or sink); the insurance will not indemnify the assured for the cost of repairing the defect (even under the extended cover afforded by the Institute Additional Perils Clause, there is no cover for the rectification of the defect unless the defect causes physical loss or damage).[37] There may also be cover under a war risks policy for deliberate third-party cyberattacks leading to the physical loss of or damage to an insured vessel, for example insofar as the policy insures against the risks of war, terrorism or persons acting maliciously.[38] If the policy insures against all risks, it seems more likely that any fortuitous loss or damage caused by a cyber risk will be covered, given the breadth of the cover afforded by all risks policies.

The application of 'latent defects', war risks and all risks cover to cyber security or safety incidents may well be complicated by untested issues, such as whether it is the cyberattack itself which constitutes or leads immediately to physical loss or damage and whether the trigger event for cover is the operation of the insured peril or the occurrence of the resulting loss or damage.[39] In the context of marine insurance policies, at least based on the Institute Clauses, it is the resultant loss or damage which usually triggers the cover, not the insured peril (if different).[40]

[34] See, eg, cl 6.2 of the Institute Time Clauses – Hulls (1995).

[35] As to this proviso, see *Sealion Shipping Ltd v Valiant Insurance Co (The Toisa Pisces)* [2012] EWHC 50 (Comm); [2012] 1 Lloyd's Rep 252, paras 94–102; aff'd [2012] EWCA Civ 1625; [2013] 1 Lloyd's Rep 108; *Versloot Dredging BV v HDI-Gerling Industrie Versicherung AG (The DC Merwestone)* [2013] EWHC 1666 (Comm); [2013] Lloyd's Rep IR 582, paras 100–104; [2014] EWCA Civ 1349; [2015] 1 Lloyd's Rep 32; [2016] UKSC 45; [2016] 3 WLR 543; *Venetico Marine SA v International General Insurance Company Ltd* [2013] EWHC 3644 (Comm); [2014] Lloyd's Rep IR 243, para 288(i).

[36] *The Caribbean Sea* [1980] 1 Lloyd's Rep 338, 348.

[37] *Arnould: Law of Marine Insurance and Average*, (19th edn, 2018), para 23–57 to 23–58.

[38] See recently *Atlasnavios-Navegação, LDA v Navigators Insurance Co Ltd (The B Atlantic)* [2018] UKSC 26; [2018] 2 WLR 1671; *McKeever v Northernreef Insurance Co SA* [2019] Lloyd's Rep IR 535, paras 83–90; *Suez Fortune Investments Ltd v Talbot Underwriting Ltd* [2019] EWHC 2599 (Comm); [2019] 2 Lloyd's Rep 485, paras 498–506.

[39] IMIA Working Group Paper 98 (16), IMIA Annual Conference 2016, para 6.1.

[40] *Promet Engineering (Singapore) Pte Ltd* v *Sturge (The Nukila)* [1997] 2 Lloyd's Rep 146, 151.

By section 55(2)(c) of the Marine Insurance Act 1906, there is generally an exclusion in all marine insurance policies in respect of 'inherent vice',[41] namely where the relevant loss or damage is solely caused by the deterioration of the subject matter insured as a result of its natural behaviour during the ordinary course of the contemplated voyage or the inability of the subject matter insured to withstand the ordinary incidents of the contemplated voyage or the ordinary use of the subject matter insured without the involvement of a fortuitous external event.[42] Accordingly, if there is an internal fault within the vessel's computer systems or networks, a loss caused by such defect might well be excluded from cover under the traditional marine hull policies.

Insofar as the cyber or computer risks originate from external sources, they might well be covered under marine, war and political risks, or protection and indemnity risks insurance, depending on the terms of cover, and any defect originating from an external source might not constitute an inherent vice, but might still constitute a latent defect. There are no express exclusions in the traditional Institute wordings which appear applicable.[43] Questions may arise as to whether the introduction of a computer virus is an inherent defect or not. It seems likely that as the virus is not an intended part of the computer system's make-up that it would not be treated as an inherent vice, although it might constitute a latent defect if it was part of the computer system at the beginning of the relevant policy period;[44] by contrast, a design flaw in the computer system or software might well be such an inherent vice.

Similarly, there is a warranty in marine voyage policies that the vessel be seaworthy at the commencement of the insured voyage.[45] There is no such warranty in time policies, but there is an exclusion introduced to time policies by section 39(5) of the Marine Insurance Act 1906 if the insured vessel is sent to sea in an unseaworthy state with the privity of the assured and the vessel suffers loss or damage by reason of that unseaworthiness.[46] A defect in the insured vessel's computer, software or network systems might render the vessel unseaworthy, meaning that the vessel is not reasonably fit in all respects to encounter the

[41] Marine Insurance Act 1906, s 55(2)(c): 'Unless the policy otherwise provides, the insurer is not liable for … inherent vice or nature of the subject-matter insured'.

[42] *Soya GmbH v White* [1983] 1 Lloyd's Rep 122, 126; *Noten BV v Harding* [1990] 2 Lloyd's Rep 283; *Global Process Systems Inc v Syarikat Takaful Malaysia Berhad* [2009] EWCA Civ 1398; [2010] 1 Lloyd's Rep 243, paras 56–63, 67–71; [2011] UKSC 5; [2011] 1 All ER 869; *European Group Ltd v Chartis Insurance UK Ltd* [2012] EWHC 1245 (Comm); [2012] 2 Lloyd's Rep 117, paras 133–39.

[43] The closest is the exclusion of 'electromagnetic weapon' in cl 31.5 of the International Hull Clauses (2003).

[44] *Promet Engineering (Singapore) Pte Ltd v Sturge (The Nukila)* [1997] 2 Lloyd's Rep 146, 151.

[45] Marine Insurance Act 1906, s 39(1).

[46] *Thomas v Tyne & Wear Insurance Association* [1917] 1 KB 938; *The Star Sea* [2001] UKHL 1; [2001] 2 WLR 170, paras 3, 23–26, 112–16; *Marina Offshore Pte Ltd v China Insurance Co (Singapore) Pte Ltd* [2006] SGCA 28; [2007] 1 Lloyd's Rep 66, paras 65–69 (Singapore CA)); *Versloot Dredging BV v HDI-Gerling Industrie Versicherung AG (The DC Merwestone)* [2013] EWHC 1666 (Comm); [2013] Lloyd's Rep IR 582, para 110; [2014] EWCA Civ 1349; [2016] UKSC 45; [2016] 3 WLR 543.

ordinary perils of the seas of the adventure insured.[47] Of course, when it comes to autonomous vessels, the absence of a crew in control on board the vessel may radically redefine what amounts to seaworthiness in this context.[48]

If, however, the marine policy expressly provides cover for loss or damage caused by 'latent defect', this would appear to override the inherent vice exception in section 55(2)(c) of the Marine Insurance Act 1906, as the marine policy in question would otherwise provide.[49] Similarly, the warranty of seaworthiness may be displaced by such 'latent defect' cover.[50]

Accordingly, existing marine hull and cargo policies might be satisfactory at least in some respects for the risks posed by the use of artificial intelligence in the conduct of a vessel both in its voyage and cargo operations, and cyber risks generally. Nevertheless, the uncertainty of the scope of cover afforded by traditional insurance wordings and the ability of the Courts to adapt such wordings to rapidly changing technological innovations make it clear that the position adopted by the insurance industry in favour of affirmative policies expressly stating that cover is provided or excluded in relation to the risks relating to autonomous vessels, and cyber risks more generally, becomes increasingly urgent.[51]

V. Affirmative Cover or Exclusions

The marine insurance contract which provides protection for a shipowner against the risks associated with the operation of a vessel either remotely or by means of artificial intelligence will not only have to define the risk being insured by reference to the insured perils, but also by reference to appropriate exclusions and promissory warranties.

In the realm of non-marine insurance policies, there is an extensive array of cover for 'cyber risks' and 'computer crime risks', in respect of both first-party losses and third-party liability risks. Such cover is designed to deal with computer and cyber risks specifically, developed as a result of the experience of corporate assureds over recent years. The cover will include compensation for loss of or

[47] Marine Insurance Act 1906, s 39(4); *Garnat Trading & Shipping (Singapore) Pte Ltd v Baominh Insurance Corporation* [2010] EWHC 2578 (Comm); [2011] 1 Lloyd's Rep 589, para 160; aff'd [2011] EWCA Civ 773; [2011] 2 Lloyd's Rep 492. The vessel is not necessarily unseaworthy just because it does not have the latest or most up-to-date technology on board: *The Westerdok* [1962] 1 Lloyd's Rep 180; *The Kriti Rex* [1996] 2 Lloyd's Rep 171, 184.

[48] See L Zhu and R Xing, 'A pioneering study of third-party liability insurance for unmanned/autonomous commercial ships' [2019] JBL 442, 452–53.

[49] *The Caribbean Sea* [1980] 1 Lloyd's Rep 338, 347; *Midland Mainline Ltd v Eagle Star Insurance Co Ltd* [2004] EWCA Civ 1042; [2004] 2 Lloyd's Rep 604.

[50] *Arnould: Law of Marine Insurance and Average*, (19th ed, 2018), paras 23–61.

[51] See M Tsimplis and M Song, 'Innovation and the law: legacy v efficiency and optimisation', *Shipping & Trade Law* (2017) 17 STL 11; J. Hjalmarsson, 'Maritime law in 2017: a review of developments in case law' 14.

damage to property, business interruption losses, reputational losses, the cost of restoring the computer systems, crisis management costs, and for legal liabilities to third-party clients and customers. Such risks may include:

i. Loss or damage to electronic data, whether caused by external risks, such as theft, computer hacking, the operation of a virus, or data breaches, or internal risks, such as the corruption of data.
ii. Cyber extortion losses which arise, for example, when a computer hacker or thief breaches the assured's computer system and makes a demand on the menace of a threat to corrupt or disrupt the computer system or to divulge confidential information.
iii. The assured's liability arising from a breach of the assured's computer network security arising from either a data breach, the inability to protect third party confidential data, or from the inability by the assured or others to access the computer system.
iv. The assured's liability for defamation, breach of confidence or invasion of personal or privacy rights.
v. The assured's losses and liabilities for programming and coding errors or software defects.
vi. Professional indemnity risks.
vii. Computer crime and fraud, electronic funds transfer frauds and cyber terrorism.
viii. The mitigation of loss resulting from such insured perils.

In a quickly developing area of artificial intelligence and the intention to exploit such technologies in the near future, the risks associated with such enterprises might well include risks which are unplanned for, unexpected and various. In such circumstances, a properly thought out and sufficiently broad range of insurance cover will become increasingly commercially important.[52]

Appropriate exclusions might include a contractual provision excluding from the insurance coverage any loss or damage caused by:

i. Any alterations made by the assured to the computer programs or algorithms which are not sanctioned by the licensed operator or manufacturer.
ii. Any known defect in the relevant computer system which has not been disclosed by the assured to the insurer.
iii. Criminal, fraudulent or dishonest conduct on behalf of the assured.
iv. The infringement or theft of intellectual property rights of third parties.
v. The disclosure of confidential information belonging to third parties or the unauthorised use of personal data.
vi. The assured's failure to implement or apply reasonable or declared security measures to prevent data breaches or unauthorised interference with the assured's computer systems.

[52] European Parliament, *Resolution on Civil Law Rules on Robotics* (16 February 2017), paras 57–59; House of Lords Report of Session 2017–19, *AI in the UK: ready, willing and able?* Select Committee on Artificial Intelligence HL Paper 100, 16 April 2018, para 305–18; S Cooper, 'Insurance and artificial intelligence: Underwriting, claims and litigation', ch 13 of B Soyer and A Tettenborn (eds), *New Technologies, Artificial Intelligence and Shipping law in the 21st Century* (Informa, 2019), 189–90.

vii. Conduct leading to the imposition of a regulatory fine.[53]
viii. The use or operation, as a means for inflicting harm, of any computer, computer system, computer software programme, malicious code, computer virus or process or any other electronic system.[54]
ix. Relevant acts or omissions which took place before the inception of the policy period.

The insurance market has developed a number of clauses for inclusion in policies to make clear whether cyber risks are insured or excluded from cover, for example:

A. **The Institute Cyber Attack Exclusion Clause – Cl. 380 (2003):** this clause provides that there is no cover for loss caused directly or indirectly by or contributed to or arising from the use or operation, of any computer, computer system, computer software program, malicious code, computer virus or process or any other electronic systems, if used as a means of inflicting injury. Accordingly, losses caused unintentionally by such means would not be expressly excluded. There is also a provision that where the relevant policy insures against war risks or terrorism, this exclusion will not exclude from cover losses arising from the use of any computer, computer system or computer software program or any other electronic system in the launch or guidance or firing of any weapon or missile.
B. **The Cyber Attack Exclusion Clause and Write-Back (JS2018-01) (2018):** this clause writes back cover against the Institute Cyber Attack Exclusion Clause where the loss or damage is caused by a '*Targeted Cyber Attack*', meaning the use or operation, as a means of inflicting harm, of any computer, computer system, computer software program, malicious code, computer virus or process or any other electronic system where the motive is to inflict harm solely on or upon the assured or the assured's property.
C. **The Electronic Data Endorsement (NMA 2914 and NMA 2915) (2015):** the clauses introduced by this endorsement provide that there is no cover in respect of loss, damage, destruction, distortion, erasure, corruption or alteration of electronic data (including software and codes instructions for the processing and manipulation of data) from any cause.
D. **IMIA Advanced Cyber Exclusion 2018 Endorsement (2018):** this clause excludes from cover any loss directly or indirectly caused by or contributed to or resulting from specified cyber incidents, namely Loss of Data, Computer Malicious Act, Computer Malware, Human Error affecting the assured's Computer Systems, a System Failure occurring on the assured's Computer Systems, a Defect in the assured's Computer Systems, or Cyber Extortion, regardless of any other cause or event contributing concurrently or in any other sequence to the loss. In addition, it is provided that where this clause is endorsed on a policy covering war risks or terrorism, the clause also excludes from cover Cyber Terrorism and Cyber War.

[53] See, eg, Data Protection Act 2018, s 196. Whether there might be cover for regulatory fines depends on considerations of public policy (*Les Laboratoires Servier v Apotex Inc* [2014] UKSC 55; [2015] 1 AC 430; *Bilta (UK) Ltd (in liquidation) v Nazir* [2015] UKSC 23; [2016] AC 1; *Patel v Mirza* [2016] UKSC 42; [2016] 3 WLR 399). See also *Sainsbury's Supermarkets Ltd v Mastercard Incorporated* [2016] CAT 11; [2016] Comp AR 33 (Competition Appeal Tribunal); [2018] EWCA Civ 1536, para 42. Many protection and indemnity policies provide cover for fines.
[54] The Institute Cyber Attack Exclusion Clause (Cl 380) (2003).

E. **IUA Cyber Loss Exclusion Clauses (IUA 09-081 / IUA 09-082) (2019):** clause IUA 09-081 excludes from cover any loss directly or indirectly caused by the use or operation of any Computer System or Network, the reduction in or loss of ability to use or operation any Computer System, Network or Data, access to, processing, transmission, storage or use of any Data, inability to access, process, transmit, store or use any Data, any threat or hoax relating to the afore-mentioned causes, or any error or omission or accident in respect of any Computer System, Network or Data. By contrast, clause IUA 09-082 excludes loss directly (not indirectly) caused by the specified perils. The IUA sought to implement a broad exclusion of cover in respect of such risks, especially clause IUA 09-081, although recognised that there could be a write-back of cover through negotiation.

The relevant marine insurance policy might include warranties by which the assured promises to ensure that cyber risks are addressed in the assured's safety management systems (as defined in the International Management Code for the Safe Operation of Ships and for Pollution Prevention (International Safety Management (ISM) Code)).[55] In *Sea Glory Maritime Co v Al Sagr National Insurance Co (The Nancy)* [2013] EWHC 2116 (Comm); [2014] 1 Lloyd's Rep 14, at paragraph 219, Blair, J held that a warranty that the insured vessel was 'ISM compliant' requiring no more than documentary compliance with the ISM, rather than actual compliance.[56] Of course, the consequences of a breach of warranty are now regulated by sections 10 and 11 of the Insurance Act 2015, which essentially provide that (1) in the event of a breach of warranty, the insurer is discharged from liability only insofar as the relevant event giving rise to the loss or damage occurs while the assured remains in breach, but if the relevant event occurs after the breach is remedied, the cover is then reinstated; and (2) the insurer is not permitted to rely on a breach of the warranty in defence of a claim under a marine insurance policy if the warranty does not define the risk as a whole, compliance with the warranty would tend to reduce the risk of loss, and non-compliance with the warranty could not have increased the risk of the loss which actually occurred in the circumstances in which it occurred.

Section 78(4) of the Marine Insurance Act 1906 provides that, in all cases, an assured is under a duty to take reasonable steps to avert or minimise a loss. However, by section 78(1), the marine policy must include a sue and labour (mitigation) clause in order to allow the assured to recover its mitigation expenses from the insurer. However, it is arguable that there might yet be a legal entitlement to recover mitigation expenses, even in the absence of a sue and labour clause.[57]

[55] IMO Maritime Safety Committee Resolution MSC.428(98) (16 June 2017); IMO Guidelines on Maritime Cyber Risk Management, MSC-FAL.1/Circ.3 (5th July 2017).

[56] See also *Transpetrol Maritime Services Ltd v SJB (Marine Energy) BV (The Rowan)* [2012] 1 Lloyd's Rep 564, para 24; *Suez Fortune Investments Ltd v Talbot Underwriting Ltd* [2019] EWHC 2599 (Comm); [2019] 2 Lloyd's Rep 485, paras 549–50.

[57] For example, under Marine Insurance Act 1906, s 64(2) (particular charges), 65 (non-contractual salvage), and 66 (general average). See also *Emperor Goldmining Co v Switzerland General Insurance Co* [1964] 1 Lloyd's Rep 348 (Sup Ct NSW); *The Netherlands Insurance Co Est 1845 Ltd v Karl Ljungberg & Co AB* [1986] 2 Lloyd's Rep 19, 22–3; *Royal Boskalis Westminster NV v Mountain* [1999] QB 674, 717–8;

The assured's duty of mitigation will have to be considered from a different perspective when considering the risks attendant on the operation of autonomous vessels and related cyber risks. There is no entitlement to recover such mitigation expenses in a non-marine insurance contract in the absence of an appropriate contractual provision.[58]

VI. The Potential Statutory Liability of Insurers

There are a number of international conventions which impose obligations on state parties to implement legislation requiring compulsory insurance on the part of shipowners in respect of a number of risks and losses, including oil pollution, bunker pollution, hazardous and noxious substances risks, and wreck removal. There is, of course, a compulsory insurance requirement in respect of motor insurance under the Road Traffic Act 1988. If autonomous vessels become a fixed part of international shipping, it is not difficult to envisage a compulsory insurance programme in connection with the operation of autonomous vessels. With the advent of autonomous vessels, the issue of compulsory insurance and compulsory insurer's liability may also be explored by Parliament, whether on its own initiative or, more probably, as a result of international conventions.

It is interesting to note that Parliament has imposed automatic liability on insurers of automated vehicles under the Automated and Electric Vehicles Act 2018.[59] The 2018 Act has not yet entered into force. The 2018 Act contains the following provisions:

i) Section 2: where an accident is caused by an automated vehicle when driving itself on a road or other public place in Great Britain, the vehicle is insured at the time of the accident, and an insured person or other person suffers damage as a result of the accident, the insurer is liable for that damage. For this purpose, damage means death, personal injury or property damage other than damage to the automated vehicle, damage to good carried for hire or reward in or on that vehicle, goods in the custody or control of the insured person or the person in charge of the automated vehicle. There is a limit to the amount of the applicable insurance under section 145(4)(b) of the Road Traffic Act 1988 (currently £1,200,000). The insurer's liability may not be excluded or limited other than under section 4 of the 2018 Act. This provision does not affect any other person's liability in respect of the accident.

Arnould: Law of Marine Insurance and Average, (19th ed, 2018), para 25–36 to 35–37; P MacDonald Eggers, 'Sue and labour and beyond: the assured's duty of mitigation' [1998] LMCLQ 228; M Clarke, 'Wisdom after the event: the duty to mitigate insured loss' [2003] LMCLQ 525.

[58] *Yorkshire Water v Sun Alliance & London Insurance Ltd* [1997] 1 Lloyd's Rep 1; *Astrazeneca Insurance Co v XL Insurance (Bermuda) Limited* [2013] EWHC 349 (Comm); [2013] Lloyd's Rep IR 290, para 137; aff'd [2013] EWCA Civ 1660.

[59] B Soyer, 'Autonomous vessels and third-party liabilities: The elephant in the room', in B Soyer and A Tettenborn (eds), *New Technologies, Artificial Intelligence and Shipping law in the 21st Century* (Informa, 2019), ch 8.

ii) Section 3: where the injured party is to any extent also responsible for the accident or the damage resulting from it, the amount of that liability may be reduced under the Law Reform (Contributory Negligence) Act 1945. The insurer is not liable under section 2 to the person in charge of the vehicle where the accident was wholly due to that person's negligence in allowing the vehicle to begin driving itself when it was not appropriate to do so.
iii) Section 4: by sub-section (1), an insurance policy in respect of an automated vehicle may exclude or limit the insurer's liability under section 2 for damage suffered by an insured person arising from an accident occurring as a direct result of 'software alterations made by the insured person, or with the insured person's knowledge, that are prohibited under the policy' or 'a failure to install safety-critical software updates that the insured person knows, or ought reasonably to know, are safety-critical'. However, where the insurer is liable for damage suffered by an insured person who is not the holder of the insurance policy, section 4(1) applies only in relation to software alterations which, at the time of the accident, the person knows are prohibited under the policy. Where the insurer pays an amount in respect of damage suffered as a result of an accident by someone who is not insured under the policy, if the accident occurred as a direct result of software alterations or a failure to install safety-critical software updates, as aforesaid, the amount paid by the insurer is recoverable from that person to the extent provided by the policy.
iv) Section 5: where the insurer is liable under section 2 and the amount of the insurer's liability to the injured party in respect of the accident is settled, any other person liable to the injured party in respect of the accident is under the same liability to the insurer. For this purpose, the amount of the insurer's liability is settled when it is established by judgment, decree, arbitral award or an enforceable agreement. If the insurer recovers more than it has agreed or has been ordered to pay to the injured party, the insurer is liable to the injured party for the difference.

The scheme imposed by the 2018 Act in respect of automated vehicles driving themselves is that the insurer is strictly liable to the injured party for death, injury, loss or damage, save for damage to the vehicle or goods carried by the vehicle or owned or in the charge of the insured person or the person in control of the vehicle. It appears that the insurer cannot escape that liability by contracting out, other than by reference to the upper financial limit of the policy (which must not be lower than the statutory limit) or where the policy excludes cover in respect of an accident directly caused by specified software alterations or failures to install safety-critical software updates. However, the insurer is entitled to rely on the injured party's contributory negligence by way of at least a partial defence and may recover relief from any person (other than the injured party) responsible for the accident.

This is a remarkably rigorous regime, although there are arguments for and against the application of such a regime to autonomous vessels.[60] If a similar regime applies in the context of autonomous sea-going vessels, there will be other

[60] B Soyer, 'Autonomous Vessels and Third-party Liabilities: The Elephant in the Room', in B Soyer and AM Tettenborn (ed), *New Technologies, Artificial Intelligence and Shipping law in the 21st Century*, (Informa, 2019), 107–10.

issues which will require consideration (not least limitation of liability).[61] In any case, such a regime might have a notable effect on the availability of such insurance. The 2018 Act does not expressly address the position where the policy in question has been procured by the assured's breach of the duty of fair presentation of the risk under the Insurance Act 2015. At least, where the policy is voidable by reason of such breach, it seems likely that the 2018 Act is not intended to affect such a remedy. However, as regards the other remedies available under the 2015 Act, in respect of a breach of the duty of fair presentation of the risk, it seems less likely that such remedies would be available to the insurer who is liable under the 2018 Act.

VII. Claims Presentation and Handling

Given the assured's access to and control over of its computer and network systems, in the event of a claim, the marine insurer's investigation of such claims will depend on gaining access to such systems. This will require clearly thought out and specific provisions in the relevant policy imposing obligations on the assured to assist and cooperate with the insurer, albeit there may also be issues which need to be addressed, such as protection for the confidentiality and proprietary nature of such systems.[62]

Moreover, with the introduction of an implied term into all insurance policies that claims will be paid within a reasonable time, the insurer will have to ensure that it has well-defined procedures for the handling of such claims, bearing in mind that the insurer will not be in breach of such a term provided that it uses a reasonable time to investigate the claim and, if it disputes a claim, it has reasonable grounds in doing so.[63]

VIII. Conclusion

Marine insurance policies and wordings have been developed over long periods of time to cater for the risks ordinarily attendant on a maritime adventure. The SG form of policy – scheduled to the Marine Insurance Act 1906 – was itself an eighteenth-century form and used until the twentieth century when the Institute Clauses began to be used. The Institute Clauses have been updated periodically since then. Nevertheless, in a rapidly changing technological environment and with the introduction of autonomous operation of vessels, there is now an array of

[61] Ibid, 113–4.
[62] IMIA Working Group Paper 98 (16), IMIA Annual Conference 2016, para 6.1.
[63] Insurance Act 2015, s 13A.

risks – in addition to the traditional maritime perils – which have not adequately been addressed in traditional marine insurance policies.

It is therefore incumbent on the insurance industry to develop new marine insurance products which cater for such risks, either by express or affirmative coverage or exclusion in respect of defined perils, as well as explaining the duties on each of the parties to the contract in the presentation and management of the risk, the making and notification of claims, the handling of claims, and the parties' cooperation and assistance. This is an exercise which will have to be undertaken in consultation with the maritime industry and with a better understanding of the legal landscape which may be imposed on insurers (having regard to the Automated and Electric Vehicles Act 2018). The traditional marine insurance policies, even if supplemented by endorsements or specific clauses, are probably no longer apt to deal with these new developments. A whole new marine insurance policy must be introduced to provide the protection needed in an age of exponential technological advancements and artificial intelligence.

PART III

The Way Forward

8

The Future of Autonomous Shipping – The Regulatory Challenge

PROFESSOR BARIŞ SOYER*

I. Introduction

It is evident from the discussion so far, that for autonomous shipping to become a reality, several regulatory challenges need to be addressed. The matter is further complicated by the fact that rules and regulations in question are embodied in several international agreements that have been put together in the last century or so, in some cases after years of negotiations conducted by the international community. Naturally, this is very different from regulating the use of autonomous cars in a particular jurisdiction, which ultimately lies in the power of the relevant government.[1] Until an international consensus on regulating this new technology is reached, it is very unlikely that autonomous ships will be operating in international waters beyond the territorial waters of any state.[2]

Even then, regulating technical aspects of this technological development is only half of the battle. Those who have a financial interest in the venture (manufacturers, programmers, shipowners and ultimately their insurers) would need to be certain of their position with regard to civil liabilities they might face if things go wrong! Obviously, this is a debate that is as important as the suitability of a regulatory framework in the context of developing autonomous vessels, essentially

* Director of the Institute of International Shipping and Trade Law, Swansea University.

[1] For example, in the UK the government has passed the Automated and Electric Vehicles Act 2018, which aims to amend the existing compulsory third party insurance framework by extending it to cover the use of automated vehicles. For the purposes of this legislation, a vehicle is 'driving itself' if it is operating in a mode in which it is not being controlled and does not need to be monitored by an individual. In the USA, as of 1 February 2020, 29 states, including California, Florida, New York, Texas, Utah and Washington, had enacted legislation relating to autonomous cars.

[2] By virtue of Arts 25(2), 211(3) and 255 of the United Nations Convention on the Law of the Sea (UNCLOS) 1982, states are entitled to ban autonomous ships from ports as well as from the state's inner waters, to the extent that it will not be contrary to general international law principles on proportionality and non-discrimination. Note too Art 300 of UNCLOS on the misuse of rights under the Convention and Art 18 of UNCLOS 1982 on innocent passage, which may be relevant.

for two reasons. First, if there is a fundamental uncertainty about the underlying liability rules, the cost of that uncertainty will be inevitably passed on to the insurers, who would reflect it with an increase in premiums.[3] This rate increase could potentially increase the operational costs, wiping out the benefits (reduction in crew wages and fuel costs) from the development of this technology. Second, inability to predict their liability costs and subsequent profits might deter manufacturers from investing in the development of autonomous vessel technology. If apart from product liability issues, there is a prospect that manufacturers could face unlimited claims from third parties in the event of a collision when a problem in the algorithms gives rise to an incident, this increases the risk of the underlying investment. In that case, the manufacturers would want to see higher returns to justify the added risk they expose themselves to, or they might pull out of this market altogether.

The International Maritime Organisation (IMO) has grappled with the regulatory challenge by establishing, in May 2018, the Maritime Autonomous Surface Ships (MASS) Working Group,[4] tasked to 'develop a framework for the regulatory scoping exercise, including aims and objectives, methodology, instruments, type and size of ship, provisional definitions and different types of concepts of autonomy, automation, operations and manning to be considered'. The scoping exercise is expected to be completed in 2021, but it should be noted that the current terms of reference do not include the development of any rules. The direction of travel in terms of determining how the regulatory challenges will be addressed will later be determined in the light of the scoping paper.

The reality is that we are only at the beginning of this journey. The aim of the concluding chapter of the book is, therefore, to make a contribution to this debate by highlighting the potential difficulties facing the regulatory process and suggesting ways in which solutions could be developed by international law makers by considering various alternatives available.

II. Problems and Challenges Facing the Regulatory Process

A. Technical Barriers

An obvious problem is that all technical shipping regulations concerning safety of navigation, protection of environment and training/watchkeeping standards have been developed on the assumption that certain functions will be performed by human beings and they will need to be reconsidered in the context of autonomous

[3] See, MG Geistfeld, 'Legal Ambiguity, Liability Insurance and Tort Reform' (2011) 60 *De Paul L Rev* 539, 559–56.

[4] IMO Doc M SC 99/WP.1, para 5.25.1.

vessels. A few examples would suffice to illustrate the problem with the existing regulatory framework. Chapter V, regulation 24 of the International Convention for the Safety of Life at Sea (SOLAS) 1974 requires 'manual control of the ship's steering' to be established immediately in 'hazardous navigational situations'. Clearly an autonomous ship with no crew on board will not be able to comply with this regulation.[5] More striking perhaps is Part 4, para 24, of the International Convention on Standards of Training, Certification and Watchkeeping for Seafarers (STCW) 1978, which provides that 'The Officer in charge of the navigational watch shall keep the watch on the bridge … [and] … in no circumstances leave the bridge until properly relieved.'[6]

This is perhaps the easy part. A more difficult issue relates to regulations that require human judgment. It remains uncertain how such rules will apply to vessels that are designed to make navigational decisions with the aid of algorithms by utilising the data obtained from their censors. Rule 2 of the International Regulations for Preventing Collisions at Sea (COLREGs) 1972, for example, states that 'nothing shall exonerate any vessel, or the owner, master or crew thereof, from the consequences of any … neglect or any precaution which may be required by the ordinary practice of seamen'. It is uncertain how such a benchmark of responsibility might be assessed if a collision occurred at a time the vessel was under the control of an autonomous navigation system. In similar vein, it is difficult to say with certainty whether the human lookout requirement stipulated by rule 5 of the COLREGs can be replaced satisfactorily by using various types of cameras, radar, audio technology and other technical devices.[7] It is unthinkable to assume that we can move forward developing autonomous technology without providing further clarification as to how such technology can be operated in compliance with requirements that are vital from a safety perspective. Those developing the new technology often remind us that deep-learning based programmes are flexible and react to and from the new patterns that they are programmed to identify – meaning that situational awareness and the subjective aspects of COLREGs could be learned by a program.[8] But even so, this poses a significant challenge to those who seek to regulate the matter.

B. The Nature of Technological Developments

Much of the analysis on autonomous ships so far has fallen prey to the initial assumption that the industry is on the verge of developing fully autonomous

[5] For more examples, see, B Eder, 'Unmanned Vessels: Challenges Ahead' [2019] *LMCLQ* 47, 54–55.

[6] See also, Pt 4, para 18 which states that 'at no time shall the bridge be left unattended'.

[7] For more examples and further technical analysis see R Veal and M Tsimplis, 'The Integration of Unmanned Ships into Lex Maritima' [2017] *LMCLQ* 303, 324–30 and L Carey, 'All Hands Off Deck? The Legal Barriers to Autonomous Ships' (2017) 23 *JIML* 202, 207–10.

[8] See, World Maritime University, *Transport 2040: Autonomous Ships: A Paradigm for Norwegian Shipping – Technology and Transformation*, (2019) Reports. 59, at 19, https://commons.wmu.se/cgi/viewcontent.cgi?article=1072&context=lib_reports, accessed 1 July 2020.

vessels which will be in operation in the near future. While fully autonomous operation with no human involvement remains an ultimate goal, the reality is that even those developing such technology are not expecting this to happen for a considerable time.[9] It is very likely that we shall see an incremental development before reaching a fully autonomous level. In all probability, in the early days, autonomous vessels will have a removable bridge which will give an opportunity for those on board to intervene if necessary. In time, it can be expected that the bridge will be removed and the vessel operated remotely from shore-based control centres when human intervention is required. Even the most optimistic supporters of the new technology do not expect a wholly autonomous operation with no human involvement for at least 20 years.

This will mean that the level of autonomy on board a vessel will vary even during a single voyage. It is possible that a vessel might rely on autonomous functions at one stage but then need to switch to human control if the circumstances require.[10] This undoubtedly creates a headache from a regulatory perspective. At this stage, even though there is no general consensus on the range of capabilities that vessels with autonomous operational capacity will have, it is essential to start the process of devising regulations in this area by taking into account the diversity in operating modes. Put differently, those developing new regulations should bear in mind that a vessel might operate at certain times with monitored autonomy, and at other times without human supervision; so they should aim to provide a comprehensive regulatory framework for all operational eventualities.

The difficulty from a regulatory perspective is apparent. On one hand, the regulatory work will inevitably start without fully appreciating the key aspects of the technology that is regulated. But at the same time there is an expectation that the regulatory framework that emerges at the end of this exercise should be at least as sound and reliable as the current one. The task is further complicated by the fact that the emerging framework should be one that provides answers for different levels of autonomy.[11] This is not an easy task by any stretch of the imagination.

[9] O Lavander, 'Autonomous Ships on the High Seas' (2017) 54 (2) *IEEE Spectrum*, 26–31.

[10] Most projects on autonomous vessels work on the assumption that the vessels will be designed so that it is possible to switch between different autonomy levels. Lloyd's Register, for example, operates on the basis that vessels might have six levels of autonomy, ranging from decision support on board (AL 1) to full autonomy (AL 6). Similarly, in the report published by the Danish Maritime Authority (December 2017), 'Analysis of Regulatory Barriers to the Use of Autonomous Ships', at 6, it has been presumed that autonomous ships will operate (at least initially) via manual steering or remote control in connection with port calls and in densely trafficked areas, whereas the vessel will switch over to fully autonomy level in open waters.

[11] It should also be noted that the IMO MASS WG has prescribed four degrees of autonomy (MSC 99/WP.9 Annex 1, para 4): 1) Ship with automated processes and decision support, but with seafarers on board to operate and control shipboard systems and functions. 2) Remotely controlled ships with seafarers on board, but controlled and operated from a distant location. 3) Remotely controlled ships without seafarers on board, controlled and operated from a distant location. 4) Fully autonomous ships, where the operating system of the ship is able to make decisions and determine actions by itself.

C. Additional Complications

The challenge of adopting the existing legal framework to technological developments is a massive one, given the number of novel matters emerging from this new technology that need to be considered by regulators. Let us consider, for example, a vessel that is remote-controlled and operated from shore. To facilitate this kind of arrangement, first of all a purpose-built electronic bridge is required. The current regulations do not specify requirements for the design and construction of such bridges: but this clearly needs to be regulated to ensure an acceptable degree of safety. Moving on to offshore-based control centres and those who will man them, naturally the current regulations are silent. Yet remote control centres are closely connected with the safety of vessels at sea and will present an important challenge for regulators aiming to achieve uniform standards. In this respect, there is a need to determine the minimum acceptable technical equipment required, including cameras, sensors and communication systems to link the vessel to a remote control centre.[12] Equally, there is no doubt that the regulators need to consider carefully the requirements for education, qualifications and certification of remote operators of such vessels, as well as watch-keeping schemes that need to be adopted to ensure a reasonable degree of safety. Considering that such vessels might have autonomous operational capacity, it will be essential to set the standards on technical equipment required to perform various significant functions, such as gaining a sophisticated situation awareness capacity and performing adequate 'lookout' functions. These will be technical issues that need to be examined and carefully debated with the aid of experts.

Perhaps, however, the prime challenge for regulators will be prescribing the technical requirements that are essential to deal with cyber risks associated with such vessels that need to be in constant contact with a remote control centre. So many things could go wrong in this context, and the cyber risks include: i) possible disruption or suppression of the radio frequency signals transmitted between autonomous and automatic systems and devices (AASD) network nodes; ii) compromising the integrity of the information conveyed between AASD nodes by altering the content, embedding content, or intercepting content; and iii) compromising the internal operation of equipment such as, for example,

[12] There will inevitably be a communication segment comprised of a satellite communication network and/or terrestrial wireless network, that routes data to and from a data source or control facility and the vessel. The control segment based in the remote control centre will include any terrestrial data source that will supply information to the vessel via the communication segment. The control segment will also need to include any terrestrial facility that monitors network configuration, bandwidth, power and antenna as necessary to comply with the service objectives and licencing obligations of the satellite or cellular network. For more comprehensive analysis and explanation as to how such systems operate, see JC Suchodolski, 'Cybersecurity of Autonomous Systems in the Transportation Sector: An Examination of Regulatory and Private Law Approaches with Recommendations for Needed Reforms' 20 (2018) *North Carolina Journal of Law & Technology* 121.

data storage and retrieval tasks or the communication functions executed at the AASD node.[13] There are industry guidelines as to how to deal with cyber risks for vessels;[14] the IMO has issued Guidelines on Cyber Risk Management,[15] and the Maritime Safety Committee adopted a Resolution[16] that encourages administrations to ensure that cyber risks are appropriately addressed in existing safety management systems (as defined in the ISM Code) no later than the first annual verification of the company's Document of Compliance after 1 January 2021. However, it is apparent that for a vessel that relies heavily on communication with the remote control centte, more detailed technical regulations are needed to ensure safe navigation at sea.

D. Different Pressures and Challenges in Regulating Different Areas of Maritime Law – Different Courses for Different Horses

In academic literature much energy has so far been devoted to elaborating how the current regulatory framework on technical rules concerning safety, environment and training/watchkeeping standards could accommodate the development of autonomous vessels.[17] This is understandable and is certainly the first vital step in the regulatory marathon. The overriding objective of any regulatory work in this area is to ensure that such vessels operate with an adequate level of 'safety' compared to vessels under the control of human beings. No doubt, once these technical rules are formulated, they will guide any discussion on related issues, in particular criminal liability of those involved in the design of such systems.[18] One should, however, not lose sight of the fact that discussion on these matters will be informed by the political and economic priorities of individual states. For example, a country at the forefront of technological development (particularly in artificial intelligence) might be more prepared to argue that the autonomous systems developed provide an efficient navigational safety system, as opposed to a country whose workforce will be significantly reduced from the introduction

[13] For a more technical analysis on the matter, see B Svilicic, J Kamahara, M Rooks and Y Yano, 'Maritime Cyber Risk Management: An Experimental Ship Assessment' 72 (2019) *The Journal of Navigation* 1108, and T Kimberly and K Jones, 'Maritime Cybersecurity Policy: The Scope and Impact of Evolving Technology on International Shipping' (2018) *Journal of Cyber Policy* 147.

[14] In particular, the following organisations issued guidelines on the matter: BIMCO, CLIA, ICS, INTERCARGO, INTERMANAGER, INTERTANKO, OCIMF, IUMI and World Shipping Council.

[15] MSC-FAL.1/Circ.3.

[16] Resolution MSC.428(98).

[17] See, E van Hooydonk, 'The Law of Unmanned Merchant Shipping – An Exploration' (2014) 20 *JIML*, 403–23; R Veal and M Tsimplis, 'The Integration of Unmanned Ships into the Lex Maritima' [2017] *LMCLQ*, 303–35; L Carey, 'All Hands off Deck: Legal Barriers to Autonomous Shipping' (2017) 23 *JIML*, 202–19; and H Ringbom, 'Regulating Autonomous Ships – Concepts, Challenges and Precedents' (2019) *Ocean Development & International Law* 141, 148–54.

[18] For a discussion on similar issues concerning the use of autonomous cars, see, G Hallevy, 'Unmanned Vehicles: Subordination to Criminal Law under the Modern Concept of Criminal Liability' 21 (2011) *Journal of Law Information and Science* 200.

of autonomous ships. In similar vein, a state which runs a very successful open ship registry might be more prepared to accept that alternative safety standards introduced are as satisfactory as the existing ones. Inevitably, the regulatory battle on introducing technical rules will come first and will be fierce. However, for this technology to become a commercial reality, this battle needs to be won, and a regulatory framework that applies all around the world needs to be implemented.

What about regulating the civil liability rules emerging from the operation of autonomous vessels? As indicated before, it is the firm view of the author that this debate is as important as the first one, but the regulatory process and challenges in this context will be rather different. Primarily, the overarching objective of any attempt to formulate uniform civil liability rules must be to ensure the formation of a coherent risk allocation mechanism between the various key players, notably manufacturers, programmers, owners, operators and insurers. Inevitably, therefore, international professional associations such as the International Shipowners' Association, the International Group of P & I Clubs and even the International Transport Workers' Federation will attempt to influence the formulation of international liability rules.[19] More significantly, however, governments will not be immune to political and social pressures coming from various interest groups. For example, in a state where such new technology is developed by its tech sector, it is natural to expect that the government will come under close scrutiny when negotiating an international agreement dealing with liability issues emanating from the use of such technology. And of course divergent approaches to justice embraced by different states could be influential in supporting a particular manner of risk allocation over another one. For example, in a case where an autonomous vessel is involved in a collision with a manned vessel and seamen on board the other vessel are injured, the basis of liability and the amount of compensation acceptable to a country will depend to a large extent on whether that country takes a generous social welfare approach to compensation for personal injury or a narrow cost-saving one emphasising liability based solely on a strict proof of fault.

These challenges aside, it is also important to note that absolute uniformity in regulating civil liability rules may be desirable but is by no means vital. As long as a solution is found to keep the main players on board, in particular insurers who need to be content that they can measure their maximum exposure with an acceptable degree of certainty, there will be no obstacle in making autonomous shipping in international waters a commercial reality from the perspective of allocation of civil liability.

[19] An appropriate example is the Hamburg Rules 1978 (contained in the United Nations International Convention on the Carriage of Goods by Sea), which aim to create a uniform liability regime for contracts concerning carriage of goods by sea in international voyages. The Convention, which has the objective of increasing the liabilities of carriers for lost or damaged cargoes, has never been embraced by key transnational maritime organisations and as a result has been adopted only by a small group of states.

III. The Shape of International Regulation – The Way Forward

It follows from the discussion carried out in the previous section that the regulatory adjustment process for technical rules concerning safety, environmental protection and training/watchkeeping standards, should be carried out in a different fashion than any consideration on private law issues (for example, shipowner's liability for collisions) that will emerge from the use of autonomous ships. This study will, therefore, follow a similar pattern taking into account various regulatory challenges identified in the previous part.

A. Technical Rules on Safety, Pollution Prevention and Training/Watchkeeping Standards

The primary international legal instrument that defines the rights and responsibilities of nations with respect to their use of the world's oceans is the UNCLOS 1982. This Convention has gained widespread acceptance and been ratified by more than 160 states.[20] It establishes that member states have a right to sail vessels flying their flag and fix the conditions for granting nationality to vessels.[21] In doing so, it avoids prescribing specific requirements and leaves it to flag states to 'take measures as are necessary to ensure safety at sea with regard to construction, equipment and seaworthiness, manning of ships, labour conditions, training of crew, the use of signals, the maintenance of communications and prevention of collisions' taking into account the applicable international instruments.[22] UNCLOS 1982 is, therefore, the framework agreement on these matters that allows the IMO, as the competent international organisation, to perform the function of setting international standards for flag states to follow on vessel construction, manning, training and safety. There are several IMO regulations and conventions in force today performing this function and requiring flag states to prescribe domestic shipping legislation reflecting the internationally agreed standards. It is, therefore, not a coincidence that the scoping exercise currently undertaken by the MASS Working Group focuses on IMO regulations and conventions dealing with such matters; and this will be our starting point as well, looking at various options and ultimately stipulating the most suitable one.

[20] For the list of ratifying countries, see www.un.org/depts/los/reference_files/chronological_lists_of_ratifications.htm, accessed 1 July 2020. The main absence from the list is the USA which is not a state party to the Convention but recognises it as a codification of customary international law.

[21] Art 90 of UNCLOS 1982.

[22] See in particular, Arts 94(2)(b), 94(3)(b) and (c) of UNCLOS 1982.

(i) Issuing Guidelines/Circulars (Soft Law)

By way of closing regulatory gaps and clarifying uncertainties arising in the scope of regulation as a result of new developments (for example, manufacturing alternative designs or using armed guards as a response to piracy), the IMO has traditionally made use of various soft law schemes, such as issuing Guidelines in the form of Circulars.[23] Such Guidelines could provide answers to key issues such as how certain IMO regulations could be satisfied for vessels that operate remotely or even perhaps autonomously.

There is no doubt that this kind of approach could dispense with some of the problems arising in this context. For example, for vessels remotely operated it can be stated in the Guidelines that the function of lookout can be performed by those officers who are located somewhere else on board the ship or even on shore.[24] Similarly, it can be clarified by the Guidelines that the relevant provisions of SOLAS that require the ship to have on board sufficient number of crew for operating the survival craft and launching arrangements required for abandonment will not be applicable in the case of an unmanned autonomously operated vessel.[25] Some might also argue that given that the technology on such vessels will be developed incrementally, Guidelines that can be developed quickly with low cost might introduce much needed flexibility to the regulatory process and help to build momentum before rolling out a hard-law package.

However, it is submitted that the above is not an appropriate regulatory method in this context, for various reasons. First, there are numerous regulations that are clearly not applicable in their current format for autonomous or remotely operated vessels, so they need to be amended; and from the perspective of international law, soft law cannot be used to achieve such results.[26] For example, Article 3 of the STCW Convention stipulates that the Convention applies only to 'seafarers serving on board seagoing ships'. The scope of this Convention could not be extended with a Guideline to apply to remote operators. Second, as indicated in the previous part, the use of such vessels will introduce several new issues, such as training and certification requirements of remote operators, and technological requirements needed to keep the remote control centre connected with the vessel, that need to be considered and regulated. On these matters, it is self-evident that existing regulations do

[23] For example, the International Code for Ships Operating in Polar Waters (Polar Code) (Safety-related Provisions) and (Environmental-related Provisions) (IMO resolution MEPC 264(68)) started its journey as a Guideline issued jointly by the Maritime Safety Committee and the Maritime Environmental Protection Committee issued on 23 December 2002 (IMO MSC/Circ. 1056 and MEPC/Circ 399).

[24] Rule 5 of COLREGs.

[25] SOLAS ch III, reg 10(3).

[26] Art 31(1) of the Vienna Convention on the Law of Treaties stipulates that 'a treaty shall be interpreted in good faith in accordance with the ordinary meaning given to the terms of the treaty in their context and in the light of its object and purpose.' It would be against the spirit of this provision to apply a treaty requirement in an instance which is clearly not contemplated by the draftsman of the relevant treaty in question.

not provide any satisfactory answers, even if adapted through Guidelines. Last but not least, it should be noted that Guidelines remain a form of soft law without any binding effect. It is, therefore, questionable whether they would be able to achieve the intended purpose of establishing a safe and uniform regime for such vessels that will give confidence to coastal states, let alone to the public which might have concerns over the use of this new technology in the world's oceans.

(ii) Utilising 'Equivalent Arrangement' Provisions in Conventions

Given the difficulties involved in amending international conventions, several IMO Conventions allow flag states to consider alternatives to existing requirements if they are at least equivalent in terms of safety to the solution provided in the relevant Convention.[27] It can be argued that once the technical capabilities of autonomous or remotely controlled ships are identified, alternatives to existing requirements (for example, setting out the technical requirements of devices that can perform certain functions that are currently undertaken by the crew) could be introduced, ideally in a coherent manner, to facilitate the use of such vessels in a safe manner.

There is a certain degree of appeal to this approach, particularly taking into account the fact that capabilities of such vessels will be developed in a progressive manner; and this model provides a great deal of flexibility. However, it is submitted that it cannot provide the desired solution either. The main difficulty is that not all IMO conventions dealing with safety of navigation, design, construction and manning include provision for the substitution of equivalents for their requirements. Take for example the COLREGs, which are prescriptive regulations setting out navigation rules to be followed by vessels to prevent collisions. If it is not possible to introduce alternative safe equivalents to the 'lookout' obligation expected to be performed by humans by 'sight and hearing' (as they require), the only alternative left is to rely on a functional interpretation technique to be able to argue that a satisfactory lookout can be performed by 'electro-optical devices' or a shoreside operator. Given that it is safe to assume that this possibility was never considered in the run-up to the adoption of the COLREGs in 1972, such a construction would be at odds with treaty interpretation principles.[28] Furthermore, this would introduce a great deal of uncertainty which could hamper the development and commercial use of such vessels.[29] Another significant obstacle to this approach is that its effectiveness is limited to existing technical arrangements on construction, design and perhaps manning. However, the new technology will introduce several

[27] See, for example, reg 1–5 of SOLAS and Art IX(1) of STCW and Art 8 of the International Convention on Loadlines 1966.

[28] See CH Allen, 'Determining the Legal Status of Unmanned Maritime Vehicles: Formalism vs Functionalism' (2018) 49 *Journal of Maritime Law & Commerce* 477, who warns against adopting such interpretation techniques that will have the effect of undermining global-based order.

[29] *Cf* R Maclaughin, 'Unmanned Navel Vehicles at Sea, USVs, UUVs and the Adequacy of Law' (2011) 21 *Journal of Law Information & Science* 100.

new problems and issues that need to be regulated (for example, the design of the remote controlling centre or programs that will be used for autonomous vessels), and this kind of requlatory technique cannot address such difficulties. A more drastic, comprehensive and permanent solution is needed.

(iii) Creating A New Convention

At the completely opposite end of the regulatory framework, an option is to consider the creation of an entirely new international convention that specifically and comprehensively addresses the legal position with regard to such vessels. At first sight, there is an instinctive appeal to this kind of project, as it can promote certainty and provides an opportunity to create a comprehensive framework not only for matters that come under the ambit of technical IMO Conventions, such as construction, design, safety and manning issues, but other significant matters that can create uncertainties with regard to the use of this type of vessels. For example, the position relating to mandatory pilotage requirements that can be imposed by coastal states to this kind of vessels, or to what extent shore-based pilotage could be acceptable for wholly autonomous vessels, could be clarified in a Convention of this nature.

There is no doubt that in an ideal world this would be the most desirable solution, but it is very likely that a project of this nature might remain no more than an academically attractive proposition. Attempts to create an overarching international legal framework in the field of maritime law on a multifaceted issue have often ended in failure. Even if there is consensus on main points, difficulties will soon emerge as economic and/or political interests of different states will require them to take a different stance on various issues. To illustrate the point, we need look no further than the CMI's well-intentioned initiative of creating a general Third Party Liability Convention to replace many existing private international law conventions with a comprehensive international instrument applying to many different kinds of marine liability. The project was soon shelved as, in addition to foreseeable drafting complexities, it was realised how difficult it would be to reconcile the competing interests of different state parties.[30]

The real danger with this approach, therefore, is that even if it proves possible to draft such a convention, it is very difficult to see widespread acceptance from the international community. For example, is it possible to ensure that a seafaring nation like the Philippines will ratify the Convention? Can it be guaranteed that the USA, which does not have a good record in ratifying international conventions, will be a contracting party? If there are significant gaps in terms of states ratifying this new Convention, it will remove the prospect of such vessels freely engaging in commercial operations in the oceans of the world. Obviously, this

[30] For more information on this venture, see PJS Griggs, 'Uniformity of Maritime Law – An International Perspective' (1999) 73 *Tul L Rev* 1551.

will defeat the purpose of attempting to provide an internationally acceptable legal framework to enable the development of the new technology. It is evident that the regulatory solution needed is the one that will gain acceptance of all nations that have a stake in maritime affairs.

(iv) Amending the Existing Legal Framework

It is submitted that the best way to tackle the regulatory challenge is working within the current legal framework, keeping in mind the objectives that we expect a new legal framework concerning such vessels to fulfil, namely: i) ensuring safe navigation; ii) protecting the marine environment; iii) introducing homogenous technical standards and equipment required for such ships; and iv) protecting the rights and working conditions of those who will work on board or in connection with such vessels. This can be achieved by creating an overarching instrument, along the lines, perhaps, of the Polar Code.[31]

Relevant parts of this Code, which is intended to deal with new types of vessels, can be made mandatory under the SOLAS – which sets minimum safety standards in the construction, equipment and operation of merchant vessels – by utilising its tacit amendment procedure.[32] This will address most of the challenges concerning construction, design and safe navigation that such vessels will present.[33] However, just like the Polar Code, it is obvious that such an overarching instrument needs to address other issues such as manning, watchkeeping and certification requirements of those who will work on board such ships or in connection with such ships. For example, the STCW requires that the bridge of a ship must at no time be left unattended.[34] This clearly poses a legal obstacle for autonomous shipping and even for periodic remote bridge operations; and new provisions in the STCW Convention need to be developed to accommodate the new technology. This should not present any significant problem, as the tacit amendment procedure exists in the STCW Convention too. Furthermore, to be able to provide a

[31] The Polar Code covers a full range of design, construction, equipment, operational, training, search and rescue and environmental protection matters relevant to ships operating in the inhospitable waters surrounding the two poles. The Code entered into force on 1 January 2017. Several provisions of the Polar Code have been made mandatory under SOLAS and MARPOL. Each of these conventions has slightly different applicability clauses, ratification and amendment procedures, so it was decided to divide the Polar Code into two parts: Part I: Safety Measures and Part II: Pollution Prevention Measures.

[32] Under SOLAS 1974, an amendment to most of the Annexes (which constitute the technical parts of the Convention) is 'deemed to have been accepted at the end of two years from the date on which it is communicated to Contracting Governments' unless the amendment is objected to by more than one-third of contracting governments, or contracting governments owning not less than 50 per cent of the world's gross merchant tonnage. This period may be varied by the Maritime Safety Committee with a minimum limit of one year.

[33] It is likely that changes should also be made in MARPOL to introduce structural and equipment requirements for remote controlled and autonomous vessels with the intention to protect seas against ship sourced pollution.

[34] See ch VIII of Pt A of the STCW.

comprehensive legal regime it is vital that this new Code goes a step further than the Polar Code and facilitates changes in the COLREGs as well by utilising its tacit amendment procedure. COLREGs is an essential part of the puzzle, given that it lays down the rules of navigation at sea and contains vital provisions that need to be considered in the context of autonomous vessels, such as how the 'lookout' function could be performed effectively by utilising sensors and other technical devices.

Amendments incorporated into these conventions through a new Code will provide the backbone of the regulatory framework required and has great advantages: a) as soon as the technical issues concerning such vessels are fleshed out in the Maritime Safety Committee of the IMO, legal matters and proposed changes can be drafted and implemented without significant delay;[35] b) there will be no few technical obstacles to autonomous navigation or use of remote control functions on ships operating in international waters once this Code comes into force; and c) the technical standards required for such ships will be standardised, providing much needed certainty for hull underwriters willing to provide cover for such ships.

In a nutshell, this solution has the advantage of providing a speedy mechanism to deal with the regulatory challenge on technical matters, and in a manner that could gain acceptance from the international community that are parties to the key IMO Conventions. Assuming that such a Code is the way forward, it is essential to deliberate on a number of related issues further.

(a) Interrelation between various Regulatory Regimes

There could be very little doubt that such a Code will be part of the extended normative framework of the UNCLOS in terms of shipping regulations, especially if it were to be developed by an international organisation (that is, the IMO), which has competence in developing rules and standards pertaining to navigation safety and environmental protection.[36] However, one difficult question remains. Article 94(4)(b) of UNCLOS stipulates that:

> each ship is in charge of a master and officers who possess appropriate qualifications, in particular, in seamanship, navigation, communications and marine engineering, and that the crew is appropriate in qualification and numbers for the type, size, machinery and equipment of the ships.

This provision does not present a difficulty for remotely operated vessels as long as the remote controller could be regarded as the master; but a fully autonomous ship without human involvement in navigation and steering will clearly be at odds

[35] It should still not be assumed that this will be a quick process. Drafting such a Code is likely to take a considerable amount of time before any discussion could begin on implementing them in relevant Conventions, namely SOLAS, MARPOL, STCW and COLREGs, through a tacit amendment procedure.

[36] Ø Jensen, 'International Code for Ships Operating in Polar Waters: Finalization, Adoption and Law of the Sea Implications' (2016) 7 *Arctic Review on Law and Politics* 60 at 71–77.

with Article 94(4)(b) of UNCLOS. Thus, the key question is whether the IMO has competency to make regulations concerning such vessels. If we proceed on the premise that the UNCLOS is a framework agreement that allows the IMO to regulate within its parameters, the IMO is clearly operating outside such parameters by opting to make regulations concerning fully autonomous vessels – unless the relevant provision of the UNCLOS is amended, which can be a very difficult process. The tension between UNCLOS and the role of the IMO is not unique to this area,[37] and it may well be addressed if member states have no objection to a clarification on the scope of Article 94(4)(b), by facilitating the simplified amendment procedure laid down in Article 313 of the UNCLOS. If not, and IMO still proceeds with the regulation, it is hard to see how the IMO could be effectively stopped from doing so by employing a judicial action.[38] Perhaps a pragmatic solution to the problem would be to argue that a fully autonomous vessel does not come under the scope of the UNCLOS, so there is actually no conflict between specifications made for such vessels under a Code and the UNCLOS. The fact that no definition of the term 'vessel' exists in the UNCLOS might render this an attractive proposition; but it should be noted, in that case, it will be rather doubtful whether a fully autonomous vessel could enjoy other privileges afforded to vessels under the Convention, such as the right of innocent passage.

Another significant matter on the interface between various international regimes is that the proposed Code might not address all the difficulties that might emerge from the use of this new technology. For example, under the Convention of Facilitation of International Maritime Traffic (FAL) 1965, the master is under an obligation to secure stowaways' 'security, general health, welfare and safety' while they are on board.[39] In the context of wholly autonomous vessels, satisfying this obligation is not possible, so this part of the Annexe might need to be amended by a resolution of the Facilitation Committee before such vessels are put into commercial use. Similarly, Chapter 12 of the Polar Code seems to presuppose that vessels operating in polar areas will be manned, and it specifies manning and training requirements for the crew on board those vessels. Again, if fully autonomous vessels will operate in such part of the world, it will be necessary to consider adjustments to the Polar Code.[40]

[37] R Beckman and S Zhen, 'The Relationship between UNCLOS and IMO Instruments' (2017) *Asia-Pacific Journal of Ocean Law and Policy* 201.

[38] The International Tribunal for the Law of the Sea (ITLOS) is an independent judicial body established by the UNCTAD to adjudicate disputes arising out of the interpretation and application of the Convention. It is envisaged that that states will be the primary users of the ITLOS. The definition of 'States Parties' in UNCLOS (Art 1(2)(2) and Arts 305–6) is not limited to states. The definition includes other entities entitled to become parties to the Convention, such as territories with full internal self-governance and international organisations with treaty-making competence such as the EU. It is not clear whether the IMO could be deemed as one of these organisations, as treaties made by the IMO could only come into force if they are ratified. Therefore, the role of the IMO in terms of treaty-making is rather different than that of the EU.

[39] Annexe, para 4.4.2, section B.

[40] The author has not identified any regulatory challenges that other major IMO Conventions such as the International Convention relating to Intervention on the High Seas in Cases of Pollution Casualties

(b) Setting Appropriate Standards

When regulating especially on technical matters, the Maritime Safety Committee of the IMO has adopted a goal-based philosophy since the early 1990s. As part of this approach, the regulations only outline the objectives to be achieved and certain functional requirements, as well as a verification process – but leave the detailed means of achieving those standards, objectives and requirements to flag states, classification societies, ship designers and builders. This was the preferred approach adopted when drafting the Polar Code, and it is submitted that it can be an appropriate method to adopt with regard to remote controlled and autonomous vessels as well, where the technology is developed on an incremental basis and the technological solutions are not yet known.

(c) Enforcement of Standards

If a goal-based approach is adopted when regulating this area, each flag state will be expected to administer and enforce the standards for vessels flying its flag. It is not uncommon in practice for special maritime authorities of a flag state to delegate these tasks to private classification societies. In such cases, classification societies together with ship building yards and marine equipment manufacturers will be the driving force behind the development of technical standards and codes of conduct for autonomous ships.[41] This will be a vital step in ensuring that such vessels achieve the goals set by the relevant regulation without falling below an internationally agreed minimum.

B. Private Maritime Law Rules

When it comes to legal principles concerning private law relationships between parties of different states, the landscape is rather different. Although several international regimes (mainly in the shape of conventions) have been developed with a view to harmonising the law, it is fair to say that this has been partially successful. For example, the International Convention on Civil Liability for Oil Pollution

(INTERVENTION) 1969, the International Convention on Tonnage Measurement of Ships 1969, and the International Convention on Maritime Search and Rescue 1979 present to autonomous shipping; but no doubt the scoping exercise will reveal other difficulties that might need to be overcome. In any event, it is submitted that these do not present an insurmountable challenge to the regulatory effort in this area.

[41] Lloyd's Register has already produced its own class guideline entitled, LR Code for Unmanned Marine Systems, in 2017, file:///C:/Users/b.soyer/Downloads/LR_Code_for_Unmanned_Marine_Systems__February_2017.pdf, accessed 1 July 2020. More recently ClassNK has released its latest guidelines for the design and operation of maritime autonomous surface ships, Guidelines for Automated/Autonomous Operation on Ships (Ver. 1.0), building on its first provisional concept design guidelines released in 2018, https://maritimecyprus.files.wordpress.com/2020/01/classnk-autonomous.pdf, accessed 1 July 2020.

Damage (CLC) 1992, designed to ensure that adequate compensation is available to persons who suffer oil pollution damage resulting from maritime casualties involving oil-carrying ships, has been ratified by 141 states. On the other hand, the International Convention on Removal of Wrecks, which places financial responsibility for the removal of certain hazardous wrecks in the EEZ and territorial waters of member states, has only 49 Member States.[42] There are numerous reasons why uniformity is lacking in this area, but it is fair to say that different political and social objectives, political systems and economic considerations play a vital role.[43] Before elaborating on the manner in which private law issues concerning the use of vessels with new technology can be best regulated, it is essential to highlight the issues that will emerge as a result of the use of the new technology.

(i) New Issues Concerning Liability

In terms of establishing the liability of a vessel utilising the new technology against third parties in case of a collision or contact with an object, the key consideration would be whose control the vessel was under at the time of the incident. If the vessel was controlled by a human being, even a remote controller, few could object that the current fault-based rules would be inappropriate. However, it is a different ball game if an accident occurs when the vessel is engaged in navigation by relying purely on artificial intelligence without human supervision. Also, more difficult legal issues might emerge in cases where the control of the vessel was supposed to be handed to a remote controller due to prevailing circumstances (for example, an emergency arising) but the system failed to do so, or the system handed over the control to a remote controller but the remote controller failed to take the appropriate steps due to a failure in the network system. The latter might also arise as a result of a cyberattack by hackers, which potentially brings a completely different dimension to the equation. In those circumstances, there could be a case for arguing that a strict liability regime would be more fitting.[44] No doubt, this will be a controversial issue and will attract considerable objection, especially from those who are affiliated with the development of new technology. However, it is a matter that needs to be considered seriously, especially if autonomous shipping becomes common.

Regardless of the debate on the introduction of a strict liability regime in certain instances, there is no doubt that autonomous navigation will introduce

[42] Information obtained from the relevant IMO web page and represents the position as of 1 May 2020, www.imo.org/en/About/Conventions/StatusOfConventions/Documents/StatusOfTreaties.pdf, accessed 1 July 2020.

[43] For a more comprehensive discussion see, W Tettley, 'Uniformity of International Private Law – The Pros, Cons, and Alternatives to International Conventions – How to Adopt an International Convention', (2000) 24 *Tul Mar LJ* 775.

[44] See, B Soyer, 'Autonomous Vessels and Third-Party Liabilities – The Elephant in the Room' in B Soyer and A Tettenborn (eds), *New Technologies, Artificial Intelligence and Shipping Law in 21st Century*, (Informa Law, 2020).

new players into the process of liability assessment. For example, manufacturers and programmers of navigation systems of autonomous vessels, as well as suppliers of communication and network solutions used by such vessels, might face liabilities, given that the systems created or operated by them will have direct influence on the decisions such vessels take during navigation. Serious thought should be given to various eventualities when determining the legal position of such parties. First, it is necessary to determine the basis of their liability: that is, will they face strict (product) liability or is their liability going to be fault-based? If the latter, will their liability be determined as part of an international regime, or will it be left to the national law? If left to the national law, in terms of direct claims from injured parties, such an action is likely to be based on the tort of negligence, as all parties involved in the manufacturing process are expected to take reasonable care to avoid foreseeable damage.[45] What amounts to reasonable care will depend essentially on industry norms and guidelines. At this precise moment no such guidelines exist. However, in line with regulatory developments, technical rules and standards based on the performance standards and additional clarification requirements for component/software developers will undoubtedly be developed. Such rules and guidelines will undoubtedly be valuable in the context of any recourse or contribution action. In an action of this nature, the claimant needs to demonstrate a fault of the manufacturer or programmers that is causative of his loss. However, a manufacturer or programmer will not be liable in tort for damage or injury arising from defects which could not be detected by due diligence on the part of the shipowner.[46] Also, in a case where negligent defect on the part of the manufacturer/programmer is deemed to have caused the accident, the manufacturer/programmer might nevertheless be exempted from liability if the ship owner has failed to carry out reasonable maintenance and inspection. So, a programming defect which could have been detected by reasonable inspection by the ship owner will possibly not give rise to a tort action against the manufacturers.

It would also require consideration whether a manufacturer or programmer should be allowed to exclude or limit its liability, especially against the party they have a contractual relationship with. For example, as far as English law is concerned, there is no obstacle in manufacturers or programmers indicating in their contracts that they only warrant their own supply to be free of defects, and they do not vouch for the integration with other onboard equipment or give a 'fit for purpose' guarantee. Not interfering with such contractual mechanisms that manufacturer or programmers could benefit from would certainly be significant to their prospect of finding liability insurance with a reasonable premium. Again, programmers or manufacturers could also put a financial limit on their liability against parties they have contracts with. However, they face unlimited liability when a claim from an injured party comes directly to the manufacturer

[45] *Donoghue v Stevenson* [1932] AC 562.
[46] *Taylor v Rover Co Ltd* [1966] 1 WLR 1491.

or programmer; as under the existing maritime conventions dealing with limitation of liability, neither of them is currently listed as one of the parties who could enjoy the right of limitation.[47] Whether the right of limitation of liability should be extended to such parties is a policy decision; but it needs to be borne in mind that if they are not given a general right to limit the liability of a manufacturer of an autonomous vessel or control system, then it will be higher than the liabilities that a shipowner will face by third parties, given that the former might be partially or fully responsible for the replacement cost of an autonomous vessel in addition to liabilities that he will face in a recourse action. This kind of outcome could affect the availability of insurance cover for product liability and its price.

To sum up, from the perspective of apportioning liability from the moment the system is authorised to act on its own without human intervention (even though this might be the case for a short period of time), there is a need to engage in a debate as to whether the current fault-based rules would be suitable or whether it is essential to introduce a strict liability system. If a strict liability system is adopted, the next question will be determining the party which the liability should be channelled to.[48] One might be tempted to argue that the 'manufacturer' of an autonomous vessel is the most suitable party for this purpose. This has an instinctive appeal at first sight. However, one should not lose sight of possible difficulties that can emerge. Given that an advanced level of technology is required to manufacture an autonomous vessel, it is very likely that several parties (for example, ship builders, various programmers, sensor manufacturers), will cooperate in the construction process. The main question will, therefore, be which corporation the liability will be channelled to. Also, channelling third-party liability to manufacturers would require them to carry acceptable liability insurance provided by a reliable insurance company. It is highly unlikely that P & I clubs would be willing to provide this kind of insurance; so manufacturers would need to seek this kind of cover from the commercial market. However, cover from the commercial market could be rather costly, considering that the current legal regime does not allow manufacturers to limit their liability for maritime claims from third parties.

Conversely, there are various reasons why the registered shipowner might be a better option for channelling of liability purposes. First, this is in line with other areas of maritime law where a party who chooses to be involved in a potentially hazardous activity also assumes liability that might emerge.[49] Second, after an autonomous vessel is delivered by the manufacturer, the owner (or his agents/employees) will be expected to maintain and inspect systems critical for the vessel's

[47] In maritime law, those exposed to liability, such as shipowners, salvors and their employees, charterers, managers and operators, are entitled to limit their liability. See Art 1 of the Convention on Limitation of Liability for Maritime Claims 1976. A similar outcome will follow under the International Convention relating to the Limitation of the Liability of Owners of Sea-Going Ships 1957.

[48] This would preclude third parties from bringing an action against any other party.

[49] For example, the registered owner of a tanker involved in carriage of oil is strictly liable to third parties for any loss and liability under the Civil Liability Convention 1992. Similarly, in the offshore sector, the operator usually assumes responsibility to third parties for losses and liabilities.

autonomous navigation, for example by installing safety-critical software updates and regularly inspecting sensors. Given the fact that the owner's active involvement is vital for an autonomous vessel to operate safely, it should not come as a surprise if the owner is expected to assume strict liability when things go wrong. Last but not least, there is a very effective and well-established liability insurance system provided by P & I clubs in place already available for shipowners; and extending the cover to autonomous vessels would not cause any significant turbulence. In fact, it can also be argued that spreading any potential liability through the P & I clubs mechanism would be a more cost-efficient way of dealing with liability insurance issues.

(ii) Appropriate Form of Regulation

It is submitted that on issues concerning private law, the most appropriate course of action is to consider the creation of a new international convention. Such a convention should aim to regulate the liability issues highlighted in the previous part, especially at periods when the vessel is in autonomous operation. A rigorous and uniform legal system for those who will be involved in such ventures – in particular, manufacturers, programmers, suppliers of communication and network solutions, owners and operators – will yield several positive results. Essentially, in international transactions and torts, uniformity of international law provides certainty and predictability; and this is critical for the insurance industry, which will be called upon to underwrite such risks. Also, creating such an order will create conditions that foster further development of technology in this field by providing certainty to those engaged in developing such technologies. Lastly, a certain and uniform system will provide assurance to third parties who might be the victims of any technical error occurring on board such vessels. Knowing that an effective and uniform legal regime is in place to provide them with compensation if things go wrong will go a long way in ensuring fairness.

When developing such an international regime, it is essential to observe the following parameters:

(i) The regulators should not attempt to provide answers to every private law matter that might be of relevance to such vessels. Having such a wide-ranging coverage is likely to reduce the prospect of consensus. More significantly, as far as many international liability regimes are concerned, the key issue is to what extent the rules of that regime are applicable to an autonomous vessel. This is a matter that can be easily addressed by courts by providing construction of relevant treaty rules. Let us provide an example. Whether an autonomous vessel can be arrested or not depends on the definition of 'vessel' for the purposes of the relevant convention regime. The 1952 Arrest Convention does not define what a 'vessel' is and leaves it to the national law to deal with the issue. So, whether an autonomous vessel could be arrested or not is a matter that the national court can easily deal with. Of course, there might be minor issues in the Arrest Convention that are not clear (that is, how the mechanics of arrest will be executed if the relevant vessel is unmanned); but these issues can certainly be addressed by national procedural rules, and there is no need to address them in the context of an international convention. At the risk of repetition, another example is in order. Whether the Nairobi Wreck Removal Convention 2007[50] – which makes shipowners liable for the cost of locating, marking and removing a wreck within a state's exclusive economic zone for safety or environmental reasons – will apply to vessels remotely controlled or autonomous vessels is a matter concerning the scope of that Convention. For the purposes of the Convention, a wreck is a ship or part of one that is sunk or stranded, or in danger of so being, and any object lost from it. A 'ship' is 'a seagoing vessel of any type whatsoever operating in the marine environment'; the term also includes 'hydrofoils, hovercraft, submersibles, floating craft and floating platforms except when such platforms are on location engaged in the exploration, exploitation or production of seabed mineral resources'.[51] It is evident that the definition provided in the Convention would not preclude the convention regime from being applicable to a ship controlled from onshore, or even an autonomous unmanned ship. Hence, there is no need to make this part of a Convention that is designed to address legal issues concerning such vessels.

(ii) Developing a convention that is designed to address private law issues concerning the use of such vessels is a venture that should not be rushed. Before attempting to regulate this area of law, we need to appreciate and fully understand the technical capability of such vessels and also the intentions of those who are behind the development of such new technologies. For example, one report that evaluates the development of such a vessel, the *Yara Birkeland*, a container ship intending to carry fertiliser products from Yara's production site in Herøya to the nearby ports in Brevik and Larvik in Norway's southern Telemark region, seems to suggest that the sole function of this vessel will be to transport a manufacturer's product along a very specific route. It is not envisaged at this stage that this vessel will move other products or will operate outside Norwegian waters.[52] Until the technology and technical regulations allow such vessels to operate in international waters, from the perspective of international maritime law we are not confronted with a significant legal vacuum. This will give us time to engage in a regulatory process in a constructive way by keeping an eye on the development of technical rules and technology.

[50] Formally the The Nairobi International Convention on the Removal of Wrecks 2007, incorporated into English law under Pt IXA of the Merchant Shipping Act 1995.

[51] See Art 1.2 of the Convention and s 255R(1) of the Merchant Shipping Act 1995.

[52] See World Maritime University, 'Transport 2040: Autonomous Ships: A Paradigm for Norwegian Shipping – Technology and Transformation' (2019) *Reports*, 59, at 16–17.

IV. Concluding Remarks

There is little doubt that technological developments will make autonomous shipping a reality in the future. It has been demonstrated by various authors in this book that the existing maritime legal framework needs to be amended to accommodate this development. This chapter has engaged with a different issue; namely what the main regulatory challenges are and how they can be tackled.

It has been argued that a different regulatory process for amending technical rules with regard to safety and manning requirements for such vessels should be followed as opposed to regulating civil liability issues emerging from the use of such vessels. With regard to the former, it is argued that a Code that makes amendments in key IMO Conventions such as SOLAS, MARPOL, and STCW by utilising tacit amendment procedures of these Conventions will provide optimal results in the shortest period of time. This will not only standardise technical requirements for such vessels but also enable them to operate in international waters. However, it should be noted that there are several new issues, such as construction and technological requirements of such vessels and remote operation centers, and training requirements of remote controllers, that need to be considered; and rules on these issues need to be developed as part of this process.

However, when dealing with liability of various parties involved in the operation and production of such vessels, a new international convention should be considered. The author is aware that achieving uniformity in this area might not be possible; and several difficult issues, for example whether a strict liability should be imposed for the owner when such a vessel operates autonomously, will need to be discussed as part of such negotiations. However, such an international regime might provide the much-needed certainty for liability insurers who will ultimately play a key role in the commercialisation process of this venture.

We are only at the beginning of this regulatory marathon. Time and energy need to be invested and technological developments need to be closely monitored during the process of developing a new legal framework. Nor should one underestimate the political challenges that lie ahead!

INDEX

www.ingramcontent.com/pod-product-compliance
Ingram Content Group UK Ltd.
Pitfield, Milton Keynes, MK11 3LW, UK
UKHW022211051026
15624UKWH00001B/109

9 781509 933358